Fourth Edition

Designing Qualitative
Research

Fourth Edition

Designing Qualitative Research

Catherine Marshall

University of North Carolina, Chapel Hill

Gretchen B. Rossman

University of Massachusetts, Amherst

SAGE Publications
Thousand Oaks ▪ London ▪ New Delhi

For information:

Sage Publications, Inc.
2455 Teller Road
Thousand Oaks, California 91320
E-mail: order@sagepub.com

Sage Publications Ltd.
1 Oliver's Yard
55 City Road
London EC1Y 1SP
United Kingdom

Sage Publications India Pvt. Ltd.
B-42, Panchsheel Enclave
Post Box 4109
New Delhi 110 017 India

Printed in the United States of America.

Library of Congress Cataloging-in-Publication Data

Marshall, Catherine.
Designing qualitative research / Catherine Marshall, Gretchen B. Rossman—4th ed.
    p. cm.
Includes bibliographical references and index.
ISBN 1-4129-2488-X (cloth)—ISBN 1-4129-2489-8 (pbk.)
    1. Social sciences—Research—Methodology. I. Rossman, Gretchen B. II. Title.
H62.M277 2006
300.72—dc22   2005026958

This book is printed on acid-free paper.

06 07 08 09 10   10 9 8 7 6 5 4 3 2

Acquiring Editor:	Lisa Cuevas Shaw
Editorial Assistant:	Karen Gia Wong
Project Editor:	Astrid Virding
Copy Editor:	Tom Lacey
Typesetter:	C&M Digitals (P) Ltd.
Indexer:	Pamela Van Huss
Cover Designer:	Janet Foulger

Contents

List of Tables

List of Figures

List of Vignettes

Preface to
Fourth Edition

Since the publication of the third edition of *Designing Qualitative Research*, the context for systematic inquiry has undergone seismic shifts. As we prepared the proposal for this edition, reviewers commented on the need to "tone down" some of the apparent defensiveness in previous editions. We listened to those gentle critics, agreeing that the climate for qualitative inquiry on many university campuses had become much more supportive. A short two years later, however, the national context supporting research, especially in education (our field), has undergone a dramatic turnaround. The current conservative federal government now stipulates that appropriate—and acceptable—inquiry can take only one form: the randomized, controlled experiment. Such a stipulation is written into policy governing research and evaluation of federally funded programs in education. We find this turn quite shocking. Hence, we have modified this edition to reflect that turn of events while also acknowledging that universities are still reasonably gentle places to find support for qualitative research.

As we now write, we find that qualitative research methodology has matured, despite the current federal climate. This fourth edition addresses the advances and challenges presented by provocative developments and new applications. The book originally met the need for advice on designing qualitative research, given the complexity, the flexibility, and the controversies of its many genres. That need persists: Doctoral students, research managers, policy analysts, and researchers anticipating multimethod team research will continue to find clear and direct guidance in this edition. Qualitative designs are currently used in health behavior, education, urban planning, public relations and communications, sociology, psychology, management, social work, nursing, and more. Our focus tends to be on research in applied fields such as these. While we acknowledge the many developments that have come from autoethnography, performance ethnography, and cultural studies, as examples, our primary audience continues to be those working in those fields that demand practical answers to complex questions.

Originally, *Designing Qualitative Research* was written because qualitative reports were intriguing but mystical. Earthy, evocative ethnographies seemed to just appear by magic. Researchers and students had no guidance for learning from such work. A few researchers provided chapters or appendixes describing their procedures. Texts extolled the philosophical stances and the cultural premises for qualitative research. We originally wrote this book to fill the void, to provide specific advice on design. Then, and now in this fourth edition, we benefit from the research experience of those who first systematically documented their designs and processes and also from the probing questions of our doctoral students. Thus, we provide readers with connections to the classics of ethnography and other qualitative genres as well as present the issues and design dilemmas of researchers with new questions for the new century. Furthermore, this edition extends and deepens the discussion in the previous edition about strategies for incorporating qualitative methodology with the challenges posed by postmodernists, feminists, and those who demand that research be directly useful to the researched.

This fourth edition continues to provide vignettes to illustrate the methodological challenges posed by the intellectual, ethical, political, and technological advances affecting qualitative research design. New vignettes include, for example, researchers' challenges designing research with refugee and immigrant populations, and new sections address issues of translating into English and dealing with internal review boards. Vignettes from the previous edition of interest include discussions of researchers' explicitly political stances toward promoting democracy while conducting evaluations of community development, and critical theorists' puzzling over reporting research without colonizing those who allowed them into their lives. Because qualitative design is not linear, different pedagogical strategies are required; the vignettes, we hope, assist readers in transferring our words about design to applications in their own research. Also new to this edition are e-mail dialogues between our quite thoughtful graduate assistants who helped with the preparation of this edition. Melanie Shofner, at UNC, and Aaron Kuntz, at UMass, engaged with many of the issues presented in the chapters of the book. They have graciously agreed to include these insightful, very real, and personal reflections as dialogues at the end of each chapter.

We have between us a total of 45 years of teaching collective qualitative methodology to graduate students! Nothing keeps us attuned to qualitative research dilemmas more than the challenges our students present in classes and dissertations. We wish to thank the many hundreds who have continuously pressed for innovative approaches and research questions fresh from real-life problems; many have graciously permitted us to use their questions in vignettes. The reviews by Cynthia S. Jacelon, School of Nursing, University of Massachusetts Amherst; Howard A. Palley, Institute for Human Services Policy, University of Maryland; Nancy J. Parezo, University of Arizona; and Karen Hult, Virginia Polytechnic Institute & State University were especially helpful. Finally, we, and our readers, benefit from the reviews of our book in scholarly journals as well as from diplomatic yet critical suggestions from our own students.

In particular, we appreciate the specific editorial contributions of Melanie and Aaron in creating and balancing the substantial revisions for this new edition. We hope our efforts will continue to provide a practical guide, assisting researchers as they craft sound, thoughtful, and sensitive proposals for qualitative inquiry that is robust and ethical.

1

Introduction

Qualitative research genres have become increasingly important modes of inquiry for the social sciences and applied fields such as education, regional planning, nursing, social work, community development, and management. Long dominated by research techniques borrowed from the experimental sciences, the social sciences now present a sometimes confusing array of alternative genres. From anthropology come ethnomethodology, ethnoscience, and the more familiar ethnography. Sociology has yielded symbolic interactionism and the Chicago School. Philosophers would have us engage in concept analysis, and interdisciplinary work has spawned sociolinguistics, discourse analysis, life histories, narrative analysis, and clinical methodology. The critical traditions, including postmodern, poststructuralist, and postcolonial perspectives, contribute critical discourse analysis, feminist research, critical race theory and analysis, cultural studies, critical and performance ethnography, and autoethnography. Action research and participatory research, often explicitly ideological and emancipatory, intend to critique and radically change fundamental social structures and processes and to reconceptualize the entire research enterprise. Many of these genres, derived from traditional and interdisciplinary scholarship, are now frequently used in

1

policy studies and professional fields. As Denzin and Lincoln (1994) note, "The extent to which the 'qualitative revolution' is taking over the social sciences and related professional fields is nothing short of amazing" (p. ix).

Each of these disciplinary traditions rests on somewhat different assumptions about what constitutes proper inquiry within the qualitative, or interpretive, paradigm. Throughout this text, we refer to *qualitative research* and *qualitative methodology* as if they were one agreed-on approach. If this were the case, it might be reassuring to the novice researcher, but unfortunately it is not. As Denzin and Lincoln (2000) write, "[Qualitative research] crosscuts disciplines, fields, and subject matters. A complex, interconnected family of terms, concepts, and assumptions surround [*sic*] the term *qualitative research*" (p. 2).

Qualitative research genres exist in great variety, and many excellent texts serve as guides to their assumptions and approaches. Most qualitative researchers, however, despite their various methodologies, espouse some common considerations and procedures for its conduct and certain habits of mind and heart. They are intrigued by the complexity of social interactions expressed in daily life and by the meanings that the participants themselves attribute to these interactions. These interests take qualitative researchers into natural settings, rather than laboratories, and foster pragmatism in using multiple methods for exploring a topic. Thus, qualitative research is pragmatic, interpretive, and grounded in the lived experiences of people. Rossman and Rallis (2003) offer five characteristics of qualitative research and four of researchers who practice it. They say that qualitative research (a) is naturalistic, (b) draws on multiple methods that respect the humanity of participants in the study, (c) focuses on context, (d) is emergent and evolving, and (e) is fundamentally interpretive. Qualitative researchers, they maintain, (a) view social worlds as holistic, (b) engage in systematic reflection on the conduct of the research, (c) remain sensitive to their own biographies/social identities and how these shape the study, and (d) rely on complex reasoning that moves dialectically between deduction and induction (see Table 1.1).

Qualitative research, then, is a broad approach to the study of social phenomena. Its various genres are naturalistic, interpretive, and increasingly critical, and they draw on multiple methods of inquiry. This book is intended to be a guide for researchers who have chosen some genre of qualitative methods in their effort to understand—and perhaps change—a complex social phenomenon and who seek to develop solid, ethical proposals as they plan their inquiry.

Table 1.1   Characteristics of Qualitative Research and Researchers

Qualitative research

   Takes place in the natural world

   Uses multiple methods that are interactive and humanistic

   Focuses on context

   Is emergent rather than tightly prefigured

   Is fundamentally interpretive

The qualitative researcher

   Views social phenomena holistically

   Systematically reflects on who she is in the inquiry

   Is sensitive to her personal biography and how it shapes the study

   Uses complex reasoning that is multifaceted and iterative

SOURCE: Adapted from Rossman and Rallis (2003, pp. 8, 10). With permission.

❖ QUALITATIVE RESEARCH GENRES

Historically, qualitative researchers have offered several typologies to organize the field. Focusing specifically on education, Jacob (1987, 1988) described six qualitative traditions: human ethology, ecological psychology, holistic ethnography, cognitive anthropology, ethnography of communication, and symbolic interactionism (see Table 1.2). Atkinson, Delamont, and Hammersley (1988) critiqued Jacob's typology and offered seven somewhat differing ones: symbolic interactionism, anthropology, sociolinguistics, ethnomethodology, democratic evaluation, neo-Marxist ethnography, and feminism. More recently, Creswell (1998) discussed biography, phenomenology, grounded theory, ethnography, and case study as the major strategies. Denzin and Lincoln (2005) recognized case studies; ethnography, participant observation, and performance ethnography; phenomenology and ethnomethodology; grounded theory; life history and *testimonio;* historical method; action and applied research; and clinical research.

   Building on the discussion provided in Gall, Borg, and Gall (1996), analysis of these categories shows a focus in three major genres: (a) *individual lived experience* exemplified by phenomenological approaches, some feminist inquiry, and life history and *testimonio;* (b) *society and culture* as seen in ethnography and action research; and (c) *language and communication*—whether spoken or expressed in text— like that in sociolinguistic approaches, including discourse analysis.

In the past two decades, a critical turn has taken place in the social sciences, humanities, and applied fields. Some qualitative researchers have espoused postmodern, post-positivist, and postcolonial theoretical perspectives that critique traditional social science (see Ashcroft, Griffiths, & Tiffin, 2000; Connor, 1989; Denzin & Lincoln, 2005; Rosenau, 1992). These scholars challenge the historic assumptions of neutrality in inquiry and assert that *all* research is interpretive and fundamentally political, "[spoken] from within a distinct interpretive community that configures, in its special way, the multicultural, gendered components of the research act" (Denzin & Lincoln, 2005, p. 21). They argue further that research involves issues of power and that traditionally conducted social science research has silenced many marginalized and oppressed groups in society by making them the passive objects of inquiry. Qualitative research is deemed especially guilty because of its historical complicity with colonialism (Denzin & Lincoln, 1994). Those espousing these critical perspectives have developed research strategies that are openly ideological and have empowering and democratizing goals.

Table 1.2   Typologies of Qualitative Research

Jacob (1987, 1988)	Atkinson, Delamont, and Hammersley (1988)	Creswell (1998)	Denzin and Lincoln (2005)
Human ethology	Symbolic interactionism	Biography	Case studies
Ecological psychology	Anthropology	Phenomenology	Ethnography, participant observation, performance ethnography
Holistic ethnography	Sociolinguistics	Grounded theory	Phenomenology and ethnomethodology
Cognitive anthropology	Ethnomethodology	Ethnography	Grounded theory
Ethnography of communication	Democratic evaluation	Case study	Life history and *testimonio*
Symbolic interactionism	Neo-Marxist ethnography		Historical method
	Feminism		Action and applied research
			Clinical research

We argue that traditional or more critical and postmodern assumptions can undergird each genre. Traditional qualitative research assumes that (a) knowledge is not objective Truth but is produced intersubjectively; (b) the researcher learns from participants to understand the meaning of their lives but should maintain a certain stance of neutrality; and (c) society is reasonably structured and is orderly.[1] Critical theory, critical race·theory, feminist theory, and postmodern perspectives also assume that knowledge is subjective but view society as essentially conflictual and oppressive. These positions critique traditional modes of knowledge production (i.e., research) that have evolved in settings structured to legitimize elite social scientists and to exclude other forms of knowing. Critical race theorists and feminists, particularly, point to the exclusion of knowledges and truths from traditional knowledge production (Harding, 1987; Ladson-Billings, 2000; Ladson-Billings & Donnor, 2005; LeCompte, 1993; Matsuda, Delgado, Lawrence, & Crenshaw, 1993). By means of such challenges, it becomes clear that the assumptions behind research questions must be questioned and sometimes dismantled and reframed (Marshall, 1997a; Scheurich, 1997). Such inquiry could contribute to radical change or emancipation from oppressive social structures, either through a sustained critique or through direct advocacy and action taken by the researcher, often in collaboration with participants in the study. All these critiques share four assumptions:

(a) Research fundamentally involves issues of *power;* (b) the research report is not transparent, but rather it is *authored* by a raced, gendered, classed, and politically oriented individual; (c) race, class, and gender [among other social identities] are crucial for understanding experience; and (d) historically, *traditional research has silenced* members of oppressed and marginalized groups. (Rossman & Rallis, 2003, p. 93)

These newer perspectives on qualitative research contain three injunctions: As researchers we (a) must examine how we represent the participants—the Other—in our work; (b) should scrutinize the "complex interplay of our own personal biography, power and status, interactions with participants, and [the] written word" (Rossman & Rallis, 2003, p. 93); and (c) must be vigilant about the dynamics of ethics and politics in our work. One implication of these concerns is that qualitative researchers pay close attention to their participants' reactions and to the *voice* they use in their work as a representation of the relationship between them and their participants.[2] Another is that the traditional criteria for judging the adequacy or trustworthiness of a work have become essentially contested. As a result, the novice researcher might be left floundering for guidance as to what *will* constitute thoughtful and ethical research. We return to these issues in Chapter 7.

Much of the critique of traditional qualitative research finds expression in narrative analysis, critical ethnography, action and participatory action research, feminist research, cultural studies, autoethnography, and performance ethnography. Each embraces the changing of existing social structures and processes as a primary purpose. Critical ethnography, participatory action research, and feminist research often have explicit emancipatory goals.

An interdisciplinary approach with many guises, *narrative analysis*, seeks to describe the meaning of experience for those who frequently are socially marginalized or oppressed, as they construct stories (narratives) about their lives. Life histories, biographies and autobiographies, oral histories, and personal narratives are all forms of narrative analysis. Each specific approach assumes that storytelling is integral to understanding lives and that all people construct narratives as a process in constructing and reconstructing identity (Sfard & Prusak, 2005). Some approaches focus on the sociolinguistic techniques a narrator uses, others on life events and a narrator's meaning-making. When framed by feminist or critical theory, narrative analysis also can have an emancipatory purpose (Bloom & Munro, 1995; Lather, 1991).

Critical ethnography is grounded in theories assuming that society is structured by class and status as well as by race, ethnicity, gender, and sexual orientation to maintain the oppression of marginalized groups. As defined by Madison, "Critical ethnography begins with an ethical responsibility to address processes of unfairness or injustice within a particular *lived* domain" (2005, p. 5). Critical ethnography developed from the commitment to radical education in several works sharply critical of accepted teaching practice (hooks, 1994; Keddie, 1971; Sharp & Green, 1975; Weis, 1990; Weis & Fine, 2000; Young, 1971). Later work of this type has focused on the constraints on adopting radical teaching practices (Atkinson, Delamont, & Hammersly, 1988). Critical ethnography can also go beyond the classroom to ask questions about the historical forces shaping societal patterns as well as the fundamental issues and dilemmas of policy, power, and dominance in institutions, including their role in reproducing and reinforcing inequities such as those based on gender and race (Anderson, 1989; Anderson & Herr, 1993; Kelly & Gaskell, 1996; Marshall, 1991, 1997a).

Action research challenges the claim of neutrality and objectivity by traditional social science and seeks full, collaborative inquiry by all participants, often to engage in sustained change in organizations, communities, or institutions (Stringer, 1999). It seeks to decentralize traditional research by staying committed to local contexts rather than to the quest for Truth and to the liberation of research from its excessive reliance on the "restrictive conventional rules of the research game" (Guba, in Stringer, 1996, p. x). When ideally executed, action research blurs the distinctions between researcher and participants, creating a democratic inquiry process. It is often practiced in organizational contexts and in education, where professionals collaboratively question their practice, make changes, and assess the effects of those changes (Kemmis & McTaggart, 1982; McKernan, 1991; McNiff & Whitehead, 2003; Miller, 1990; Sagor, 2005). Also active in social work, business management, and community development (Hollingsworth, 1997), researchers who engage in action research do so to improve their practice.

More visible in international work, *participatory action research* draws on the precept of emancipation, as articulated by Friere (1970), that sustainable empowerment and development must begin with the concerns of the marginalized (Park, Brydon-Miller, Hall, & Jackson, 1993). In addition to an explicit commitment to action, the hallmark of participatory action research is full collaboration between researcher and participants in posing the questions to be pursued and in gathering data to respond to them. It entails a cycle of research, reflection, and action. Examples include research by Maguire (2000) on battered women, by Phaik-Lah (1997) in Malaysia on World Bank projects, and by Titchen and Bennie (1993) on training for nursing. McTaggart (1997) described it well.

Feminist theories frame research across issues and disciplines. One of their key commitments is to place women at the center and to identify patriarchy as the key structure for understanding experience. Feminist perspectives "uncover cultural and institutional sources and forces of oppression. . . . They name and value women's subjective experience" (Marshall, 1997a, p. 12). Feminist work examines gender differences in schools (Clarricoates, 1980, 1987), the development of adolescent girls (Griffin, 1985; Lees, 1986), and the challenges made by Indonesian women to the male dominance of shaman rituals (Tsing, 1990). By combining feminist and critical perspectives, scholars dismantle traditional policy analysis that has failed to incorporate women (Marshall, 1997a) and create research agendas that challenge the legitimacy of the dominant order and turn critical thought into emancipating action (Lather, 1991). Different feminisms frame different research goals (Collins, 1990; Marshall, 1997a; Tong, 1989). For example, socialist, so-called women's-ways feminisms focus on women in leadership positions to expand leadership theory; power-and-politics feminisms examine the state-imposed oppression of women in welfare, medical, and other systems the state regulates, grounding "research, policy and action [in] the political choices and power-driven ideologies and embedded forces that categorize, oppress, and exclude" (Marshall, 1997a, p. 13).

The domain of *cultural studies* is broad and diverse, encompassing a set of theoretical and political commitments in research. It takes culture as the central, organizing concept while it problematizes that notion by questioning the historical essentializing tendencies of studies of culture by cultural anthropology and the sociology of culture. Originating after World War II and generated in part by burgeoning media (especially television), cultural studies has concentrated on "the ordinary culture . . . of its own society" (Frow & Morris, 2000, p. 329). Researchers challenge totalizing conceptions of culture but still focus on groups and identity, often as people construct and reconstruct notions of identity in the mundane aspects of their lives.

We should note here the recent development of postcritical ethnography, which moves beyond critical ethnography to explicitly incorporate postmodern perspectives. This discourse community develops critical social narratives that are ethnographies in the traditional sense but in which the involved social scientist explicitly takes a political stand (Everhart, 2005). Postcritical ethnographers use narrative, performance, poetry, autoethnography, and ethnographic fiction as their forms of representation. Their goal is to take a stand (like participatory action researchers) and have greater impact than that allowed by a 20-page article in an academic journal or a book read by 40 people (Noblit, Flores, & Murillo, 2005). An example closely linked to the more familiar autobiography is the genre of *autoethnography,* which has evolved over the past two decades. Using the self as both subject and object, its inquiry proceeds through "multiple layers of consciousness, connecting the personal to the cultural" (Ellis & Bochner, 2000, p. 739). The self is deployed as an exemplar through which social processes and identities are constructed and contested, changed and resisted.

Another of postcritical ethnography's forms of representation that has entered the lexicon of qualitative scholars is the notion of performance. *Performance ethnography* has become a critical mode of representing ethnographic materials, "the staged reenactment of ethnographically derived notes" (Alexander, 2005, p. 411). Embodying cultural knowledge through performance not only depicts cultural practice but might lead to social change, as actors and audience reconceptualize their social circumstances. This genre also evokes cultural performance: the methods and resources available to members of a community or social identity group to construct and reconstruct (perform) those identities. (See Denzin, 2005, for an example.)

The preceding discussion is intended to provide ways of categorizing a variety of qualitative research genres and approaches as well as to depict the current critical, feminist, and postmodern critiques of traditional social science inquiry. As we note, systematic inquiry in each genre occurs in a natural setting rather than an artificially constrained one, such as a laboratory. The approaches, however, vary depending on theory and ideology, the focus of interest (be it individual, group or organization, or a communicative interaction, such as a text), the degree of interaction between researcher and participants in gathering data, and the participants' role in the research. The discussion was intended to provide some sense of the array of paradigms and approaches under the qualitative research umbrella. This text, however, cannot do justice to the detailed and nuanced variety of qualitative methods; we refer you to additional sources at the end of this chapter. Some of these sources are classic—the "grandmothers and grandfathers" in the field; others reflect emergent perspectives. Our purpose in this book is to describe the generic process of designing qualitative research that immerses researchers in the everyday life of a setting chosen for study. These researchers value and seek to discover participants' perspectives on their worlds and view inquiry as an interactive process between the researcher and the participants. The process is both descriptive and analytic and uses people's words and observable behavior as the primary data. Whether or not some single methodological refinement is qualitative could be debated in another arena. We hope to give practical guidance to those embarking on an exciting, sometimes frustrating, and ultimately rewarding journey into qualitative inquiry.

* * * * *

The evocative case study, the rich description of ethnography, the narratives of complex personal journeys all are the products of systematic inquiry. In their beginnings, however, they were modest research proposals. Qualitative researchers have had to search hard to find useful guidelines for writing thorough, convincing research proposals.[3] Too often, policy studies offer findings and recommendations with little sense of how the research led to them. Some written reports of qualitative research lack sufficient detail to provide strong examples of how they were designed; beginning qualitative researchers have difficulty learning how to write proposals from such reports. Others are written as if the process unfolded smoothly, with none of the messiness inherent in this research. These versions are also difficult to learn from. This book provides specific guidance for writing strong, convincing proposals for research grounded in the assumptions and practice of qualitative methodology.

Although qualitative research has an accepted place in formal research arenas—the amazing takeover described above—dissertation committees and reviewers for funding agencies still need to see proposals that are well developed, sound, rigorous, and ethical. This book, organized as a guide through the process of writing a qualitative research proposal, shows how to write a proposal that reassures reviewers by defining explicit steps to follow, principles to adhere to, and rationales for the strengths of qualitative research.

Sociologists, community psychologists, criminologists, anthropologists, political scientists, regional planners, and others from a range of the social sciences and applied fields will find this guide useful. Although many of the examples come from education (because our own backgrounds are there), the principles, challenges, and opportunities are transferable across disciplines and into other applied fields.

This book does not replace the numerous texts, readers, and journal articles that are important for learning qualitative methodology. It is meant to complement those resources that explicate the philosophical bases, history, and findings of qualitative studies. Its purpose is to give practical, useful guidance for writing proposals that fit within the qualitative paradigm and that are successful.

We should mention here, as a cautionary note, that many of the examples presented here—indeed, the entire structure and organization of the book—suggest that the processes of proposal development are linear and transparent. As we note throughout the text, this is not the case. The vignettes are written in well-polished prose, often because they are the final versions of sections in successful proposals. The structure of the book may suggest that one proceed from point A to point B in a seamless and quite logical manner. Such are the challenges of presenting an iterative, recursive process in formal academic writing. The looping back and forth, the frustrations are masked. We trust that the reader will keep this in mind.

❖ THE CHALLENGES

Researchers who would conduct qualitative research face three challenges: (a) developing a conceptual framework for the study that is thorough, concise, and elegant; (b) planning a design that is systematic and manageable, yet flexible; and (c) integrating these into a coherent document that convinces the proposal readers (a funding agency or a dissertation committee) that the study should be done, can be done, and will be done.

"Should-Do-Ability"

The first challenge is to build an argument that the study will contribute to theory and research: that is, to the ongoing conversation in a social science discipline or an applied field. The researcher should argue that the study will be significant to policy and practice and address the familiar question, *So what?* She should respond cogently and knowledgeably when asked why the study should be conducted.

"Do-Ability"

The second challenge is to demonstrate the feasibility, the "do-ability," of the study. This depends on judgments about resources (time, money), access to the site or population of interest or both, ethical considerations, and the researcher's knowledge and skills. Proposals seeking external funding and those for dissertation research *must* include a discussion of resources. Strategies to gain access to a site or to identify participants for the study should also be discussed. Both the generic ethical issues in qualitative research and those specific to the site or the participants should be analyzed thoughtfully and sensitively. Throughout the proposal, the researcher should demonstrate her[4] competence to conduct a thorough, ethical, qualitative research study. In citing the methodological literature and discussing pilot studies or previous research, the researcher demonstrates her experience in conducting qualitative research and familiarity with the ongoing discourse on methodology and situates her own work within the evolving context of research.

"Want-to-Do-Ability"

In contrast, "want-to-do-ability" is solely a function of the researcher's engagement in the topic. Far removed from the days of dispassionate science, the qualitative researcher cares deeply about the substance of the inquiry at hand. Qualitative research, however, is neither naively subjectivist nor biased (criticisms that are all too common). Rather, it acknowledges that *all* research in social science may well be subjective and shifts the discourse to a discussion of epistemology and to strategies for ensuring trustworthy and credible studies. The proposal, then, is an argument that makes the case that the study can and should be done and that there is sufficient energy and interest to sustain it.

❖ DEVELOPING AN ARGUMENT

Central to this book is the premise that developing a proposal is a process of building an *argument* that supports the proposal. Like the logic of formal debate or the reasoning in a position paper, a research proposal is intended to convince the reader that the research holds potential significance and relevance, that the design of the study is sound, and that the researcher is capable of conducting the study successfully. The proposal writer must, therefore, build a logical argument for the endeavor, amass evidence in support of each point, and show the entire enterprise to be conceptually integrated. As Maxwell (2005) notes, "A proposal is an argument *for* your study. It needs to explain the logic behind the proposed research, rather than simply describe or summarize the study, and to do so in a way that nonspecialists will understand" (p. 119).

Research proposals consist of two major sections: the conceptual framework and the design and research methods. Roughly corresponding to the *what*—the substantive focus of the inquiry—and the *how*—the means for conducting it—these two sections of the proposal describe in detail the specific topic or issue to be explored and the proposed means of exploration. In a sound, well-developed, well-argued proposal, the sections are integrally related: They share common epistemological assumptions; research questions and methods chosen to explore the topic are congruent and related to one another organically.

Conceptual Framework

The first section of the proposal—the conceptual framework—demands a solid rationale. In examining a specific setting or set of individuals, the writer should show how she is studying a case in a larger phenomenon. By linking the specific research questions to larger theoretical constructs or to important policy issues, the writer shows that the particulars of the study serve to illuminate larger issues and therefore hold potential significance for that field. The doctoral student in economics, for example, who demonstrates that his qualitative case studies of five families' financial decision making are relevant for understanding larger forces in the marketplace has met this condition. The case studies are significant because they illuminate in detail larger economic forces while focusing on individuals.

A research design also can stipulate phenomenological, in-depth interviewing as the sole method of data collection. By linking that approach to socialization theory, one can begin to build a case for the proposal, a case that grounds it in important theoretical and empirical literatures. We develop the logic undergirding the conceptual framework in Chapter 2.

Design Soundness

The second area in which to build a sound argument for the proposal is its design. The writer should show that the design is the result of a series of decisions she has made based on knowledge gained from the methodological literature and previous work. Those decisions should not derive just from the methodological literature, however. Their justification should also flow logically from the research questions and from their conceptual framework.

Because qualitative research proposals are at times unfamiliar to reviewers, the logic supporting the choice of those methods must be sound. Ensuring a clear, logical rationale in support of qualitative methods entails attention to seven topics:

1. the assumptions of qualitative approaches;

2. the logic for selecting a site, a sample, the participants, or any combination of these;

3. the choice of overall design and data collection methods;

4. an acknowledgment of the intensive aspects of fieldwork;

5. a consideration of ethical issues;

6. the resource needs; and

7. attention to the trustworthiness of the overall design.

The first five of these areas are considered in detail in Chapters 1 through 5; resource needs are discussed in Chapter 6; and ensuring the trustworthiness of the study is elaborated in Chapter 7.

Researcher Competence

Finally, in developing an argument to support the proposal, the writer should explicitly and implicitly demonstrate competence. The exact standard of competence applied for evaluating the proposal depends on the purpose and scope of the research. Standards applied to a dissertation proposal will likely differ from those used to evaluate a multiyear-funded project written by established researchers. Paradoxically, even though dissertation research is intended to provide an opportunity for learning the craft, careful scrutiny will be given to all portions of the dissertation proposal. Writers will be expected to show their capability by thorough attention to every facet of the conceptual framework and the research design. Established researchers, on the other hand, may not receive such careful scrutiny because their record of previous work engenders trust, and the logic of good faith preserves standards for research. Although this may seem unfair, it nevertheless is the reality of proposal evaluation.

To demonstrate competence, then, proposal writers should refer to their previous work and discuss the strengths and weaknesses of a pilot study as well as their course work and other relevant education. The high quality of the proposal's organization and its conceptual framework must be discussed, along with the relevant literature and design.

To illuminate this process of building an argument to support qualitative research, we offer two fictitious vignettes. The first describes a doctoral student in sociology convincing her dissertation committee that qualitative methods are best suited for exploratory research on the culture of a hospital. She intends to uncover patterns in the work lives of participants that will lead to important improvements in the treatment of patients. Vignette 2 shows researchers building a rationale based on the strengths of qualitative methods for policy analysis. The researchers had to convince legislators that qualitative methods would yield useful, vivid analyses that could inform the policy-making process. Following the vignettes, we develop the implications for building an argument in support of qualitative proposals and provide an overview of the rest of the book.

VIGNETTE 1

Justifying Fieldwork to Explore Organizational Culture

As O'Brien reviewed the notes she had written to help with the proposal defense, she realized that her strongest argument rested on two aspects of the proposed study's significance: its exploratory purpose and its commitment to improving patient treatment in large urban hospitals. She realized that the latter aspect might be construed as biased, but if she kept the rationale grounded in the need to better understand complex interactions, tacit processes, and often-hidden beliefs and values, she could demonstrate the study's clear potential to improve practice.

Her committee was composed of two quantitatively trained sociologists and a medical anthropologist. She knew she had the support of the anthropologist, whose advice had been crucial during the several proposal drafts she had written. The sociologists, however, were more likely to be critical of the design.

O'Brien decided to begin her presentation with an explication of the four purposes of research (exploration, explanation, description, and prediction) to link the purpose of her proposed study to general principles regarding the conduct of inquiry. She could then proceed quite logically to a discussion of the ways in which exploratory research serves to identify important variables for subsequent explanatory or predictive research. This logic could allay the concerns of the two quantitatively oriented sociologists, who would search the proposal for testable hypotheses, instrumentation and operationalization of variables, and tests of reliability.

The second major justification of the study would develop from its significance for practice. O'Brien recalled how she had reviewed empirical studies indicating that organizational conditions had a significant effect on wellness and hospital leaving rates. What had not been identified in those studies were the specific interactions between hospital staff and patients, the widely shared beliefs about patients among the staff, and the organizational norms governing patient treatment. Her research, she would argue, would help identify those tacit, often hidden, aspects of organizational life. This, in turn, could be useful both for policy regarding health care and for practice in health care facilities.

That O'Brien would be engaging in exploratory research where the relevant variables had not been identified and uncovering the tacit aspects of organizational life strongly suggested qualitative methods. Fieldwork would be most appropriate for discovering the relevant variables and building a thorough, rich, detailed description of hospital culture. By linking her proposed research to concepts familiar to the quantitative sociologists, O'Brien hoped to draw the sociologists into the logic supporting her proposal and to convince them of its sound design.

A researcher's first task, even before formulating the proposal, is quite often to convince critics that the research will be useful. O'Brien faces this challenge and develops a rationale supporting her choice of qualitative research methods. In many cases, and especially in policy research, one can appeal to policymakers' frustration with previous research. The researcher should convince them that qualitative research will lead to strong, detailed conclusions and recommendations. The next vignette shows how two policy analysts convinced their superiors that they could answer pressing questions with qualitative methods.

VIGNETTE 2

Convincing Policymakers of the Utility of Qualitative Methods

Why, 6 months after state legislators had allocated $10 million to provide temporary shelters, were homeless families still sleeping in cars? Keppel and Wilson, researchers in the legislative analyst's office, knew that the question demanded qualitative research methodology. Convincing their skeptical superiors, however, would be a real challenge. They scoured their texts on research methods, selected convincing phrases and examples, and prepared a memo to demonstrate the viability of qualitative research and to build the capacity of the legislative analyst's office in that direction. They argued that, too often, the office's research and evaluations missed the mark. The memo began with a quote about how an approximate answer to the right question is better than an exact answer to the **wrong** question. The winning points, though, in their presentation to their superiors came from two major points. They first pointed out the numerous implementation questions concerning homelessness that needed to be explored in the real-world setting. Second, they pointed out that certain subtleties of the policy implementation process had to be explored to understand fully what was happening. They spoke of needing to discover the right questions to ask so that the systematic collection of data would follow. Thus, Keppel and Wilson convinced their superiors that their findings would help define the important questions, describe patterns of implementation, and identify the challenges and barriers that could lead to more effective policy outcomes.

In Vignette 2, we see researchers convincing others that a qualitative study was needed. This underscores the notion that researchers proposing qualitative inquiry do best by emphasizing the promise of quality, depth, and richness in the findings. They may, however, encounter puzzlement and resistance from those accustomed to surveys and quasi-experimental research and may need to translate between qualitative and quantitative paradigms. Researchers who are convinced that a qualitative approach is best for the question or problem at hand should make a case that "thick description" (Geertz, 1973, p. 5) and systematic and detailed analysis will yield valuable explanations of processes.

❖ OVERVIEW OF THE BOOK

The remainder of the book takes the reader through the sections of a qualitative research proposal. Chapter 2 discusses the complex task of building a conceptual framework around the study. This process entails moving beyond the initial puzzle or intriguing paradox by embedding it in appropriate traditions of research, linking the specific case to larger theoretical domains. The argument also should demonstrate the proposed study's significance for larger social policy issues, concerns of practice, and people's everyday lives or to some combination of these. Thus, the study's general focus and research questions, the literature, and the significance of the work are interrelated. We call this the substantive focus of the study—the *what*.

Chapter 3 presents a detailed discussion of the *how* of the study. Having focused on a research topic with a set of questions or a domain to explore, the proposal should describe how systematic inquiry will yield data that will respond to the questions. The writer should discuss the logic and assumptions of the overall design and the methods, linking these directly to the focus of the study and justifying the choice of qualitative methods.

Chapter 4 describes primary and secondary methods of data collection. This chapter is not intended to replace the many exemplary texts that deal in great detail with methods; rather, we present a brief discussion of various alternatives and their strengths and weaknesses. Chapter 5 describes procedures for managing, recording, and analyzing qualitative data. This discussion is necessarily brief because, although the writer cannot specify the exact categories and themes for analysis at the proposal stage, he can describe the strategy he will use and link this to the conceptual framework of the study.

Chapter 6 describes the complex, dialectical process of projecting the resources necessary for the study. Time, personnel, and financial resources should be considered. Finally, Chapter 7 revisits the image introduced here of the proposal as an argument. We discuss criteria for evaluating the soundness and competence of a qualitative proposal, with special attention to building a logical rationale and answering challenges from critics.

Throughout the book, we use vignettes to illustrate our points. Most of these are drawn from our own work and that of other social scientists; a few are fictitious with no references to published work. The principles depicted in the vignettes apply to research grounded in several disciplines as well as in the applied fields; they challenge you, the reader, to apply them to your own design.

Two themes run through this book. The first is that *design flexibility* is a crucial feature of qualitative inquiry, even though demands for specificity in design and method seem to preclude such flexibility. We urge the researcher to think of the proposal as an initial plan: one that is thorough, sound, well-thought-out, and based on current knowledge. The proposal reveals the researcher's sensitivity to the setting, the issues to be explored, and the ethical dilemmas sure to be encountered, but it also reminds a reader that considerations as yet unforeseen may well dictate changes in this initial plan. Therefore, the language used in discussing the design and methods is sure, positive, and active, while reserving for the researcher the right to modify what is currently proposed.

The second theme, which we have already introduced, is that the *proposal is an argument*. Because its primary purpose is to convince the reader that the research is substantive and will contribute to the field, that it is well conceived and that the researcher is capable of carrying it through, the proposal should rely on reasoning and evidence sufficient to convince the reader: the logic undergirding it should be carefully argued. All this will demonstrate a thorough knowledge of both the topic to be explored and the methods to be used. At times, we give guidance and use terminology that should assist in translating qualitative design assumptions for more quantitatively oriented audiences. In thinking of the proposal as an argument, we often mention the reader of the proposal to remind you, the reader of this book, that a sense of audience is critically important in crafting a solid research proposal. Finally, at the end of each chapter you will find a dialogue between two graduate students that we hope will provide a model of the kind of dialogues you will have with others learning about qualitative proposals.

DIALOGUE BETWEEN LEARNERS

Hi Aaron,

So, if we're to work together during the book revision, I suppose we should introduce ourselves! I'm Melanie, Catherine Marshall's research assistant, and a doctoral candidate in UNC-CH's education program. I'm in the dissertation phase right now–just finished my data collection–and I'm working on my analysis now. Not surprisingly, I chose to do a qualitative study. Because I'm focused on teacher education, reflection, and technology, for my study I chose to follow a group of student teachers who agreed to maintain Weblogs during their year of graduate study. I am looking at the "results" of their Weblogs for reflectivity, ownership, attitude toward technology, so on and so forth. A qualitative approach really supports my desire to include the students' voices in the study, while providing a framework that encourages multiple answers and flexible methods–and I know I'm lucky that there is support for these factors in my program.

What about you? What are your research interests? Are you focusing on qualitative approaches? What helped you make the decision one way or the other? Do you have support for that decision?

Looking forward to working with you,

Melanie

Melanie,

Great to hear from you. Like you, I'm also in the dissertation phase, only just barely. I'm working on narrowing down my proposal and thinking through the many choices that reveal themselves to someone beginning a qualitative research project. I'm interested in merging two interests of mine in my dissertation: the philosophical assumptions we make when we structure universities along disciplinary lines and faculty activism. Though they both might seem rather disparate, I'm hoping to bring them together by examining the effect (if any) of the disciplines on how faculty define and render activism in their daily work. I have support for looking at this qualitatively, though I think mainly because I've made it known from the day I started here that I don't have much love for quantitative work; my values simply don't match up with the overarching assumptions that make quantitative work possible.

I'm looking forward to e-mailing a bit more.

Take care,

Aaron

❖ NOTES

1. Burrell and Morgan (1979) provide one useful way for understanding research paradigms and the assumptions they embrace; Rossman and Rallis (2003) rely on their conceptualization to help situate various qualitative research genres. The discussion here draws on the work of Rossman and Rallis.

2. We address this more fully in Chapters 3 and 7, but here we note that participants may disagree with the researcher's report and that passive constructions ("the research was conducted") suggest anonymity and distance, whereas active ones ("we conducted the research") claim agency.

3. Recent works, in addition to this text, provide guidance. See, for example, *Research Design: Qualitative, Quantitative, and Mixed Methods Approaches* (2nd ed.), by J. W. Creswell (2003), and *Qualitative Research Design: An Interactive Approach* (2nd ed.), by J. A. Maxwell (2005).

4. Throughout the text, we alternate between *he* and *she* when referring to the qualitative researcher.

❖ FURTHER READING

Introductions to Qualitative Research

Bogdan, R. C., & Biklen, S. K. (2003). *Qualitative research for education: An introduction to theory and methods* (4th ed.). Boston: Allyn & Bacon.

Eisner, E. W. (1991). *The enlightened eye: Qualitative inquiry and the enhancement of educational practice.* New York: Macmillan.

Glesne, C. (1999). *Becoming qualitative researchers: An introduction* (2nd ed.). New York: Longman.

Lincoln, Y. S., & Guba, E. G. (1985). *Naturalistic inquiry.* Beverly Hills, CA: Sage.

Rossman, G. B., & Rallis, S. F. (2003). *Learning in the field: An introduction to qualitative research* (2nd ed.). Thousand Oaks, CA: Sage.

Schwartz, H., & Jacobs, J. (1979). *Qualitative sociology: A method to the madness.* New York: Free Press.

Silverman, D. (2005). *Doing qualitative research* (2nd ed.). Thousand Oaks, CA: Sage.

Strauss, A., & Corbin, J. (1990). *Basics of qualitative research.* Newbury Park, CA: Sage.

Taylor, J. J., & Bogdan, R. (1984). *An introduction to qualitative research: The search for meanings* (2nd ed.). New York: John Wiley.

On Narrative Analysis

Clandinin, D. J., & Connelly, F. M. (2000). *Narrative inquiry: Experience and story in qualitative research.* San Francisco: Jossey-Bass.

Hatch, J. A., & Wisniewski, R. (Eds.). (1995). *Life history and narrative.* London: Falmer.

Josselson, R. (Ed.). (1996). *Ethics and process in the narrative study of lives.* Thousand Oaks, CA: Sage.

Josselson, R., & Lieblich, A. (Eds.). (1993). *The narrative study of lives.* Newbury Park, CA: Sage.

Riessman, C. (1993). *Narrative analysis.* Newbury Park, CA: Sage.

On Action Research

Heron, J. (1996). *Co-operative inquiry: Research into the human condition.* Thousand Oaks, CA: Sage.

Hollingsworth, S. (Ed.). (1997). *International action research: A casebook for educational reform.* London: Falmer.

Kincheloe, J. L. (1991). *Teachers as researchers: Qualitative inquiry as a path to empowerment.* London: Falmer.

McNiff, J., & Whitehead, J. (2003). *Action research: Principles and practice.* London: Routledge.

Sagor, R. (2005). *Action research handbook: A four-step process for educators and school teams.* Thousand Oaks, CA: Corwin.

Stringer, E. T. (1999). *Action research: A handbook for practitioners* (2nd ed.). Thousand Oaks, CA: Sage.

On Critical and Postcritical Ethnography

Carspecken, P. F. (1996). *Critical ethnography in educational research: A theoretical and practical guide.* New York: Routledge & Kegan Paul.

Gitlin, A. (Ed.). (1994). *Power and method: Political activism and educational research.* New York: Routledge.

Madison, D. S. (2005). *Critical ethnography: Method, ethics, and performance.* Thousand Oaks, CA: Sage.

Marcus, G., & Fischer, M. (1986). *Anthropology as cultural critique: An experimental moment in the human sciences.* Chicago: University of Chicago Press.

Morrow, R. A., with Brown, D. D. (1994). *Critical theory and methodology.* Thousand Oaks, CA: Sage.

Noblit, G. W., Flores, S. Y., & Murillo, E. G. Jr. (Eds.). (2005). *Postcritical ethnography: Reinscribing critique.* Cresskill, NJ: Hampton Press.

Weis, L. (1990). *Working class without work: High school students in a de-industrializing economy.* New York: Routledge.

Weis, L., & Fine, M. (Eds.). (2000). *Construction sites: Excavating race, class, and gender among urban youth.* New York: Teachers College Press.

On Participatory Action Research

Cooke, B., & Kothari, U. (Eds.). (2001). *Participation: The new tyranny?* London: Zed Books.

Hart, R. A. (1997). *Children's participation: The theory and practice of involving young citizens in community development and environmental care*. London: Earthscan.

Hickey, S., & Mohan, G. (Eds.). (2004). *Participation: From tyranny to transformation?* London: Zed Books.

Maguire, P. (2000). *Doing participatory research: A feminist approach*. Amherst, MA: Center for International Education.

McTaggart, R. (Ed.). (1997). *Participatory action research: International contexts and consequences*. Albany: State University of New York Press.

Park, P., Brydon-Miller, M., Hall, B., & Jackson, T. (Eds.). (1993). *Voices of change: Participatory research in the United States and Canada*. Ontario, Canada: Ontario Institute for Studies in Education Press.

Selener, D. (1997). *Participatory action research and social change*. Cornell, NY: Cornell Participatory Action Research Network.

Whyte, W. F. (Ed.). (1991). *Participatory action research*. Newbury Park, CA: Sage.

On Feminist Research

Harding, S. (Ed.). (1987). *Feminism and methodology*. Bloomington: Indiana University Press.

Lather, P. (1991). *Getting smart: Feminist research and pedagogy with/in the postmodern*. New York: Routledge & Kegan Paul.

Marshall, C. (Ed.). (1997). *Feminist critical policy analysis: A perspective from primary and secondary schooling*. London: Falmer.

Marshall, C., & Young, M. (2006). Gender and methodology. In C. Skelton, B. Francis, & L. Smulyan, *Handbook of Gender and Education*. Thousand Oaks: Sage.

Nielson, J. (Ed.). (1990). *Feminist research methods: Exemplary readings in the social sciences*. Boulder, CO: Westview.

2

The What of the Study

Building the Conceptual Framework

W hat is research? What is a research proposal? How do the two relate to each other? For the social scientist or researcher in applied fields, research is a process of trying to gain a better understanding of the complexities of human experience and, in some genres of research, to take action based on that understanding. Through systematic and sometimes collaborative strategies, the researcher gathers information about actions and interactions, reflects on their meaning, arrives at and evaluates conclusions, and eventually puts forward an interpretation, most frequently in written form. Quite unlike its pristine and logical presentation in journal articles—"the reconstructed logic of science" (Kaplan, 1964)—real research is often confusing, messy, intensely frustrating, and fundamentally nonlinear. In critiquing the way journal articles display research as a supremely sequential and objective endeavor, Bargar and Duncan (1982) describe how "through such highly standardized reporting practices, scientists inadvertently hide from view the real inner drama of their work, with its intuitive base, its halting time-line, and its extensive recycling of concepts and perspectives" (p. 2).

The researcher begins with interesting, curious, or anomalous phenomena that he observes, discovers, or stumbles across. Like the detective work of Sherlock Holmes or the best traditions in investigative reporting, research seeks to explain, describe, explore, and/or critique the phenomenon chosen for study. Emancipatory genres, such as those represented by some critical, feminist, or postmodern work, also make explicit their intent to act toward the change of oppressive circumstances. The commitment of these emancipatory genres to social justice is increasingly present in all genres of qualitative inquiry. Thus, the research proposal is *a plan for engaging in systematic inquiry* to bring about a better understanding of the phenomenon and/or to change problematic social circumstances. As discussed in Chapter 1, the finished proposal should demonstrate that (a) the research is worth doing, (b) the researcher is competent to conduct the study, and (c) the study is carefully planned and can be executed successfully.

A proposal for the conduct of any research represents *decisions* the researcher has made that a theoretical framework, design, and methodology will generate data appropriate for responding to the research questions and will conform to ethical standards. These decisions emerge through intuition, complex reasoning, and the weighing of a number of possible research questions, possible conceptual frameworks, and alternative designs and strategies for gathering data. Throughout, the researcher considers the "should-do-ability," "do-ability," and "want-to-do-ability" of the proposed project (discussed in Chapter 1). This is the complex, dialectical process of designing a qualitative study. This chapter discusses how, in qualitative design, you are deciding among possible research questions, frameworks, approaches, sites, and data collection methods. Building the research proposal demands that the researcher consider all elements of the proposal *at the same time*. As noted in Chapter 1, this recursive process is complex and intellectually challenging because the researcher needs to consider multiple elements—multiple decisions and choices—of the proposal simultaneously. But how to begin? This is often the most challenging aspect of developing a solid proposal.

Our experience suggests that research interests may have their origins in deeply personal interests, professional commitments and concerns, intriguing theoretical frameworks, methodological predilections, and/or recurring social problems. Whatever their source, these interests must be transformed into a logical proposal that articulates key elements and demonstrates competence. We offer one model for those elements, recognizing that much thought and drafting have preceded this formal, public writing.

❖ SECTIONS OF THE PROPOSAL

Proposals for qualitative research vary in format but typically include the following three sections: (a) *the introduction,* which includes an overview of the proposal, a discussion of the topic or focus of the inquiry and the general research questions, the study's purpose and potential significance, and its limitations; (b) *a discussion of related literature,* that situates the study in the ongoing discourse about the topic and develops the specific intellectual traditions to which the study is linked; and (c) *the research design and methods,* which detail the overall design, the site or population of interest, the specific methods for gathering data, a preliminary discussion of strategies for analyzing the data and for ensuring the trustworthiness of the study, a biography of the researcher, and ethical and political issues that may arise in the conduct of the study. In all research, these sections are interrelated, each one building on the others. They are listed in Table 2.1. In qualitative inquiry, the proposal should reserve some flexibility in research questions and design because these are likely to change. The next section provides some strategies for building a clear conceptual framework while retaining the flexibility to allow the unanticipated to emerge.

Table 2.1   Sections of a Qualitative Research Proposal

Introduction

Overview
Topic and purpose
Potential significance
Framework and general research questions
Limitations

Review of related literature

Theoretical traditions
Essays by experts
Related research

Design and methodology

Overall approach and rationale
Site or population selection
Data gathering methods
Data-analysis procedures
Trustworthiness
Personal biography
Ethical and political considerations

Appendixes

❖ BUILDING THE CONCEPTUAL FRAMEWORK:
    TOPIC, PURPOSE, AND SIGNIFICANCE

The purposes of this section of the proposal are (a) to describe the substantive focus of the research—the topic—and its purpose; (b) to frame it in larger theoretical, policy, social, or practical domains and thereby develop its significance; (c) to pose initial research questions; (d) to forecast the literature to be reviewed; and (e) to discuss the limitations of the study. The proposal writer should organize the information so that a reader can clearly ascertain the essence of the research study. This section, along with the review of related literature, forms the conceptual framework of the study and informs the reader of the study's substantive focus and purpose. The design section then describes how the study will be conducted and showcases the writer's ability to conduct the study.

Although separated into sections by convention, the narrative of the first two sections—the introduction and the review of related literature—is derived from a thorough familiarity with the literature on relevant theory, empirical studies, reviews of research, and informed essays by experts. A careful reading of the related literature serves two purposes. First, it provides evidence for the significance of the study for practice and policy and for its contribution to the ongoing discourse about the topic (often referred to as contributing to "knowledge"). Second, it identifies the important intellectual traditions that guide the study, thereby developing a conceptual framework and refining an important and viable research question.

Because of the interrelatedness of the sections and because writing is developmental and recursive—a "method of inquiry" itself (Richardson, 2000, p. 923)—the writer may find it necessary to rewrite the research questions or problem statement after reviewing the literature or to refocus the significance of the research after its design is developed. Bargar and Duncan's (1982) description of "extensive recycling of concepts and perspectives" (p. 2) captures this dialectical process. Our advice is that the writer be sensitive to the need for change and flexibility and not rush to closure too soon. Sound ideas for research may come in a moment of inspiration, but the hard work is in developing, refining, and polishing the idea, the intellectual traditions that surround the idea, and the methods for exploring it.

Overview

The first section of the proposal provides an overview of the study for the reader. It introduces the topic or problem and the purpose of the study, the general research questions it will answer, and how it is designed. This section should be crisply written, engage the reader's interest, and anticipate sections to follow. First, the topic or problem that the study will address is introduced, linking this to practice, policy, social issues, and/or theory, thereby forecasting the study's significance. Next, the broad areas of theory and research to be discussed in the literature review are outlined. Then, the design of the study is sketched, focusing on the principal techniques for data collection and the unique features of the design. Finally, the introduction provides a transition to a more detailed discussion of the topic, the study's significance, and the research questions.

The Topic

The curiosity that inspires qualitative research often comes initially from observations of the real world, emerging from the interplay of direct experience with emerging theory, of political commitment with practice, as well as from growing scholarly interests, as noted above. At other times, a topic derives from the empirical research and traditions of theory. Beginning researchers should examine journals specifically committed to publishing extensive reviews of literature (e.g., *Review of Educational Research*, the *Annual Review of Sociology*, the *American Review of Public Administration*, the *Annual Review of Public Health*), peruse policy-oriented publications to learn about current or emerging issues in their fields, and talk with experts about crucial issues. They might also reflect on the intersection of their personal, professional, and political interests.

Inquiry cycles between theory, practice, research questions, and personal experience. A research project may begin at any point in this complex process. Considering possible research questions, potential sites, and individuals or groups to invite to participate in the research may lead to a focus for the study. Imagining potential sites or groups of people to work with may reshape the focus of the study. Thinking about sites or people for the study also encourages the researcher to think about her positionality and possible strategies for gathering data. The researcher may know of a site where intriguing issues of practice capture her imagination. Thinking about this site and the issues and people in it will foster analysis about which research questions are likely to be significant for practice. These questions then shape decisions about gathering data. Developing the research project proceeds dialectically as possible focuses of the research, questions, sites, and strategies for gathering data are considered.

Figure 2.1   Shiva's Circle of Constructivist Inquiry

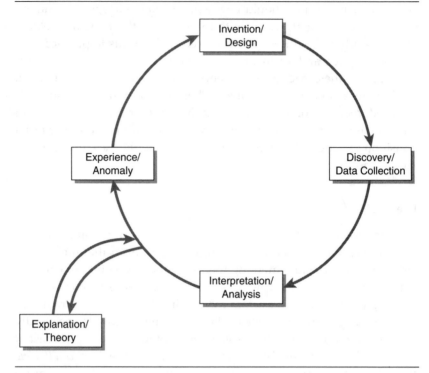

SOURCE: Crabtree and Miller (1992, p. 10). Reprinted by permission.

Crabtree and Miller (1992) offer useful conceptualizations of the *cycle of inquiry*. They argue that a metaphor for the process of much qualitative research is embedded in "Shiva's circle of constructivist inquiry," Shiva being the Hindu god of dance and death (see Figure 2.1). The researcher enters a cycle of interpretation with exquisite sensitivity to context, seeking no ultimate truths. She must be faithful to the dance, but she also stands apart from it, discovering and interpreting the "symbolic communication and meaning . . . that helps us maintain cultural life" (p. 10). A more radical process of inquiry is captured in Figure 2.2, which expresses critical, feminist, and some postmodern perspectives. Both models depict the researcher looking critically at experience and the larger social forces that shape it. She searches for expressions of domination, oppression, and power in daily life. Her goal is to unmask this "false consciousness" and create "a more empowered and emancipated

Figure 2.2   Global Eye of Critical/Ecological Inquiry

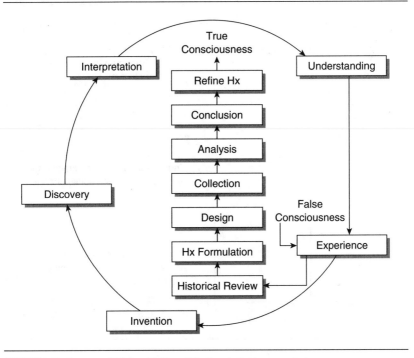

SOURCE: Crabtree and Miller (1992, p. 11). Reprinted by permission.
NOTE: Hx = hypotheses.

consciousness by reducing the illusions" of experience (Crabtree & Miller, pp. 10–11). Figures 2.1 and 2.2 provide somewhat differing images of the cycle of inquiry; note, however, that each entails question posing, design, data collection, analysis, and interpretation.

Especially in applied fields, such as management, nursing, community development, education, and clinical psychology, a strong autobiographical element often drives the study. A doctoral student in international development education, for example, studied insider-outsider tensions and dilemmas in refugee and immigrant groups in the United States because of her own professional work with similar groups in community development (Jones, 2004). A student in social psychology, deeply committed to the protection of the environment, studied environmental attitudes from the perspective of adult development theory (Greenwald, 1992). Another, a student in international development education, studied Indonesian farmers' views on land use because of her political commitment to indigenous peoples (Campbell-Nelson, 1997).

Figure 2.3   The Conceptual Funnel

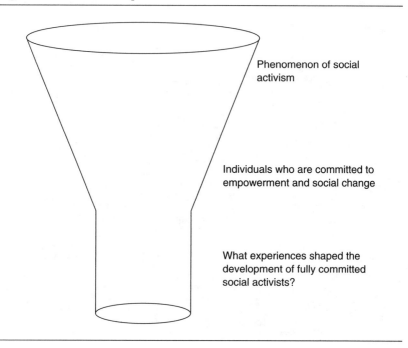

Phenomenon of social activism

Individuals who are committed to empowerment and social change

What experiences shaped the development of fully committed social activists?

The qualitative researcher's challenge is to demonstrate that this personal interest—increasingly referred to as the researcher's *positionality*—will not bias the study. Sensitivity to the methodological literature on the self and one's social identities in conducting inquiry, interpreting data, and constructing the final narrative helps accomplish this. Knowledge of the epistemological debate about what constitutes knowledge and knowledge claims, especially the critique of power and dominance in traditional research, is also valuable (see Chapter 1 on critical ethnography, feminist research, participatory action research, and postmodern perspectives). When direct experience stimulates the initial curiosity, the researcher needs to link that curiosity to general research questions. The mouth of the conceptual funnel, if you will, contains the general, or "grand tour," questions the study will explore; the specific focus for the proposed study is funneled from these questions.

Figure 2.3 illustrates the funnel as a metaphor, drawing on Benbow's (1994) study about the development of commitment to social action. The mouth of the funnel represents the general conceptual focus—the issue of social activism and its role in ameliorating oppressive circumstances.

The focus narrows, as a funnel does, to a concern with individuals who have demonstrated and lived an intense commitment to social causes or, possibly, to a focus on social movements as group phenomena. A research question (or set of questions) about how life experiences help shape and develop a lifelong, intensive commitment to social activism will slip through the funnel.

People develop personal theories—theories-in-use or tacit theories (Argyris & Schön, 1974)—about events as ways to reduce ambiguity and explain paradox. Those who conduct inquiry, however, should be guided by systematic considerations, such as existing theory and empirical research. Tacit theory (one's personal understanding) together with formal theory (from the literature) help bring a question, a curious phenomenon, or a problematic issue into focus and raise it to a level at which one might generalize about it. The potential research moves from a troubling or intriguing real-world observation (e.g., these kids won't volunteer in class no matter how much it's rewarded!), to personal theory (they care more about what other kids think than they do about grades), to formal theory, concepts, and models from literature (students' behavior is a function of the mediation of formal classroom expectations by the informal expectations of the student subculture). These coalesce to frame a focus for the study in the form of a research question: What are the expectations of the student subculture concerning class participation?

This complex process of conceptualizing, framing, and focusing a study typically begins with a personally defined question or identified problem. Personal observations are then transformed into systematic inquiry by reviewing the work of other scholars and practitioners on the topic, thereby building a theoretical rationale and conceptual framework to guide the study. Research questions can then be refined and the design of the study can be more tightly focused; decisions about where to go, what to look for, and how to move to real-world observations become more specific. As the researcher moves back and forth through these various stages, there are pertinent questions to pose:

- Personal observations:
  - How do I move from casual observations to systematic inquiry?
  - What previous research can help to frame my interests?
- Conceptual framework:
  - What is my specific focus?
  - What are useful and/or creative questions?
  - How do I connect the literature to real-life observations?

- Research design:
  - Where can I do this study? With whom?
  - How will I actually gather data?
  - What will I do with the data?
- Data analysis:
  - How will I manage the data?
  - Will I use software?
  - What themes might be there? How can the literature help here?
- Reporting:
  - Who is my audience?
  - What form should this take? How can I be creative?
  - How can I ensure the trustworthiness of my assertions? What canons do I use?
  - Who might want to use this research? How do I make it accessible to them?

This framework and these questions are intended to be suggestive of others to pose when going through this difficult process of conceptualizing and designing. However, as generic principles, the ideas apply to research in an urban neighborhood, with a legislative body, in a rural village in West Timor, Indonesia, or with newly arrived immigrant groups.

This early work of conceptualizing is the most difficult and intellectually rigorous of the entire process of proposal writing. It is messy and dialectical, as alternative frames (scholarly traditions) are examined for their power to illuminate and sharpen the research focus. As noted earlier, exploring possible designs and strategies for gathering data also enters into this initial process. The researcher must let go of some topics and captivating questions as he fine-tunes and focuses the study to ensure its do-ability. Although this entails loss, it bounds the study and protects the researcher from impractical ventures.

Intuition in this phase of the research process cannot be underestimated. Studies of eminent scientists reveal the central role of creative insight—intuition—in their thought processes (Briggs, 2000; Hoffman, 1972; Libby, 1922; Mooney, 1951). By allowing ideas to incubate and maintaining a healthy respect for the mind's capacity to reorganize and reconstruct, the researcher finds that richer research questions evolve. This observation is not intended to devalue the analytic process but, instead, to give the creative act its proper due. Bargar and Duncan (1982) note that research is a process "that religiously uses logical analysis as a critical tool in the *refinement* of ideas, but which often begins at a very different place, where imagery, metaphor and analogy, intuitive hunches, kinesthetic feeling states, and even dreams and dream-like states are prepotent" (p. 3).

Initial insights and recycled concepts begin the process of bounding and framing the research by defining the larger theoretical, policy, or social problem or issue of practice that the study will address. This complex thinking also begins to establish the study's parameters (what it is and what it is not) and to develop the conceptual framework that will ground it in ongoing research traditions.

Purpose of the Study

The researcher should also describe her intent in conducting the research—its purpose. Generally embedded in a discussion of the topic (often only a sentence or two but important nonetheless), a statement of the purpose of the study tells the reader what the research is likely to accomplish. Historically, qualitative methodologists have described three major purposes for research: *to explore, explain,* or *describe* a phenomenon. Synonyms for these terms could include *understand, develop,* or *discover.* Many qualitative studies are descriptive and exploratory: They build rich descriptions of complex circumstances that are unexplored in the literature. Others are explicitly explanatory: They show relationships (frequently as perceived by the participants in the study) between events and the meaning of the relationships. These traditional discussions of purpose, however, are silent about critique, action, advocacy, empowerment, or emancipation—the purposes often found in studies grounded in critical, feminist, or postmodern assumptions. The researcher can assert *taking action* as part of the intention of the proposed study, as in action research. He can assert *empowerment* (the goal of participatory action research) as a goal. But he can only, at best, discuss how the inquiry *may* create opportunities for empowerment (see Table 2.2).

The discussion of the topic and purpose also articulates the *unit of analysis*—the level of inquiry on which the study will focus. Qualitative studies typically focus on individuals, dyads, groups, processes, or organizations. Discussing the level of inquiry helps focus subsequent decisions about data gathering.

Significance and Potential Contributions

Convincing the reader that the study is significant and should be conducted entails building an argument that links the research to important theoretical perspectives, policy issues, concerns of practice,

Table 2.2   Matching Research Questions and Purpose

Purpose of the study	General research questions
Exploratory:	
To investigate little-understood phenomena	What is happening in this social program?
To identify or discover important categories of meaning	What are the salient themes, patterns, or categories of meaning for participants?
To generate hypotheses for further research	How are these patterns linked with one another?
Explanatory:	
To explain the patterns related to the phenomenon in question	What events, beliefs, attitudes, or policies shape this phenomenon?
To identify plausible relationships shaping the phenomenon	How do these forces interact to result in the phenomenon?
Descriptive:	
To document and describe the phenomenon of interest	What are the salient actions, events, beliefs, attitudes, and social structures and processes occurring in this phenomenon?
Emancipatory:	
To create opportunities and the will to engage in social action	How do participants problematize their circumstances and take positive social action?

or social issues that affect people's everyday lives. Think of it as an opportunity to discus ways that the study is likely to contribute to policy, practice, or theory or for taking social action. Who might be interested in the results? With what groups might they be shared: scholars? policymakers? practitioners? members of similar groups? individuals or groups usually silenced or marginalized? The challenge here is to situate the study as addressing an important problem; defining the problem shapes the study's significance. A clinical psychologist might identify a theoretical gap in the literature about isolation and define the topic for an ethnography of long-distance truck drivers. Such a study may be relatively unconcerned with policy or practice; its contributions to theory, however, are preordained. A feminist sociologist could frame a study of discriminatory thinking among business executives for policy and practice by addressing the problem of persistent sexism in the workplace. A study of the impact of welfare reform on the lives of adult learners in basic education courses could focus either on policy issues or on how this recurring social problem plays out in the lives of the learners. In that event, theory is less significant. The researcher develops the significance of the study by defining the problem.

Funding opportunities often focus a question. A welfare-to-work grants program calling for a multisite evaluation of programs for the so-called hard to employ provides other opportunities for the researcher. It also has significance for policy. Be wary of research opportunities focused on policy for their potential to seduce the researcher into agendas serving primarily the powerful elite (Anderson, 1989; Marshall, 1997a; Scheurich, 1997). Recall the discussion of explicitly ideological research in Chapter 1. For further discussion of these issues, see Smith (1988).

A study may well be able to contribute understanding and opportunities for action in all four domains, but it is unlikely to contribute equally to all four; the statement of the topic should thus emphasize one of them. For example, a study of the integration of children with disabilities into regular classrooms could be significant for both policy and practice. Framing this as a policy study requires that the topic be situated in national and state policy debates on special education. Framing it as most significant for practice would require the researcher to focus on structures supporting inclusive classrooms. Both frames are legitimate and defensible; the researcher's challenge is to argue for the study's potential contributions to the domains in which he is most interested. This, in turn, has implications for the literature review and the design of the study.

Significance for Theory

The discussion of the study's significance for theory is often an intellectual odyssey the researcher can pursue more fully in the review of related literature. At this point in the proposal, the researcher should outline the project's potential contribution to knowledge by describing how it fits into theoretical traditions in the social sciences or applied fields in ways that will be new, insightful, or creative. The significance statement should show how the study will contribute to research traditions or foundational literatures in new ways.

Often, the proposal identifies gaps in the literature to which the study will contribute. If the research is in an area for which theory is well developed, the study may be a significant test or expansion of the theory. The researcher may use concepts developed by previous researchers and formulate questions similar to those used in previous research. Data collection, however, may be in a different setting, with a different group, and certainly at a different time. Thus, the results of the research will constitute an extension of theory that will expand the generalizations or more finely tune theoretical propositions. The contribution of such research is the expansion of previous theory. When researchers conceptualize the focus of the study and generate the research questions, they may draw on a body of theory and related research that is different from previous research. Significance of this sort, however, generally derives from an extensive and creative review of related literature. Having developed that section of the proposal, the writer then incorporates references to and summaries of it in the significance section. This type of significance is treated fully in the next section on the review of related literature. Generally, by answering the question, *How is this research important?* the researcher can demonstrate the creative aspects of the work.

The development of theory takes place by incremental advances and small contributions to knowledge through well-conceptualized and well-conducted research. Most researchers use theory to guide their own work, to locate their studies in larger scholarly traditions, or to map the topography of the specific concepts they will explore in detail. In addition, some very creative research can emerge when a researcher breaks theoretical boundaries and reconceptualizes a problem or relocates the problem area. For example, Bronfenbrenner (1980) reconceptualized children's learning processes by applying the concept of *ecology* to child development theory. Weick's (1976) metaphor of schools as *loosely coupled systems* profoundly altered theoretical conceptualizations of educational organizations. Often researchers follow a theoretical pragmatism, being "shamelessly eclectic" in the creative application of concepts from one discipline to another (Rossman & Wilson, 1994).

Significance for Policy

The significance of a study for policy can be developed by discussing formal policy development in that area and presenting data that show how often the problem occurs and how costly it can be. For example, to demonstrate the significance of a study of the careers of women faculty, the researcher could present statistics documenting persistently lower salaries for women than men at comparable ranks; this is the problem that the study will address. The study's potential contributions for university compensation policies could then be spelled out. Contributions to university degree program policy could then be articulated. In another example, the researcher could describe recent changes in welfare law and discuss how this reform was developed with little regard for those most affected—the problem the study will address. Potential contributions of the study to further reform of welfare law could then be described. In developing the topic and how the study might contribute to policy in that area, the researcher would demonstrate that the general topic is one of significant proportions that should be studied systematically.

A study's importance can also be argued through summaries of the writings of policymakers and informed experts who identify the topic as important and call for research pursuing the general questions. Statistical presentations of incidence and persistence of the problem as well as calls for research by experts demonstrate that the study addresses an important topic, one of concern to policymakers in that area. In applied fields such as education, health policy, management, regional planning, and clinical psychology, for example, demonstrating a study's significance to policy—whether international, national, state, regional, or institutional—may be especially important.

Significance for Practice

Situating a study as significant for practice follows the same logic as developing significance for policy. The argument here should rely on a discussion of the concerns or problems articulated in the literature. This will involve citing experts, referencing prior research, and summarizing incidence data. Recall the preceding discussion of a study about the inclusion of children with disabilities. The researcher who wants this study to focus on issues of practice would discuss the literature detailing the concerns of teachers about meeting the needs of children with disabilities in their classrooms. The study's potential contributions, then, would be improvement in teachers' classroom practice. Shadduck-Hernandez's proposal for her dissertation research (1997) about immigrant and refugee college students' sense of ethnic identity summarized incidence data on enrollment and the paucity of culturally relevant experiences for them in the college curriculum. She then detailed the study's potential contributions to pedagogical practice in university classrooms.

Significance for Social Issues and Action

Finally, a study may be significant for its detailed description of life circumstances that express particular social issues. Such a study may not influence policy, contribute to scholarly literature, or improve practice; it may illuminate the lived experiences of interest by providing rich description and foster taking action. Action research and participatory action research genres stipulate *taking action* as central to their work. In these cases, researchers should argue that the proposed inquiry and its attendant action will likely be valuable to those who participate, as well as to others committed to the issue. The challenge here is to identify how and in what ways.

Maguire's (2000) study with battered women was a participatory action research project. Her study's primary contributions were not intended for scholarly traditions, policy, or practice per se; rather, they were for the women involved in the work and for others committed to alleviating the abuse of women. The work was important because it focused on a major social issue. Extending this work (although not explicitly linked to it), Browne's (1987) study of battered women who kill their assailants provided a critique of the legal system that does little to protect women under threat; it led to increased activism for women in these circumstances. Lather and Smithies's (1997) study collaborating with HIV-positive women invited the reader to enter into the women's lives so as to create new connections and the possibilities for action.

Through a discussion of relevant scholarship and the concerns of practice, the significance section articulates the topic to be studied and argues that further investigation of this problem has the potential to contribute to scholarship, policy, practice, or a better understanding of recurring social issues. This section defines who is likely to have an interest in the topic and therefore how and in what ways the study may contribute.

Of course, researchers preparing proposals for funding should adjust their statements about significance to the needs and priorities of the funding agencies. The foundation that takes pride in funding action projects or interventions will want to see statements about how the proposed research will directly help people or change a problematic situation. On the other hand, when seeking funds from an agency whose goals include expanding knowledge and theory (e.g., the National Science Foundation), to demonstrate the significance of the research, the researcher should emphasize the undeveloped or unsolved theoretical puzzles to be addressed.

❖ POSING RESEARCH QUESTIONS

Qualitative approaches to inquiry are uniquely suited to uncovering the unexpected and exploring new avenues. This demands flexibility in the proposal so that data gathering can respond to increasingly refined research questions. Herein lies a dilemma, however. The proposal should be sufficiently clear, both in research questions and design, so that the reader can evaluate its do-ability; on the other hand, the proposal should reserve the flexibility that is the hallmark of qualitative methods. This suggests that the research questions should be general enough to permit exploration but focused enough to delimit the study—not an easy task.

Focusing the study and posing general research questions are best addressed in a developmental manner, relying on discussions of related literature to help frame and refine the specific topic. Often, the primary research goal is to discover those very questions that are most probing and insightful. Most likely, the relevant concepts will be developed during the research process, but the research proposal must suggest themes based on one's knowledge of the literature.

Initial questions should be linked to the problem and its significance and should forecast the literature to be reviewed. Questions may be theoretical ones, which can be studied in a number of different sites or with different samples. They may focus on a population or class of individuals; these too can be studied in various places. Finally, the questions may be site-specific because of the uniqueness of a specific program or organization. The study of refugee and immigrant college experiences (Shadduck-Hernandez, 2005) could have been conducted in any setting that had newcomer students; the theoretical interest driving the research was not linked to a particular organization. A study of an exemplary sex education program, however, can be studied only at that site because the problem identified is one of practice. Thus, the questions posed are shaped by the identified problem and, in turn, constrain the design of the study.

Examples of *theoretical questions* include the following:

- How does play affect reading readiness? Through what cognitive and affective process? Do children who take certain roles—for example, leadership roles—learn faster? If so, what makes the difference?
- How does the sponsor-protégé socialization process function in professional careers? Does it work differently for women? For minorities? What processes are operating?

Questions focused on *particular populations* could include the following:

- How do neurosurgeons cope with the reality that they hold people's lives in their hands? That many of their patients die?
- What happens to women who enter elite MBA programs? What are their career paths?

- What is the life of the long-distance truck driver like?
- How do school superintendents manage relations with school board members? What influence processes do they use?
- What happens to change-agent teachers during their careers? Do organizational socialization processes change or eliminate them? Do they burn out early in their careers?

Finally, *site-specific* research questions might take the following form:

- Why is the sex education program working well in this school but not in the others? What is special about the people, the plan, the support, the context?
- How do the school-parent community relations of an elite private school differ from those in the neighboring public school? How are the differences connected with differences in educational philosophies and outcomes?
- What are the ways in which lobbying groups influence pollution control policy in the Massachusetts legislature?
- Why is there a discrepancy in the perceptions of the efficacy of affirmative action policy between university officials and groups of students of color at the University of North Carolina? What explains the discrepancy?

These are typical examples of initial questions developed in the proposal. They serve as boundaries around the study without unduly constraining it. The questions focus on interactions and processes in sociocultural systems and in organizations and thus link to important research literature and theory, but they are also grounded in everyday realities. The goal of this section of the proposal is to explicate the questions, thereby further focusing the study, and to forecast the literature to be discussed in the next section. Vignette 3 shows early development of an introductory statement for a pilot-study proposal.

VIGNETTE 3

An Initial Statement

A doctoral student from China, Fan Yihong (2000), became deeply concerned about the fundamental purposes of education, especially as enacted in universities. Her experiences in universities in China and the United States led her to see that much of the organizational practice—procedures, norms, disciplinary boundaries—on both continents was deadening human spirit and creativity. She immersed herself in organizational theory, science and technology, and the development of the "new sciences" and complex systems theory in relation to Eastern philosophy. During this journey, she came upon the emerging theories of the holographic universe and the holotropic mind (Capra, 1975, 1982, 1996; Senge, 1990; Wilber, 1996) that stress the wholeness of people, events, nature, and the world, and the innate capacity of the mind to comprehend reality in a holistic manner. Based on these interests, she posed four overarching research questions that would allow her to integrate the various complex intellectual traditions that framed her study:

1. What serves as triggers and preconditions for individuals to change their worldviews?

2. What processes have they undertaken to enable them to transform their changed ways of knowing to their changed ways of doing, and then to their changed ways of being, and to finally becoming transformed human beings?

3. What characterizes these change processes?

4. How does individual awakening, recognizing the need for change, help bring about collective and organizational transformational change?

The potential significance of the study was described in terms of its contributions to understanding how personal and organizational transformation are possible, through rich descriptions of people and organizations that were radically different from traditional ones. Thus the study would potentially contribute theory and practice, building a thoughtful and detailed analysis of the processes of transformation.

Fan Yihong has introduced the topic—the persistent problem of confining versus liberating educational environments—posed the preliminary general research questions, and forecast the study's potential significance. While this approach is not at all typical, it represented congruence with her theoretical framework and personal epistemology and cosmology. Following are two examples of other introductory paragraphs. Each states the topic, discusses the purpose, stipulates the unit of analysis, and forecasts the study's significance:[1]

Children with physical handicaps have unique perceptions about their "bodiedness." Grounded in phenomenological inquiry, this study will explore and describe the deep inner meaning of bodiedness for five children. The study will result in rich description through stories of these children's relationships with sports. The central concept of bodiedness will be explicated through the children's words. Those working with children with physical handicaps, as well as policymakers framing programs that affect them, will find the study of interest.

The Neighborhood Arts Center in Orange, Massachusetts, is an award-winning program that serves all members of its community. The purpose of this study is to explain the success of this program in bringing arts to members of this low-income community. The study will use an ethnographic design, seeking detailed explanations of the program's success. The study will help decision makers and funders design similar programs that involve groups historically underrepresented in the arts.

❖ LIMITATIONS OF THE STUDY

All proposed research projects have limitations; none is perfectly designed. As Patton (2002) notes, "There are no perfect research designs. There are always trade-offs" (p. 223). A discussion of the study's limitations demonstrates that the researcher understands this reality—that she will make no overweening claims about generalizability or conclusiveness about what she has learned.

Limitations derive from the conceptual framework and the study's design. A discussion of these limitations early on in the proposal reminds the reader what the study is and is not—its boundaries—and how its results can and cannot contribute to understanding. Framing the study in specific research and scholarly traditions places limits on the research. A study of land use in Indonesia, for example, could be situated in development economics; reminding the reader that the study is framed this way helps allay criticism. The overall design, however, indicates how broadly applicable the study may be. Although no qualitative studies are generalizable in the probabilistic sense, their findings may be transferable. A discussion of these considerations reminds the reader that the study is bounded and situated in a specific context. The reader, then, can make decisions about its usefulness for other settings.

❖ REVIEW OF RELATED LITERATURE

A thoughtful and insightful discussion of related literature builds a logical framework for the research and locates it within a tradition of inquiry and a context of related studies. The literature review serves four broad functions. First, it demonstrates the underlying assumptions behind the general research questions. If possible, it should display the research paradigm that undergirds the study and describe the assumptions and values the researcher brings to the research enterprise. Second, it demonstrates that the researcher is knowledgeable about related research and the scholarly traditions that surround and support the study. Third, it shows that the researcher has identified some gaps in previous research and that the proposed study will fill a demonstrated need. Finally, the review refines and redefines the research questions by embedding them in larger traditions of inquiry. We describe the literature review as a *conversation* between the researcher and the related literature.

As the researcher conceptualizes the research problem, he locates it in a tradition of theory and related research. Initially, this may be an intuitive locating, chosen because of the underlying assumptions: how the researcher sees the world and how he sees the research questions fitting in. As the researcher explores the literature, however, he should identify and state those assumptions in a framework of theory. This could be child development theory, organizational theory, adult socialization theory, critical race theory, or whatever body is appropriate. This section of the literature review provides the framework for the research and identifies the area of knowledge the study is intended to expand.

The next portion of the review of literature should, quite literally, review and critique previous research and scholarly writing that relates to the general research question. This critical review should lead to a more precise problem statement or refined questions because it demonstrates a specific area that has not yet been adequately explored or shows that a different design would be more appropriate. If a major aspect of the significance of the study arises from a reconceptualization of the topic, it should be developed fully here. Cooper (1988) provides a discussion of the focus, goal, perspective, coverage, organization, and audience for a literature review. An extended example of integrating and dovetailing the significance and the review sections is provided in Vignette 4. Look for the ways the literature review led Marshall (1979, 1981, 1985b) to find new possibilities for pursuing the research questions.

VIGNETTE 4

Building Significance Through the Literature

When Marshall was researching the general problem of women's unequal representation in school administration careers, she first reviewed the work of previous researchers. Many researchers before her had conducted surveys to identify the attributes, the positions, and the percentages of women in school administration. A few researchers had identified patterns of discrimination.

In a significant departure from this tradition, Marshall reconceptualized the problem. She looked at it as a problem in the area of adult socialization and looked to career socialization theory. From a review of this body of theory and related empirical research on the school administrative career, including recruitment, training, and selection processes, and on women in jobs and careers, Marshall framed a new question. She asked, "What is the career socialization process for women in school administration? What is the process through which women make career decisions, acquire training and supports, overcome obstacles, and move up in the hierarchy?"

This reconceptualization came from asking the significance question: Who cares about this research? The question encouraged a review of previous research that demonstrated how other research had already answered many questions. It showed that women were as competent as men in school administration. But a critical review of this literature argued that this previous research had asked different questions. Marshall could assert that her study would be significant because it would focus on describing a process about which previous research had only guessed. The new research would add to theory by exploring career socialization of women in a profession generally dominated by men. It would also identify the relevant social, psychological, and organizational variables that are part of women's career socialization. This established the significance of the research by showing how it would add to knowledge.

The literature review also established the significance of the research for practice and policy with an overview of the issues of affirmative action and equity concerns. Thus, the research question, literature review, and research design were all tied in with the significance question. Responding to this question demanded a demonstration that this was an area of knowledge and practice that needed exploration. To ensure exploration, qualitative methods were the most appropriate for the conduct of the study.

As the preceding vignette shows, the literature review can identify established knowledge and, more important, develop significance and new questions and often turn old questions around. This "initiating function" (Rossman & Wilson, 1994) of the literature review can be quite creative. The review, moreover, provides intellectual glue for the entire proposal by demonstrating the sections' conceptual relatedness. The researcher cannot write about the study's significance without knowledge of the literature. She cannot describe the design without a discussion of the general research topic. The dissertation proposal is divided into sections because of tradition and convention, not because of a magical formula. To organize complex topics and to address the three critical questions posed at the beginning, however, the structure provided here is recommended. Vignette 5 illustrates how the conceptualization of a study can be creative and exciting, as the researcher forges links among historically disparate literatures.

VIGNETTE 5

Creative Review of the Literature

When research questions explore new territory, a single line of previous literature and/or theory may be inadequate for constructing frameworks that usefully guide the study. A case in point is that of Shadduck-Hernandez (2005), a graduate student in international development education, who searched the literature for a way to frame her study of a community service learning initiative serving refugee and immigrant youth and undergraduate students at a major research university.

Shadduck-Hernandez's forays into the literature on community service learning and the relationships between institutions of higher education and the communities they serve identified a substantial gap. Previous studies described demographics about participants in community service learning projects, noting that typical projects involved white, middle-class undergraduate students working with communities of color. However, few critiqued the hegemonic practice embodied in such projects or called into question the continuing Eurocentric values in university and community relations. It became clear that previous research failed to conceptualize the problem in terms of a sustained critique of the university, from the perspectives of those often marginalized from mainstream university discourse: refugee and immigrant students of color.

Having established that the study was situated in scholarly writing and research on community service learning and university-community relations, Shadduck-Hernandez still felt incomplete. This literature helped to establish the context for her study, but did not provide theoretical concepts or propositions that would help illuminate students' experience. She turned to the literature on critical pedagogy to more fully frame the principles of the project. She also discussed situated learning theory with its key notions of context, peer relations, and communities of practice to provide analytic insights into the learning milieu of the project. Finally, she relied upon the anthropological concept of funds of knowledge—"the strategic and cultural resources that racially and ethnically diverse and low-income students and communities possess" (pp. 115–116). Her discussion of these literatures was tested against their usefulness in understanding community service learning among similar and familiar ethnic groups and for developing a gentle but quite pointed critique of the university.

Vignette 5 shows a creative blending of several strands of literature for framing the research. The integration of literatures helped shape a research focus that was theoretically interesting yet could help inform policy and practice in universities. Broad reading and knowledge of the history of institutions of higher education relative to their local communities—richly augmented by more theoretical literature on critical pedagogy, situated learning, and funds of knowledge—created a variegated and highly creative synthesis. Rather than narrowly constructing the study to focus on only one topic, the researcher searched widely for illuminating constructs from other disciplines. This work, although at times tedious, confusing, and ambiguous, enhances the research to follow and demonstrates that the researcher has engaged in significant intellectual work already.

The literature review serves many purposes for the research. It supports the importance of the study's focus and may serve to validate the eventual findings in a narrowly descriptive study. It also guides the development of explanations during data collection and analysis in studies that seek to explain, evaluate, and suggest linkages between events. In grounded-theory development, the literature review provides theoretical constructs, categories, and their properties that can be used to organize the data and discover new connections between theory and phenomenon.

* * * * *

The sections of the proposal discussed thus far—introduction, discussion of the topic and purpose, significance, general research questions, and literature review—stand together as the conceptual body of the proposal. Here, the major (and minor) ideas for the proposal are developed, their intellectual roots are displayed and critiqued, and the writings and studies of other researchers are presented and critiqued. All of this is intended to tell the reader what the research is about (its subject), who ought to care about it (its significance), and what others have described and concluded about the subject (its intellectual roots). All three purposes are interwoven into these sections of the proposal.

The final major section—research design and methods—must flow conceptually and logically from all that has gone before; these are discussed in Chapters 3, 4, and 5. In the design and methods section, the researcher makes a case, based on the conceptual portion of the proposal, for the particular sample, methods, data analysis techniques, and reporting format chosen for the study. Thus, the section on design and methods should build a rationale for the study's design and data collection methods. Here, the researcher should develop a case for using qualitative methods. These topics are also discussed in Chapters 3, 4, and 5.

Although there are parallels, qualitative and more traditional quantitative proposals differ. In the development of a qualitative proposal, the researcher first orients the proposal reader to the general topic to be explored. This will not involve a statement of specific research questions, propositions to be tested, or hypotheses to be examined. It can include a general discussion of the puzzle, the unexplored issue, or the group to be studied. Discussion becomes more focused through the literature review because, in exploratory studies, it is hard to predict which literature will be most relevant; the focus of the study may best be served by an intersection of literatures.

In some cases, the literature review yields cogent and useful definitions, constructs, concepts, and even data collection strategies. These may fruitfully result in a set of preliminary guiding hypotheses. Using the term *guiding hypothesis* may assist readers accustomed to more traditional proposals. It is essential, however, that the researcher explain that guiding hypotheses are tools used to generate questions and to search for patterns; they may be discarded when the researcher gets into the field and finds other exciting patterns of phenomena. This approach retains the flexibility needed to permit the precise focus of the research to evolve. By avoiding precise hypotheses, the researcher retains her right to explore and *generate* questions. The guiding hypotheses illustrate for the reader some possible directions the researcher may follow, but the researcher is still free to discover and pursue other patterns.

We do not intend to suggest that proposal development proceeds in a linear fashion, as we have noted. Specifically, in Chapter 1, we argue that conceptualizing a study and developing a design that is clear, flexible, and manageable is dialectic, messy, and just plain hard work. As the researcher plays with concepts and theoretical frames for the study, she often entertains alternative designs, assessing them for their power to address the emerging questions. Considering an ethnography, a case study, or an in-depth interview study as the overall design will, in turn, reshape the research questions. So the process continues as the conceptual framework and specific design features become more and more elegantly related. The challenge is to build the logical connections between the topic, the questions, and the design and methods.

DIALGOUE BETWEEN LEARNERS

Melanie,

In reading through the first few chapters, I'm struck with the trials of striving to give a sense of order to the messiness of qualitative research. We try to imagine that there is some type of logical order to our work, only to find that different aspects of our research designs bump into and merge with one another. I think about this often when we talk about conceptual framework in our classes. As a student, I feel that I'm often looking for the "right" theoretical lens with which to make sense of my qualitative work. It is, of course, a hopeless quest. There doesn't ever seem to be a perfect fit to our own research contexts. Yet in classes, we try one on and see how it fits, and then we try on another and see how the fit may be different. And then, of course, we begin our own work on dissertations and such and suddenly we're meant to, in some way, construct our own. Perhaps we piece a few theoretical perspectives together, finding links and overlaps that others might not have intuited. And it's all so very messy and, at times, disconcerting. I'm just beginning work on my dissertation and am (obviously) struggling a bit with this desire (hope?) for clarity.

   Sorry to ramble so. Hope all is well,

Aaron

Aaron,

I completely agree with you about the messiness of qualitative research. I'm in the dissertation phase now, too, you know, and the theoretical piece is killing me! In theory (no pun intended), I understand what we mean by conceptual framework but I have such a hard time articulating that in my own work. How do I pull from disparate works to create a logical whole? At what point does the framework stand on its own? How do I successfully craft a framework when the pieces are still coming together as I dig into the analysis?

One thing I've slowly realized about qualitative research—and I hope this is a legitimate understanding!—is that the process is not only nonlinear but hopelessly intertwined, almost like we're struggling to unravel a Gordian knot of our own making. Sometimes the interest in my research subject is the only thing that keeps me picking away at my confusion! Like you said, it's messy and it's complex and it's frustrating—perhaps that's part of the appeal?

I'm afraid I'm rambling now, as I'm quite tired and rather hungry. So, time for a late dinner and bed!

Melanie

❖ NOTE

1. These paragraphs are adapted from Rossman and Rallis (2003).

❖ FURTHER READING

Creswell, J. W. (1998). *Qualitative inquiry and research design: Choosing among five traditions.* Thousand Oaks, CA: Sage.

Creswell, J. W. (2003). *Research design: Qualitative, quantitative, and mixed methods approaches* (2nd ed.). Thousand Oaks, CA: Sage.

Glesne, C. (1999). *Becoming qualitative researchers: An introduction* (2nd ed.). New York: Longman.

Janesick, V. J. (1994). The dance of qualitative research design. In N. K. Denzin & Y. S. Lincoln (Eds.), *Handbook of qualitative research* (pp. 209–219). Thousand Oaks, CA: Sage.

Locke, L. F., Spirduso, W. W., & Silverman, S. J. (2000). *Proposals that work: A guide for planning dissertations and grant proposals* (4th ed.). Thousand Oaks, CA: Sage.

Madison, D. S. (2005). *Critical ethnography: Method, ethics, and performance.* Thousand Oaks, CA: Sage.

Maxwell, J. A. (2005). *Qualitative research design: An interactive approach* (2nd ed.). Thousand Oaks, CA: Sage.

Piantanida, M., & Garman, N. B. (1999). *The qualitative dissertation: A guide for students and faculty.* Thousand Oaks, CA: Corwin Press.

Silverman, D. (2005). *Doing qualitative research* (2nd ed.). Thousand Oaks, CA: Sage.

Strauss, A., & Corbin, J. (1990). *Basics of qualitative research.* Newbury Park, CA: Sage.

3

The How of the Study

Building the Research Design

T he section of the research proposal devoted to a description of the design and methods serves three major purposes. First, it presents a plan for the conduct of the study. Second, it demonstrates to the reader that the researcher is capable of conducting the study. And third, it asserts the need for and offers strategies to preserve the flexibility of design that is a hallmark of qualitative methods. The latter purpose is often the most challenging.

Eight major topics are addressed in this section: (a) the qualitative genre, overall strategy, and rationale; (b) site selection, population selection, or both; (c) the researcher's role; (d) data collection methods; (e) data management; (f) data analysis strategy; (g) trustworthiness; and (h) a management plan or time line. Woven into these is the challenge of presenting a clear, doable plan—with concrete, specific details—while maintaining flexibility in its implementation. After discussing this challenge, we address the first three topics. Chapter 4 describes data collection methods, followed by a discussion of strategies for managing, analyzing, and interpreting qualitative data in Chapter 5. Because managing the entire research process (using a management plan and time line) and trustworthiness require full elaboration, those considerations are presented in Chapters 6 and 7, respectively.

❖ MEETING THE CHALLENGE

How do researchers maintain the needed flexibility of design, so that the research can "unfold, cascade, roll, and emerge" (Lincoln & Guba, 1985, p. 210), and still present a plan that is logical, concise, and thorough, meeting the criterion of do-ability? The research design section should demonstrate to the reader that the overall plan is sound and that the researcher is competent to undertake the research, capable of employing the methods arrayed, and sufficiently self-aware and interested to sustain the effort necessary for the successful completion of the study. This design and the researcher's defense of it must stand up to questioning. After all, the design must convince reviewers that the researcher is able to handle a complex and personal process, often making decisions in the field during the unfolding, cascading, rolling, and emerging.

The researcher should demonstrate to the reader that she reserves the right to modify the original design as the research evolves: building flexibility into the design is crucial. The researcher does so by (a) demonstrating the appropriateness of and the logic of using qualitative methods for the particular research question, and (b) devising a proposal that includes many of the elements of traditional models. At the same time, she reserves the right to change the implementation plan during data collection. As mentioned earlier, this section of the proposal should discuss the rationale for and logic of the particular qualitative genre in which the study is grounded, the overall strategy, and the specific design elements. At times, however, the researcher may need to justify qualitative research, in general, before situating the proposed study in a genre. We address the reality of this issue first and then focus on specific genres and approaches.

❖ JUSTIFYING QUALITATIVE RESEARCH

In recent years, the value and prestige of qualitative inquiry have risen in some fields. Still, given the historic domination of social science research by traditional, quantitative models and the current conservative climate of the federal government, the researcher may well have to develop a justification for qualitative methods in general. Before describing the specific genre and approach, he should show how and why the research questions will be best addressed in a natural setting, using exploratory approaches. To accomplish this, the strengths of qualitative methodology should be emphasized by elaborating the value of such studies for the following types of research (Lincoln & Guba, 1985; Marshall, 1985a, 1987):

- Research that seeks cultural description and ethnography;
- Research that elicits multiple constructed realities, studied holistically;
- Research that elicits tacit knowledge and subjective understandings and interpretations;
- Research that delves in depth into complexities and process;
- Research on little-known phenomena or innovative systems;
- Research that seeks to explore where and why policy and local knowledge and practice are at odds;
- Research on informal and unstructured linkages and processes in organizations;
- Research on real, as opposed to stated, organizational goals;
- Research that cannot be done experimentally for practical or ethical reasons; and
- Research for which relevant variables have yet to be identified.

Further support is found in the many excellent introductory texts on qualitative methods that describe the characteristics and strengths of qualitative methods (see the Chapter 1 reference list). Drawing on these sources, the researcher proposing a study in a particular setting (e.g., hospital ward or social service agency) could argue that human actions are significantly influenced by the setting in which they occur and that one should therefore study that behavior in those real-life situations. The social and physical setting—schedules, space, pay, and rewards—and internalized notions of norms, traditions, roles, and values are crucial aspects of an environment. Thus, for qualitative studies, context matters. The researcher could argue that the study should be conducted in the setting where all this complexity operates over time and where data on the multiple versions of reality can be collected. For a study focusing on individuals' lived experience, the researcher could also argue that human actions cannot be understood unless the meaning that humans assign to them is understood. Because thoughts, feelings, beliefs, values, and assumptive worlds are involved, the researcher needs to understand the deeper perspectives that can be captured through face-to-face interaction.

Critiquing and demonstrating the limitations of quantitative, positivist approaches can be an excellent strategy for justifying use of qualitative methodology. The researcher might argue that the objective scientist, by coding the social world according to operational variables, destroys valuable data by imposing a limited worldview on the subjects (a consideration for all studies, qualitative or otherwise, we would argue). The researcher might further critique experimental models by noting that policymakers and practitioners are sometimes unable to derive meaning and useful findings from experimental research and that the research techniques themselves have affected the findings. The lab, the questionnaire, and so on have become artifacts. Subjects are either suspicious and wary or they are aware of what the researchers want and try to please them. And the researcher could describe the ways in which stories—complex narratives of personal experience—are masked by quantitative methods or, worse, displaced by them.

In short, the strengths of qualitative studies should be demon-strated for research that is exploratory or descriptive and that stresses the importance of context, setting, and participants' frames of reference. A well-reasoned and convincing explanation for qualitative methods should include a concise but strong rationale firmly grounded in the conceptual framework, and for the specific data collection methods. The rationale should show how the selection of methods flows from the research questions. Two examples illustrate. For Glazier's (2004) ethno-graphic study on the ability of collaborative work of Arab and Jewish teachers in Israel to influence understanding of the Other, the com-pelling argument was that triangulation of qualitative data allows for multiple perspectives. Mishna (2004) also made a strong argument that a study using interviews with children and parents about bullying needs a qualitative methodology to capture context, personal interpre-tation, and experience. As Mishna pointed out,

> [Q]ualitative data ... privileges individuals' lived experience ... Increasing our understanding of the views of children and adults is key to developing effective interventions. ... We know surpris-ingly little about the dynamics of school bullying relationships. ... It is vital to have children's perspectives when trying to identify the processes involved in problematic peer relations. (p. 235)

Notice how this researcher first presented what was already known, then what was still needed, and then why this topic needed a qualitative approach.

❖ THE QUALITATIVE GENRE AND OVERALL APPROACH

Although acceptance of qualitative inquiry is currently widespread, at times it is necessary to provide a rationale for the particular genre in which a study is situated. Recall the discussion in Chapter 1 in which we argued that the many nuanced traditions of qualitative research can be categorized into those focusing on (a) *individual lived experience,* (b) *society and culture,* and (c) *language and communication.* The most compelling argument emphasizes the unique strengths of the genre for research that is exploratory or descriptive, that accepts the value of context and setting, and that searches for a deeper understanding of the participants' lived experiences of the phenomenon under study. One assumption common to all genres is that people express meaning about some aspect of their lives. This follows Thomas's (1949) classic proposition that, in the study of human experience, it is essential to know how people define their situations: "If men [sic] define situations as real, they are real in their consequences" (p. 301). Explicating the logical and compelling connections—the epistemological integrity—between the genre, the overall strategy, the research questions, the design, and the methods is often quite convincing.

Overall Strategies

The richness and diversity of overall design strategies in qualitative research are evident in the literature detailing specific studies. Analysis of this richness yields three distinct strategies, each associated with the genres mentioned earlier (see Table 3.1). A study focusing on individual lived experience typically relies on an *in-depth interview strategy.* Although this may be supplemented with journal writing by the participants or other forms of data, the primary strategy is to capture the deep meaning of experience in the participants' own words. Studies focusing on society and culture in a group, a program, or an organization typically espouse some form of *case study* as a strategy. This entails immersion in the setting and rests on both the researcher's and the participants' worldviews. Research focusing on language and communication typically involves *microanalysis or textual analysis* through which speech events, including text, and subtle interactions are recorded (often on videotape) and then analyzed. Directly linked to the qualitative genre and research questions, each strategy stipulates the focus of the inquiry (individual, group, interactions) and the overall approach to collecting data.

The distinctions among these three broad strategies rest on two continua: the *complexity* of design and the *degree of close interaction* between researcher and participants. In-depth interview strategies are elegant in design, relying on a single primary method for gathering data. Microanalyses frequently encompass more of the complexities of context than in-depth interview strategies, relying on some form of

Table 3.1   Qualitative Genre and Overall Strategy

Genre	Main strategy	Focus of inquiry
Individual lived experience	In-depth interviews	Individuals
Society and culture	Case study	Groups or organizations
Language and communication	Microanalysis or text analysis	Speech events and interactions

observation often complemented by interviews. Case study, the most complex strategy, may entail multiple methods—interviews, observations, document analysis, even surveys. Following the same logic, interview strategies require close, personal interactions between researcher and participants, often over long periods of time. Case studies are less intimate than those involving participant observation (discussed in Chapter 4), which fosters close relationships. With their focus on observation, microanalyses tend to lie somewhere in the middle of this continuum. These continua are presented in Figure 3.1.

The strategy is a road map, a plan for undertaking a systematic exploration of the phenomenon of interest; the research methods are the specific tools for conducting that exploration. In-depth interview strategies stipulate a primary method for gathering data—interviewing. In case studies and microanalyses, the combination of methods proposed for responding to the research questions may be quite complex. A case study of the impact of welfare reform, for example, could rely on an array of methods, ranging from in-depth interviewing to analysis of work experiences. A microanalysis study of classroom interactions might choose direct observation (through videotape) supplemented by interviews and analysis of student work. The strategy frames the study by placing boundaries around it, identifying the analytic focus. The research strategy is a product of major decisions made by the researcher to determine the best approach to the questions posed in the conceptual portion of the proposal.

In developing the strategy, the researcher needs to consider its *informational adequacy* and *efficiency* (Zelditch, 1962) and an array of ethical considerations. To discern the adequacy of the strategy, ask whether this research design can be carried out without harming people or significantly disrupting the setting. Ask whether it is likely to foster responses to the research questions thoroughly and thoughtfully. Will this strategy elicit the information one seeks? (See questions of the study's do-ability in Chapter 1.) Does this plan allow adequate data to be collected, given constraints of time, financial resources,

Figure 3.1   Complexity of Design and Interaction

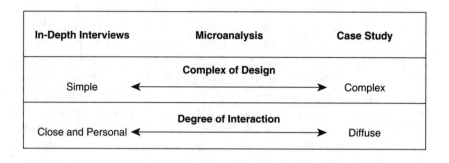

access, and cost to participants and researcher? To these, we would add ethical considerations. Will the proposed strategy violate the participants' privacy or unduly disrupt their everyday worlds? Are they putting themselves in danger or at risk by participating in the study? Will the study violate their human rights in some way? (We address these ethical issues more fully later in this chapter.) The range of possible qualitative strategies is small. Which is chosen depends on the research questions, on the genre, on ethics, and on the time frame possible for the study.

To buttress the argument and rationale for a genre and strategy, discussion of a pilot study can be quite important. When the researcher proclaims that she is capable of conducting the proposed research and provides a description and assessment of a qualitative pilot study with intriguing preliminary data, doubters are often persuaded. As Sampson (2004) notes,

> [W]hile pilots can be used to refine research instruments such as questionnaires and interview schedules, they have greater use still in ethnographic approaches to data collection in foreshadowing research problems and questions, in highlighting gaps and wastage in data collection, and in considering broader and highly significant issues such as research validity, ethics, representation, and researcher health and safety. (p. 383)

Pilot interviews help in understanding oneself as a researcher. In his research on the fears of social workers, Smith (1999) shows how piloting helps eliminate barriers such as resistances to tape recorders and mistrust of the researcher's agenda.

Even without a pilot study, the researcher can demonstrate her ability to manage qualitative research by describing initial observations or interviews. These experiences usually reveal fascinating questions and intriguing patterns. A description of initial observations demonstrates not only an ability to manage this research but also the strengths of the genre for generating enticing research questions. Thus, describing a pilot study or initial observations strengthens a proposal.

In addition to developing a strong, supported rationale for the genre and strategy, this section of the proposal should preserve the right to modify aspects of the design as the research proceeds. Early investigations of a phenomenon can also demonstrate the benefits of maintaining some flexibility. Illustrating this is Geer's (1969) description of first days in the field. She describes the qualitative researcher's immersion in the setting, beginning with some analytic concepts that were identified in previous research, guided by the theoretical framework and related research questions. These help the researcher determine what situations to observe, whom to interview, and what to ask. The researcher should establish the need and right to determine the precise focus of the research after these first days in the field when new insights begin to clarify patterns and focus the relevant themes.

One purpose of the research design section is to demonstrate that the researcher is capable of conducting qualitative research. Materials from courses in qualitative methodology or from independent reading will provide a wealth of rich and appropriate quotations and citations of other researchers' work. They are used not merely to impress readers with the number of the citations but to provide solid evidence that the researcher has entered into the critical conversation about methodology. This demonstrates a knowledge of the historic and ongoing methodological discourse about qualitative inquiry and of the specific genre in which the study is situated. Such quotations and citations situate one's study in an established tradition of research methodology. An increasing number of researchers have provided descriptions of the rationale for an evolving research design; both classical and newer works are referenced at the end of this chapter. Those that provide appendixes on methodology are particularly useful.

Reflection on one's identity and one's sense of voice and perspectives and considering assumptions and sensitivities are key to a discussion of the researcher's choice of questions and of researcher role. The schema presented in Figure 3.2 usefully portrays the range of questions to consider, both for proposals and for final reports.

Once the overall approach and supporting rationale have been presented, the proposal outlines the setting or population of interest and plans for more specific sampling of people, places, and events. This outline provides the reader with a sense of the scope of the proposed

Figure 3.2   Reflexive Questions: Triangulated Inquiry

**Those studied
(participants):**

How do they know what
they know? What shapes and
has shaped their worldview?
How do they perceive me?
Why? How do I know?
How do I perceive them?

Reflexive screens:

Culture, age, gender, class,
social status, education,
family, political praxis,
language, values

**Those receiving
the study (audience):**

How do they make
make sense of what I give
them? What perspectives
do they bring to the findings
I offer? How do they perceive
me? How do I perceive them?

Myself (as qualitative inquirer):

What do I know?
How do I know what I know?
What shapes and has shaped my perspective?
With what voice do I share my perspective?
What do I do with what I have found?

SOURCE: Patton (2002, p. 66). Reprinted by permission.

inquiry and of whether the intensity, amount, and richness of the data
will encourage full responses to the research questions. The researcher
may devise a chart showing questions to explore, potential rich settings,
and specific data collection strategies to display the logic of the design.
In addition, the proposal should address the issue of the researcher's
role, including (a) entry, reciprocity, and ethics; (b) specific planned data
collection techniques; (c) how the data will be recorded and managed;
(d) preliminary strategies for data analysis; (e) design features for ensuring the trustworthiness of the study; and (f) a management plan with a
time line for the conduct and final reporting of the study.

The research design section draws supporting evidence for the
decisions from the relevant quotations of researchers who have written
about these issues, thereby allaying fears that dilemmas encountered in
the field will be unmanageable. For example, to explain researcher
ethics concerning participants, the experience of Krieger (1985) studying a lesbian community is useful and compelling. Or the researcher can
cite Chaudhry's (1997) example of handling complex role dilemmas as
she studied Pakistani Muslim immigrants. The researcher can use concepts from her conceptual framework and citations from her literature
review to suggest possible categories or themes for data analysis.

Finally, when possible, it is useful to include a list of preliminary
or tentative interview questions as well as observation and coding

categories. Many human subject review committees in universities require these. Funding agencies will find them useful in assessing the quality of the proposal. These can be developed from a pilot study or from the literature review. Such an outline demonstrates that the researcher has the ability to make connections between sensitizing concepts, from the literature review to the research design. It also underscores that the researcher understands how to start gathering data as she begins the study and that she has an initial approach to analyzing the data. As one illustration, Vignette 6 is derived from Basit's (2003) recounting of planning for data analysis in her study of the aspirations of British Muslim girls.

VIGNETTE 6

Anticipating the Initial Coding Categories

Anticipating the arduous, yet creative, dynamic process of inductive reasoning, thinking, and theorizing, Tehima Basit knew that prior planning for data coding was crucial. She read all the warnings and advice of Miles (1979), Gough and Scott (2000), and Delamont (1992), who cautioned against shortcuts. As she prepared to describe how she would handle "data condensation" and "data distillation" (Tesch, 1990), she knew she must provide some concrete examples of how she would proceed. She recalled that "category names can come from the pool of concepts that researchers already have from their disciplinary and professional reading, or borrowed from technical literature, or are the words and phrases used by informants themselves" (Basit, 2003, p. 144). From her interviews with adolescent girls, parents, and teachers, she elicited 67 codes and themes: ethnicity, language, freedom, control, gender, family patterns, marriage and career, further education, homework, unrealistic aspirations, and so on. With these as a start, she referred to her literature review for concepts to elicit deeper connections. Thus, her evolving coding categories had evolved from her literature review but also from the interviews, which provided context and ways of altering, distilling, and refining themes.

   Plunging into data collection and analysis with a good sense of initial themes and with a firm sense of the need to value the unstructured, nonnumerical nature of qualitative data provided Basit (and her reviewers) with needed guidance and reassurance. With confidence, she answered the questions, How is such voluminous rich data managed? and Which parts of your literature review frame your analysis?

―――――――〰―――――――

One must include good statements of the overall approach in the proposal. Once this grounding is established, the proposal continues with the more focusing design decisions.

❖ THE SETTING, SITE, POPULATION, OR PHENOMENON

Unless a study is quite narrowly construed, researchers cannot study all relevant circumstances, events, or people intensively and in depth. Instead, they select samples. The first and most global decision— choosing the setting, site, population, or phenomenon of interest—is fundamental to the design of the study and serves as a guide for the researcher. This early, significant decision shapes all subsequent ones and should be clearly described and justified.

Some research is site specific. For example, research that asks, By what processes do women's studies programs become incorporated into universities? must focus on a setting where this takes place. In contrast, research that asks, By what processes do innovative units become incorporated into educational organizations? has a choice of many sites and many different substantive programs. Questions such as, By what processes have Peace Corps volunteers been able to effect long-term health improvements in communities? can be pursued in many sites throughout the world.

The decision to focus on a specific setting (e.g., the Women's Studies Program at the University of Massachusetts or a street gang in Cincinnati) is somewhat constraining; the study is defined by and intimately linked to that place. Choosing to study a particular kind of population (faculty in women's studies programs or street gangs) is somewhat less so: the study can be conducted in more than one place. Studying a phenomenon (the socialization of new faculty) is even less constrained by either place or population. In these latter instances, the researcher determines a sampling strategy that is purposeful and representative.

If the study is of a specific program, organization, place, or region, some detail regarding the setting is crucial for the reader. A rationale should also be provided that outlines why this specific setting is more appropriate than others for the conduct of the study. What is unique? What characteristics of this setting are compelling and unusual? Justify this early and highly significant decision.

What about research in your own setting? While access to the site is automatic since you are native to it, the following concerns are associated with such access: the expectations of the researcher based on familiarity with the setting and the people; the transition to researcher from a more familiar role within the setting; ethical and political dilemmas; the risk of uncovering potentially damaging knowledge; and struggles with closeness and closure (Alvesson, 2003). There are also positive aspects: relatively easy access to participants; reduced time expenditure for certain aspects of data collection; a feasible location for research; the potential to build trusting relationships; and, as Kanuha (2000) says, "being drawn to study 'my own kind'" (p. 441). Closeness to the people and the phenomenon through intense interactions provides subjective understandings that can greatly increase the quality of qualitative data (Toma, 2000). A realistic site is where (a) entry is possible; (b) there is a high probability that a rich mix of the processes, people, programs, interactions, and structures of interest is present; (c) the researcher is likely to be able to build trusting relations with the participants in the study; (d) the study can be conducted and reported ethically; and (e) data quality and credibility of the study are reasonably assured. Although this ideal is seldom attained, the proposal nonetheless describes what makes the selection of a particular site especially sound. A site may be perfect for its representativeness and interest and for providing a range of examples of the phenomenon under study, but if the researcher cannot gain access to the site or to a range of groups and activities within it, the study cannot succeed. Likewise, if the researcher is very uncomfortable or endangered in the site, or if the data gathering or the findings of the research would do harm, then that site will be risky and the research process will be hampered.

One cannot study the universe—everything, every place, all the time. Instead, the researcher makes selections of sites and samples of times, places, people, and things to study. When the focus of the study is a particular population, the researcher should present a strategy for sampling that population. For example, in her study of forced terminations of psychotherapy, Kahn's (1992) strategy was to post notices in local communities asking for participants. Much discussion ensued at her proposal hearing about the feasibility of this strategy. Given assurances about the soliciting of participants using this method previously, the committee agreed; the strategy was ultimately successful.

Sample size in qualitative research depends on many complex factors. Case studies may be of a single person, like the classic *The Man in the Principal's Office* (Wolcott, 1973), or of roles, interactions, and sentiments in a bar, like *The Cocktail Waitress* (Spradley & Mann, 1975). In health research (which is more likely to be well funded), recent qualitative or mixed-method studies averaged one to four informants. Ten groups was the average in focus groups; 16 to 24 months of fieldwork was the norm in observational studies (Safman & Sobal, 2004). *Ambiguous Empowerment: The Work Narratives of Women School Superintendents* (Chase, 1995) is based on 92 tape-recorded interviews with policymakers, selection consultants, school board members, and superintendents, as well as observations in work settings.

While funding and time constraints affect sample size, the weightier concerns center on the question of research purpose. An unknown culture or profession studied in-depth over time may be composed of one case study or ethnography. A study of new mothers' receptivity to training for breast-feeding could have a huge sample, in a vast array of settings, with good funding and a large research team. A small sample would be useful as thick cultural description. The large sample in disparate and varied settings with diverse participants would also be seen as very useful since its transferability would be great.

In the proposal, the researcher should anticipate questions about the credibility and trustworthiness of the findings; poor sampling decisions may threaten these findings. To justify a sample, one must know the universe of possible samples and all of their relevant variables. Since this is an impossible task, the best compromise is to include a sample with reasonable variation in the phenomenon, settings, or people (Dobbert, 1982).

Long ago, scholars in community studies dealt with sampling issues. When the famous Yankee City study seemed to demand a parallel study of the Deep South, Warner (reported by Gardner in Whyte, 1984) pondered identifying a city representative of the Deep South. After selecting several cities that fit the criteria of size and history, he met with leaders and established contacts in the communities, eventually selecting Natchez, Mississippi, as the site for *Deep South: A Social Anthropological Study of Caste and Class* (Davis, Gardner, & Gardner, 1941). Natchez would work for negotiating access to various levels of the caste system. The use of two wife-husband teams, one black and one white, also eased access. Because they were all raised in the South and familiar with appropriate behavior within the caste system, they could observe, interview, and participate in activities, interactions, and sentiments representing all levels of the Natchez community.

The reports demonstrated that Natchez, although not exactly like all other Southern communities, was not atypical. Setting abstract criteria, checking out sites in advance, and carefully planning entry ensured that (a) the research team could move throughout the community to gather data, and (b) Natchez was not an unrepresentative pocket of the research universe. Researchers had identified the site that would maximize comparability and permit access to a wide range of behaviors and perspectives. Clearly, the selection of site and sample are critical decisions.

In another community study, of "Elmtown," a typical Midwestern community, the ease of establishing contacts with civic leaders enabled the team to act as full members of the community. They then gained access to parents and institutional functionaries through their interest in adolescent character development. This interest brought them invitations to speak before a variety of community organizations, resulting in additional contacts. They spent a considerable amount of time in informal settings with young people as well. They were at a high school before classes started, at noon, and after school; they attended most school activities, church affairs, Scout meetings, dances, and parties; and they skated, bowled, shot pool, played poker, and generally "hung out" where youth were known to gather. "The observational technique of being with them as often as possible and not criticizing their activities, carrying tales, or interfering overcame the initial suspicion in a few weeks" (Hollingshead, 1975, p. 15). The researchers' ability to gain access to a range of groups and activities was enhanced by their ability to blend in. Site and sample selection should be planned around practical issues, such as the researcher's comfort level, ability to fit into some role during participant observation, and access to a range of subgroups and activities. In some proposals, particularly those for multisite studies conducted with several researchers or for studies of organizations, it is wise to make even finer-grained decisions about sampling. This is discussed next.

❖ SELECTING A SAMPLE OF PEOPLE, ACTIONS,
     EVENTS, AND/OR PROCESSES

Once the initial decision has been made to focus on a specific site, a population, or a phenomenon, waves of subsequent sampling decisions are made. The proposal describes the plan, as conceived before the research begins, that will guide sample selection, the researcher being always mindful of the need to retain flexibility. As Denzin says, "All sampling activities are theoretically informed" (1989, p. 73). Thus, the sensitizing concepts from the literature review and the research questions provide the focus for site and sample selection; if they do not, the researcher at the very least makes the procedures and criteria for decision making explicit.

Well-developed sampling decisions are crucial for any study's soundness. Making logical judgments and presenting a rationale for these decisions go far in building the overall case for a proposed study.

Decisions about sampling people and events are made concurrently with decisions about the specific data collection methods to be used and should be thought-through in advance. When faced, for example, with the complexity of studying the meaning that women managers attach to computer-mediated communications, Alvarez (1993) had to decide what individuals and events would be most salient for her study.

VIGNETTE 7

Focusing on People and Events

The general question guiding Alvarez's (1993) study was in what ways computer-mediated communications, specifically electronic mail, alter human communications within an organizational context. She was interested in the power equalization potential of e-mail communications among persons of unequal status within the organization and in the socioemotional content of messages sent and received in a medium of reduced social cues.

The sampling strategy began as a search for information-rich cases (Patton, 1990) to study individuals who manifested the phenomenon intensely. A related concern was to have both men and women participants in the study, given that the theoretical literature suggested that there are significant differences between men and women in ease of computer usage. Once she had identified participants and they had agreed to engage in the study with her, Alvarez had to make decisions about which specific events she wanted to observe or learn more about. She reasoned that observing the sending or receiving of a message would yield little; she therefore asked participants to share sets of correspondence with her and to participate in two in-depth interviews. The first request proved quite sensitive because Alvarez was asking people to share their personal and professional mail with her. She reassured them of the confidentiality of the study and also showed them how to send copies of e-mail directly to her without revealing the direct recipient of the message. This reassured them sufficiently so that she was able to obtain a substantial set of messages that could then be content-analyzed.

In designing studies with multiple sites, with a team of researchers, or with both, plans for systematic sampling are crucial. Miles and Huberman (1994) provide excellent guidance for such planning. Vignette 8 illustrates the greater need for a sound, sampling plan in a multisite study involving more than one researcher. This plan is taken from a study of high school cultures (Rossman, Corbett, & Firestone, 1984) and depicts extensive thinking about the places, circumstances, and people that the researchers would have to learn about to respond thoughtfully and sensitively to the research questions.

VIGNETTE 8

Sampling People and Behaviors

To plan for the study, the researchers identified those events, settings, actors, and artifacts that would have the greatest potential to yield good data on each of five cultural domains: collegiality, community, goals and expectations, action orientation, and knowledge base for teaching. Items within each category provided parameters to frame data collection and represented the core data the researchers believed would be useful. The researchers started with settings because these were the most concrete, as they were collecting data in the public places (main office, hallways, parking lot), the teachers' lounge or lunchroom, classrooms, meeting rooms, private offices, department offices or workrooms, the gymnasium or locker room, and the auditorium.

In the disciplinarian's office, they expected the handling of routine infractions, suspensions, or expulsions; in the counselor's office, there might be crisis interventions. In general, the researchers expected that the events of importance would include those during which professionals interacted. These would include formal routines such as faculty and department meetings, evaluations, and union meetings; informal routines such as lunch or coffee breaks, preparation periods, recess, morning arrivals; and events during which professionals interacted with students, including teaching acts, extracurricular activities, suspensions and expulsions, roster changes, crisis counseling, postsecondary counseling, and assemblies and pep rallies.

The first category—events during which professionals interact—would provide major data on collegiality, goals and expectations, and the knowledge base for teaching. Faculty and department meetings would be crucial. In these meetings, norms governing the local definition of teaching and norms regarding how teachers should relate to one another in a meeting setting would be evident. Morning routines and other informal encounters—requests for help, supportive gestures, queries about how a particular concept or skill is best taught—would also reveal these norms and reflect notions of collegiality but in less structured settings.

Table 3.2 Data Collection: Sampling Plan

	Collegiality	Community	Goals and expectations	Action orientation	Knowledge base
Setting					
Public places (main offices, hallways)	X	X	X	X	X
Teachers' lounge or lunchroom	X	X			X
Classrooms		X	X	X	X
Meeting rooms	X		X	X	
Private offices					
Counselor's		X	X		
Disciplinarian's		X	X		
Vice principal's for scheduling			X		
Coaches'		X	X		
Principal's			X		
Department office or workroom	X		X	X	X
Gymnasium or locker room		X	X		
Auditorium		X			
Events					
Events during which professionals interact					
Faculty/department meetings	X		X		X
Lunch/coffee break/recess	X	X			X
In-service sessions	X				X
After school (local pub?)	X	X			

(Continued)

67

Table 3.2 (Continued)

	Collegiality	Community	Goals and expectations	Action orientation	Knowledge base
Events during which professionals and students interact					
Teaching acts		X	X	X	X
Extracurricular activities		X	X	X	
Suspensions and expulsions		X	X	X	
Roster changes		X	X	X	
Crisis counseling		X	X	X	
Assemblies and pep rallies		X	X	X	
Actors					
Administrators					
Principal			X	X	X
Vice principal for discipline		X	X	X	
Vice principal for curriculum	X		X	X	X
Vice principal for schedule/roster		X	X	X	
Vice principal for activities			X	X	
Counselors		X	X	X	
Coaches		X	X	X	
Teachers					
Department heads	X	X	X	X	X
Different tenure in building	X	X	X	X	X
Different departments	X	X	X	X	X

Table 3.2 (Continued)

	Collegiality	Community	Goals and expectations	Action orientation	Knowledge base
Students					
Different ability levels		X	X	X	
Different visibility		X	X	X	
Artifacts					
Documents					
Newspapers		X	X		X
Policy statements			X	X	X
Attendance records		X	X		
Disciplinary records		X	X		
Achievement test scores			X		
Objects					
Logos	X	X			
Mascots	X	X			
Trophies			X		
Decorations		X			
Art work		X			
Physical arrangements	X	X			

SOURCE: Rossman, Corbett, and Firestone (1984, p. 54). Reprinted by permission.

The second category—events during which professionals and students interact—would provide data about community, goals and expectations, and action orientation. Both in the classroom and outside of it, when teachers and students interacted, they would reveal whether or not there was a sense of community, what their expectations were for one another regarding behavior and achievement, and whether teachers felt it was important to translate ideas and concepts into actions, such as lesson and courses.

As data collection progressed, the researchers planned to sample the perceptions of key actors both within and external to the school. Finally, the researchers planned to collect or to be able to describe certain artifacts that would provide data for each of the five domains. In the above plan, the emphasis was on observation, because many of the domains the researchers were trying to understand were implicit. Thus, they inferred norms and values from behavior patterns and from naturally occurring conversations. Interviews helped them understand the settings and reconstruct the history of change in the high schools.

The sampling plan shown in Vignette 8 tried to ensure that events, rituals, resources, and interactions would be observed at each site. Purposive and theoretical sampling, which is guided by the theoretical framework and concepts, is often built into qualitative designs. For example, research on professional cultures would suggest that the researcher should sample among individuals, events, and sentiments in the early stages of initiation into a profession. Often, however, researchers' site selection and sampling begin with accessible sites (convenience sampling) and build on insights and connections from the early data collection (snowball sampling).

Miles and Huberman (1994) usefully describe different approaches to sampling in Table 3.3. Although such plans are often subject to change, given the realities of field research, at the proposal stage, they demonstrate that the researcher has thought-through some of the complexities of the setting and has made some initial judgments about how to deploy her time. Such plans also indicate that the researcher has considered both the informational adequacy and efficiency of these methods. Related to these considerations, however, are the ethical issues of the researcher's role with participants.

Table 3.3   Typology of Sampling Strategies in Qualitative Inquiry

Type of Sampling	Purpose
Maximum variation	Documents diverse variations and identifies important common patterns
Homogeneous	Focuses, reduces, simplifies, facilitates group interviewing
Critical case	Permits logical generalization and maximum application of information to other cases
Theory based	Finds examples of a theoretical construct and thereby elaborates and examines it
Confirming and disconfirming cases	Elaborates initial analysis, seeks exceptions, looks for variation
Snowball or chain	Identifies cases of interest from people who know people who know what cases are information rich
Extreme or deviant case	Learns from highly unusual manifestations of the phenomenon of interest
Typical case	Highlights what is normal or average
Intensity	Involves information-rich cases that manifest the phenomenon intensely, but not extremely
Politically important cases	Attracts desired attention or avoids attracting undesired attention
Random purposeful	Adds credibility to the sample when the potential purposeful sample is too large
Stratified purposeful	Illustrates subgroups, facilitates comparison
Criterion	Includes all cases that meet some criterion, useful for quality assurance
Opportunistic	Follows new leads, takes advantage of the unexpected
Combination or mixed	Involves triangulation and flexibility, meets multiple interests and needs
Convenience	Saves time, money, and effort but at the expense of information and credibility

SOURCE: Miles and Huberman (1994, p. 28). Reprinted by permission.

❖   THE RESEARCHER'S ROLE: ISSUES OF ENTRY,
    RECIPROCITY, PERSONAL BIOGRAPHY, AND ETHICS

In qualitative studies, the researcher is the instrument. Her presence in the lives of the participants invited to be part of the study is fundamental to the methodology. As mentioned in Chapter 1, the genre in which a study is situated may include postmodern or more traditional assumptions affecting the researcher's role and position. A more traditional qualitative researcher learns from participants' lives but maintains a stance of "empathic neutrality" (Patton, 2002, p. 49). Critical and postmodern genres, though, assume that all knowledge is political and that researchers are not neutral since their ultimate purposes include advocacy and action.

Whether the presence of the researcher in the setting is sustained and intensive, as in long-term ethnographies, or relatively brief but personal, as in in-depth interview studies, the researcher enters the lives of the participants. This brings a range of strategic, ethical, and personal issues that do not attend quantitative approaches (Locke, Spirduso, & Silverman, 2000). The research proposal should include an extensive discussion of a plan for dealing with issues before they present dilemmas and also as they may arise in unanticipated ways in the field, using the advice and experience of previous scholars. The issues range from technical ones that address entry and efficiency in terms of role to interpersonal ones that capture the ethical and personal dilemmas that arise during the conduct of a study (Rossman, 1984). Clearly, the considerations overlap and have reciprocal implications; for clarity, however, we address each set of issues in turn.

Technical Considerations

At the proposal stage, technical considerations include decisions about the deployment of the researcher's time and other resources and about negotiating access.

Situating the Self

Patton (2002) develops a series of continua for thinking about one's role in planning the conduct of qualitative research. This section relies on that work considerably. First, the researcher may plan to have a role that entails varying degrees of *participantness*—that is, the degree of actual participation in daily life. At one extreme is the full participant, who goes about ordinary life in a role or set of roles constructed in the setting. At the other is the complete observer, who engages not at all in social interaction and may even shun involvement in the world being studied. Of course, all possible complementary mixes of these roles along the continuum are available to the researcher. Our experience is that some sort of direct and immediate participation in the research environment usually becomes important to building and sustaining relationships. The researcher may help out with small chores (or large ones), learn more about a particular activity (and hence enter into that activity), or feel compelled to engage in daily activities to meet the demands of reciprocity. Such interaction is usually highly informative while remaining informal.

Next, the researcher's role may vary as to its *revealedness* or the extent to which the participants know that there is a study going on. Full disclosure lies at one end of this continuum; complete secrecy at the other. The ethical issues surrounding covert research can be reduced to one fundamental question: Is the potential advancement of knowledge worth deceit? (See Taylor & Bogdan, 1984, Chapter 3, for a provocative discussion.) Many researchers follow Taylor and Bogdan's advice to be "truthful but vague" (p.25) in portraying a research purpose to participants. Patton (2002), however, advises "full and complete disclosure. People are seldom deceived or reassured by false or partial explanations— at least not for long" (p. 273). The researcher should discuss in the proposal the issues concerning revealing or concealing the purpose of the study.

Third, the dimensions of a researcher's role may vary in *intensiveness* and *extensiveness*—that is, the amount of time spent daily in the setting and the duration of the study. Various positions on both dimensions demand certain role considerations by the researcher. For example, an intensive and extensive study requires the researcher to devote considerable time early on to developing trusting relations with the participants. Gathering pertinent data is secondary at that point. On the other hand, when the researcher will be minimally intrusive and present for a short period of time, building trusting relations must proceed in conjunction with gathering good data. In our view, this is difficult for novice researchers.

Finally, the researcher's role may vary depending on whether the focus of the study is specific or diffuse. When the research questions are well developed beforehand and data appropriate to address those questions have been identified, the researcher's role can be managed efficiently and carefully to ensure good use of the available time (both the researcher's and the participants'). Even when well specified, however, sound qualitative design protects the researcher's right to follow the compelling question, the nagging puzzle that presents itself once in the setting. When the research questions are more diffuse and exploratory, the plan for deploying the self should ensure access to a number of events, people, and perspectives on the social phenomenon chosen for study.

Fortunately, some researchers who have used participant observation have provided extensive descriptions of their plans, rationales, and actual experiences. Notable among these are researchers who have engaged in significant reflection on the research endeavor and their lives as researchers. References to these works are listed at the end of this chapter.

Negotiating Entry

The research design section of a proposal should contain plans for negotiating access to the site and/or participants through formal and informal gatekeepers in an organization, whether the organization is an urban gang or an Ivy League university. We recommend that, rather than trying to be inauthentic by adopting a contrived role, qualitative researchers be themselves, true to their social identities and their interests in the setting and/or topic. The energy that comes from a high level of personal interest (called *bias* in traditional research) is infectious and quite useful for gaining access. Access may be a continuous issue when the researcher moves around in various settings within an organization. The researcher should reveal a sensitivity to participants' testing of her and their reluctance to participate, unquestionably respecting their right not to participate in a study. Excellent discussions of access issues can be found in general texts about qualitative research referenced at the end of this chapter. Of particular interest is Anderson's (1976) experience in becoming accepted for an ethnographic study of an urban cultural group, detailed in Vignette 9.

VIGNETTE 9

Negotiating Entry

A bleak corner of urban life. A bar and liquor store named Jelly's that also serves as a hangout for African American men in south Chicago. In such a place, an angry man pulls a knife on another, a wino sleeps off his last bottle, police cars cruise without stopping, all within the sight of children at play.

Jelly's and its countless urban counterparts "provide settings for sociability and places where neighborhood residents can gain a sense of self-worth" (Anderson, 1976, p. 1).

Anderson determined that he was going to study this particular setting, but how was he to gain entry? His first observations indicated that "visitors" received special treatment, because the next person might prove to be "the police," "the baddest cat in Chicago," or someone waiting to follow another home and rip him off. In the words of the regular clientele at Jelly's, "unknown people bear watching" (p. 5).

Anderson accepted visitor treatment for several weeks, being unobtrusive yet sociable, acquainting himself with the unwritten social rules. Being African American was insufficient justification for immediate acceptance by the regulars. Enter Herman. Anderson cultivated a relationship with Herman that became a means for mutual protection of each other's "rep and rank" in the social status system at Jelly's. Anderson responded openly to Herman's persistent questioning, and several days later, Herman reciprocated by introducing Anderson to Sleepy, TJ, and Jake: "He all right. Hey this is the study I been tellin' you about. This cat getting his doctor's degree." With this introduction to the regulars, Anderson's place in the social system had been defined. In short, it provided Anderson with a license to be around. Herman used Anderson to gain credibility at his on-the-job Christmas party, introducing Anderson as "cousin" and getting him to tell the regulars at Jelly's how well Herman got along with "decent folks and intelligent folks" (p. 20).

Anderson's role evolved naturally from the low-key, nonassertive role he initially assumed to prevent unwieldy challenges from those who might have felt threatened by a more aggressive demeanor, especially from a stranger. It is the kind of role any outsider must play—is forced into—if he is not to disrupt the "consensual definition of social order in this type of setting" (pp. 22–23).

Anderson's experience is typical of those proposing long-term ethnographic studies of particular groups. At times, the best entry is one, like this one, when there is an insider who provides sponsorship and helps the researcher seem nonthreatening. There are circumstances, however, when sponsorship can backfire, setting the researcher up for difficulties in accessing other groups within the organization. For those conducting studies of organizations, negotiating access may require perseverance and persistence with formal leaders within the organization, as Vignette 10 depicts.

VIGNETTE 10

Negotiating and Maintaining
Access with a Transient Vulnerable Population

A study of socially marginalized women (former crack cocaine users and sex workers who became politically active after contracting HIV/AIDS) required great sensitivity on the part of the researcher. Berger (2003) found that negotiating access to such a vulnerable, transient population required conversations with people in agencies such as homeless shelters, courthouses, the Department of Health, and substance-abuse facilities. Gatekeepers in these agencies didn't always agree readily to participate in the study. They were often protective of their clientele (as well they should be) and of their own views of the relevant issues. Thus, when Berger spoke of her desire to understand the complexities of drug-related behaviors and of the lives of sex workers, gatekeepers were reluctant to cooperate. Their expressed views were that drugs explain most of the women's behaviors and that prostitution is dangerous and degrading. To them, learning about the subtleties and complexities of this social world had no immediate use. Although they were accustomed to survey research, they simply could not see the value (to them) of long hours of oral histories. Yet these gatekeepers' assistance was essential. What to do?

With a new approach and a new set of gatekeepers, Berger introduced her study thus: Eliciting the women's stories would confirm what gatekeepers knew about the challenging lives of these women who frequently felt victimized by larger social structures and often felt at the mercy of their drug addiction. As she recounts, "A hook is better when it is short and simple . . . it's helpful to try to categorize the type of rejection . . . [and to] plan ahead to counter or redirect assumptions" (p. 67).

Although they still regarded Berger as quite strange, gatekeepers eventually perceived her as a "nice black girl" (p. 67) who reminded them of some distant cousin. This fictive kin status served well so she began to purposefully incorporate the naïve fictive kin performance to maintain access, to encourage participants to help her get the record straight, and to help her tell outsiders how their real stories differed from televised stereotypes.

Tensions do arise when researchers are involved over the long term and the short term. We recommend that researchers plan strategies for easing those tensions that arise from relationships with research participants. Researchers may also need to think about strategies to maintain themselves. Research designs should include strategies to protect the physical and emotional health and safety of the researcher by providing plans for quiet places in which he can write notes, reassess roles, retreat from the setting, or question the directions of the research. Rager (2005) suggests several strategies for dealing with sometimes overwhelming emotional involvement, such as journal writing, peer debriefing, and personal counseling, as ways to maintain balance when data collection "can break your heart" (p. 23). In some settings, the researcher's planning may go well beyond considerations of comfort to planning to stay safe. Unfamiliar settings where strangers are unwelcome, where illegal activities may be observed, or where the researcher's race or gender makes her unwelcome require careful sensitivities (Lee, 1995; Warren, 2001). In anticipating such potential difficulties, proposals should cite the experiences of previous researchers and apply them to the current research to think-through role strategies; some excellent sources are provided at the end of this chapter.

Gaining access to sites—receiving formal approval, like Herman's sponsorship, a principal's approval—requires time, patience, and sensitivity to the rhythms and norms of a group. At the proposal stage, the researcher should indicate that negotiations have begun and formal approval is likely or that she has knowledge about the nuances of entry and a healthy respect for participants' concerns.

Efficiency

In qualitative studies, the researcher should think-through how he will deploy the resources available for the study to ensure full responses to the research questions. Although this consideration overlaps directly with decisions about data gathering, issues of role also arise here. The researcher should think carefully about how he can deploy the self, as it were, to maximize the opportunities for gathering data. This consideration should be balanced against the resources available for the study, most notably time and energy. We would caution the novice, moreover, that once a study is begun, tantalizing puzzles and intriguing questions mushroom. Even though the researcher reserves the right to pursue those, he should remain mindful of the goal of the project. Doctoral students often need to be gently prodded back into a structure for the completion of the work. Also, a priori but tentative statements about boundaries will help: A discussion of goals and limitations (e.g., five life histories; observations in one school for one year) and reminders of practical considerations (e.g., dwindling funds, the need to get a "real" job), serve as reminders that the research must be finite. One should design the study to be "reasonable in size and complexity so that it can be completed with the time and resources available" (Bogdan & Biklen, 2003, p. 51).

Interpersonal Considerations

One could argue that the success of qualitative studies depends primarily on the interpersonal skills of the researcher. In general qualitative research texts, this caveat is often couched as building trust, maintaining good relations, respecting norms of reciprocity, and sensitively considering ethical issues. These entail an awareness of the politics of organizations as well as a sensitivity to human interaction. Because the conduct of the study often depends exclusively on the relationships the researcher builds with participants, interpersonal skills are paramount. We would go so far as to dissuade a would-be qualitative researcher from using a qualitative approach if she cannot converse easily with others—being an active, patient, and thoughtful listener and having an empathetic understanding of and a profound respect for the perspectives of others. It is important to acknowledge that it is difficult for some people to become good qualitative researchers, despite sensitive and thoughtful training in courses and through pilot studies.

Further, some of the traditions of social science create a kind of *academic armor* that prevents the intimate emotional engagement often required in qualitative research (Lerum, 2001). The use of obscure academic language (linguistic armor), professional clothing and demeanor (physical armor), assumptions of theoretical privilege (ideological armor), and the effort to avoid "going native" (to be objective and detached), all create this academic armor. Dropping the academic armor allows richer, more intimate acceptance into the ongoing lives and sentiments of participants; it is a visceral way of moving beyond seeing to understanding (Denzin, 1997). Still, the researcher needs protection at times. Researchers planning their roles and their degree of engagement—whether for research on sex workers, snake handlers, or on professions where sexual harassment is allowed—will want to plan for some deployment of academic armor at times (Lerum, 2001). Researchers' respect and caring for participants can, if unguarded, go so far that they lose their ability to separate from personal entanglements (Wolcott, 2002). (We discuss this notion of having an exit strategy later in the chapter.)

Discussions of one's role in the setting and consideration of how participants' willingness to engage in thoughtful reflection may be affected help provide evidence that the researcher knows enough about the setting and the people, their routines, and their environments to anticipate how she will fit in. Researchers benefit from carefully thinking through their own roles because most participants detect and reject insincere, inauthentic people.

In addition, researchers may have to educate the participants about the researcher's role. They should describe their likely activities while in the setting, what they are interested in learning about, the possible uses of the information, and how the participants can engage in the research. Norms of reciprocity suggest that the researcher cannot be simply a spongelike observer, as Thorne (1983) describes in compelling detail in her reflections on studying war resistance in the 1960s, because many people will not respond to or trust someone who will not take a stand. Providing further illustration of these ideas, Vignette 11 describes how Rosalie Wax (1971) went about the complex task of building trust in her study of Native Americans.

VIGNETTE 11

Building Trust

The extensive writing of anthropologist Rosalie Wax (1971) has emphasized the importance of the researcher's initial contacts with members of the society or group chosen for study. The reciprocal relationship between host and field-worker enables the latter to avoid foolish, insulting, and potentially dangerous behavior, to make valuable contacts, and to understand the acceptance and repayment of obligations. "The most egregious error that a field-worker can commit," according to Wax (p. 47), is assuming that tolerance by hosts also implies their high regard and inclusion.

In her ethnographic community study of Native American reservation society, Wax found the women embarrassed and hesitant to open their poor, bare homes to the scrutiny of a researcher. Their trust and cooperation were essential to her study because Wax sought to understand the relationship between cultural patterns expressed in the home and poor adjustment and underachievement by the children in school. In her account of the slow uncovering of answers, Wax reveals her method of making others comfortable with her presence. She permitted children to play with her typewriter. She employed some of the women as interviewers. Avoiding the social-worker or Bureau-of-Indian-Affairs do-gooder image, Wax interacted as woman to woman, always exploring but doing so with an interest in the welfare of the women's children.

———————————— ⑈ ————————————

Vignette 11 demonstrates that researchers should allow time and be sensitive to the need for time to pass, for flexibility in their roles, and for patience because confidence and trust emerge over time through complex interactions. Roles and relationships do emerge in the field. At the proposal stage, however, the researcher should demonstrate a logical plan that respects the need for time to build relationships. It is not enough to state that trust and relationships are important. The researcher should also display the skills and sensitivities to deal with complexities in relationships that inevitably emerge during fieldwork. Moving on to another site is another way to manage—politically and ethically—a difficult situation: There are times when, even with the best planning, the researcher cannot gain entry to a site, as Vignette 12 shows.

VIGNETTE 12

Moving On

Wanting to explore the interaction between the political demands of a community and access to leadership in a school district by women and people of color, Marshall (1992) designed comparative case studies and identified two sites—two cities in the same region of the country with similar political cultures, demographic composition, and comparatively large numbers of women and people of color in leadership positions. The sites were chosen for comparability along those dimensions but with one significant difference: "Change City" showed evidence of a political structure undergoing substantial change, whereas "Avondale" represented a more placid political climate.

At Avondale, Marshall encountered no more than the typical bureaucratic barriers to gaining access: letters to gatekeepers, meetings with district research directors, assurances of compliance with district monitoring of the research. Pleased with this response, she began the access process in Change City by subscribing to the local newspaper to learn about local politics and by placing phone calls to the superintendent, a newly hired African American man from another state. Weeks passed. Months passed. Her politely persistent calls resulted in a telephone relationship with the secretary! She devised other strategies: letters flattering to the superintendent, reassurances of the value of the research for the district, name-dropping, emphasizing the university letterhead in her written correspondence and the study's connection to a national center on school leadership. Still no response.

Searching for insights behind the scenes, Marshall learned that this new superintendent was extremely careful about controlling information as he dealt with an explosive dispute about resources, people of color in administrative positions, and political maneuvers to support incumbent white administrators.

Intrigued, Marshall tried one last tactic: the "chance" meeting. With a little help from the superintendent's secretary, she got herself invited to a conference that the superintendent planned to attend and was able to engage him in conversation during a coffee break. In the context of conference-related talk, she mentioned casually that she hoped to talk with him about doing research in the district. Gracious, interested, and promising to talk at length at the next break, the superintendent appeared open. Much to Marshall's chagrin, however, his assistant apologized that the superintendent had been called back to the office to manage some emergency. Foiled again!

Marshall resumed the phone calls and letters but the silence from his office was deafening. It was time to face facts. The political controversies about people of color in leadership positions—the very question that she wanted to study—was the tense and difficult issue that kept this superintendent from risking exposure in this political maelstrom. Marshall went back to the library to find another Change City.

Sometimes, because the politics in a setting are so explosive, researchers must simply move on. At some point, they decide that the efforts to get around the barriers to entry are excessive, and they must respect the needs of key actors in the setting. With topics that are politicized and sensitive, the researcher should identify several potential sites so she can move to an alternative site with little delay if need be.

Reciprocity and Ethics

A thorough research proposal also demonstrates the researcher's awareness of reciprocity issues. Qualitative studies intrude into settings as people adjust to the researcher's presence. People may be giving their time to be interviewed or to help the researcher understand group norms; the researcher should plan to reciprocate. When people adjust their priorities and routines to help the researcher, or even just tolerate the researcher's presence, they are giving of themselves. The researcher is indebted and should be sensitive to this. Reciprocity may entail giving time to help out, providing informal feedback, making coffee, being a good listener, or tutoring. Of course, reciprocity should fit within the constraints of research and personal ethics and of maintaining one's role as a researcher.

Ethics

The qualities that make a successful qualitative researcher reveal themselves as an exquisite sensitivity to the ethical issues surrounding any moral act. Ethical considerations are generic—informed consent and protecting participants' anonymity—as well as situation-specific. The research design anticipates the array of ethical challenges that will occur. As Lerum (2001) says, emotionally engaged researchers must continuously evaluate and construct their behavior. If anticipated in the design, these challenges will be less dilemma-laden in the field and may provide opportunities for ways of reasoning that may help negotiate such dilemmas when they do arise.

Several authors discuss ethical considerations in qualitative research, describing the dilemmas they have encountered. Role, reciprocity, and ethical issues must be thought-through carefully in all settings but especially in those that are particularly sensitive or taboo. In developing the section of the proposal that addresses role and reciprocity issues, the qualitative researcher should draw on the advice and experience of her predecessors.

The competent research proposal, then, anticipates issues of negotiating entry, reciprocity, role maintenance, and receptivity and, at the same time, adheres to ethical principles. The researcher must demonstrate awareness of the complex ethical issues in qualitative research and show that the research is both feasible and ethical. If the researcher will be playing a deceptive role, she should demonstrate that this will not be harmful to the participants. If she will require people to change their routines or donate their time, doing so must be voluntary for them. What is routine and acceptable in one setting may be harmful in another; what is volunteered in one may be withheld in another. The researcher cannot anticipate everything, but she must reveal an awareness of, an appreciation for, and a commitment to ethical principles for research. Several authors have explored these issues in the general texts and articles referenced at the end of this chapter as well as in the studies described in the following vignettes.

VIGNETTE 13

Ethics and Ethnographic Fieldwork

Ethnographic research has traditionally been undertaken in fields that, by virtue of the contrast between them and the researcher's own culture, could be described as exotic. The researcher's goal is to describe the symbols and values of such a culture without passing judgment based on his cultural context. Soloway and Walters (1977), however, point out that when a researcher studies those whose acts are considered criminal, profound ethical dilemmas arise: "When one decides to attempt to enter their world and to study it, the field-worker arrives at a true moral, ethical, and legal existential crisis" (p. 161).

One option is to carry out studies of criminal subcultures from within institutions such as prisons or treatment centers. Critical of such a procedure, Soloway and Walters note that "if addicts are studied at Lexington [a federal hospital], then the result is a study of patients. If addicts are studied in jail, the result is a study of prisoners" (p. 163).

To understand addiction, Soloway chose to enter the addicts' natural habitat. Entry was aided by his affiliation with a methadone treatment program and by the fact that he was doing his research within the neighborhood where he had spent his childhood. One of his contacts during observation of the weekly distribution of methadone was Mario, an old neighborhood friend and a patient at the treatment center.

Mario saw this relationship as a source of status both within the program and on the street. He chose to test this relationship at one point, coming in "high" for his weekly dose. When he was refused the methadone because of his condition, he sought out his friend the ethnographer to intercede with the nurses. Not only did the researcher refuse to intercede, he rebuked Mario, saying, "I'm no lame social worker from the suburbs; you're high and everybody knows it" (p. 165). Even though he risked jeopardizing the researcher-informant relationship, the risk paid off because Mario eventually introduced Soloway to other addicts. This involvement with urban heroin addicts enabled him to observe them in the context of their total social milieu, where junkie was only part of their identity.

Was Soloway taking advantage of his friendship with Mario? Is the participant observer a friend to participants? Can the researcher be both observer and friend? How does one juggle the objectivity of the stranger and the desire for the well-being of a friend? "The bind on the ethnographer's personal ethic," according to Soloway and Walters, "is that his total integrity cannot be maintained in either role" (p. 166). What represents a researcher's ethical response when observing or possibly becoming involved in criminal activity? Polsky (1969) insists that to study adult criminals in their natural settings, one must "make the moral decision that in some ways he will break the law himself" (pp. 133–134). On the other hand, Yablonsky (1965) asserts that participant observation among the criminally deviant merely serves, by way of the researcher's interest in the subject, to reinforce the criminal behavior.

In the exchange with Mario, the researcher attempted to strike a balance by employing the principle of relativism. According to this principle, ethnographers are not expected to renounce their own culturally formed consciences, nor are they to project those values on their subjects. "Relativism operationally guards against two dangers, the ethnographer's own ethnocentrism and an equally dangerous inverted ethnocentrism—that is, going native and personally identifying with the studied value system" (Soloway & Walters, 1977, p. 168).

Manning (1972) recounted advising a student designing research on police. He noted that the student could walk the beat with the police officer, ride in the patrol car with the police officer, even tag along when an arrest is about to be made. But he could not be a police officer, wear the uniform, take the risks, make the arrests, or adopt the police officer's perspective. How do researchers go about courting the cooperation of individuals whose social ecology is so very different from their own? Must researchers assume identities other than their own? According to Westley (1967), a critical norm among law enforcement personnel is the maintenance of secrecy:

> It is carefully taught to every rookie policeman. . . . The violator is cut off from vital sources of information and the protection of his colleagues in times of emergency. Secrecy means that policemen must not talk about police work to those outside the department. (p. 774)

Thus, he had to consider whether it is ethical to encourage police officers to talk about their work. He had to anticipate dilemmas if he should observe an incidence of police brutality. Complying with the law and turning the officer in would risk the destruction of the study. Remaining silent would gain the trust of those he was observing along with some leverage. This student planned ahead, deciding to opt for the benefits of silence.

Not all qualitative studies present such extreme ethical dilemmas. It is, however, quite difficult to maintain the role of researcher when caught in the middle of events that seem to call for action. Researchers must anticipate more routine ethical issues and be prepared to make on-the-spot decisions that (one hopes) follow general ethical principles (see, especially, Christians, 2000, 2005; Punch, 1994; Welland & Pugsley, 2002). Reading other researchers' discussions of ethical problems and using case material to prepare for hypothetical situations can illuminate so-called standard ethical considerations and refine the researcher's abilities to reason through moral argument. Vignette 14 draws from the work of a Chicana ethnographer as she struggled with the challenges of conducting research to fulfill her own goals while respecting those with whom she had conducted the study. The political and ethical dilemmas she confronted were acute, as she found herself co-opted by the dominant Anglo leaders in the community where she conducted her research.

VIGNETTE 14

Ethics, Power, and Politics

In her work, Villenas (1996) describes being caught between her role as a Chicana ethnographer, the marginalized Latino community she studied, and the Anglo groups in power within the community. She examined the educational histories of Latina mothers who were recent immigrants in the small rural community of Hope City in North Carolina. She focused on telling the women's stories about how they created educational models for raising their children.

Villenas focused on how to overcome the Latino community's perception of her as a privileged ethnographer from an elite university. However, she found herself being co-opted by the dominant English-speaking community, who spoke of Latino family education and child-rearing practices as problematic and "lacking." By using and not challenging the language of the community leaders, she was complying with this negative representation.

Concerned about gaining access to community leaders, she censored herself when she spoke to the Anglo leaders and did not point out their racist language and demeaning depictions of the Latino community. In addition, the community leaders assumed that she shared their fear of poor persons and people of color and that she also saw the Latino community as a "problem." Because there were no Latinos/as in the community in leadership positions with whom Villenas could align herself, she became the sole Latina accepted by community leaders. In this role, she was accepted as an insider in the Anglo community while, at the same time, seen as an outsider by the Latino community.

To counter this co-opted role, she started "to engage in small subversive strategies and acts of resistance" (p. 725). For example, she used opportunities to speak at meetings to present a positive depiction of the Latino community and chose not to sit at the head table with community leaders, sitting in the audience with friends she had made in the Latino community instead.

Vignette 14 shows that a researcher's role can be co-opted by people in positions of power. Although the intent of the research may be to show the positive aspects of a culture, it is easy for an inadequately self-reflexive researcher to be appropriated by and become complicit in the process by which marginalized groups are negatively depicted as a problem.

Potential dilemmas can be addressed at the proposal stage. For example, in a phenomenological study of gay, lesbian, and straight youth who participate in gay/straight alliances in high schools, Doppler (1998) described the issues involving ethics and human subjects in her study in some detail. To provide details of how to write about ethics, we include excerpts from Doppler's proposal as well as her consent letter for students.

The discussion she referred to as Informed Consent included the following

"Because participants will be high school students, some of whom may be especially vulnerable because of being lesbian or gay or due to status as a heterosexual ally of lesbian and gay youth, it will be particularly important to protect them from any potential harm . . . Participants will have the opportunity to read transcripts of each interview in which they share their reactions and will be asked to modify the transcript."

Doppler's Appendix included the consent letter shown in Figure 3.3. (She constructed a similar informed consent letter to be signed by willing parents.)

Doppler's discussion of Reciprocity included

"[Participants] will have an opportunity to voice their experiences and feelings in a safe setting with someone who **will** validate the importance of their participation in a GSA [gay/straight alliance]. Lesbian or gay students may receive the greatest benefit because they will have an opportunity to voice feelings and thoughts about which they may usually remain silent. Also, interacting with a lesbian educator who is happy and well-adjusted to life as a lesbian can provide a positive role model. . . . On a cursory level, I will share power with participants by encouraging them to modify interview transcripts to make them fully accurate. Much more important is the power dispensed by providing opportunity for students to give voice to their experiences."

In her section entitled Right to Privacy, Doppler wrote

"Pseudonyms will be used to protect the anonymity of participants. It is possible for this study, however, that some participants will want to have their names used as a rite of passage out of the closet. In that case, the implications of the use of actual names versus

Figure 3.3   Informed Consent: Students

**Informed Consent for Dissertation Research Project Participation:
Gay/Straight Alliance Participants in Public High Schools**

Dear Gay/Straight Alliance Member:

I am a graduate student in the School of Education at the University of Massachusetts, Amherst. I would like to invite you to participate in a research project about the benefits and costs of participating in a gay/straight alliance. I am interested in exploring the experiences of self-identified lesbian, gay, and heterosexual students who participate in GSAs.

Your participation will include being interviewed twice for 45 minutes to an hour each time. A third interview of the same length may be added if it seems necessary after the first two interviews.

You may be vulnerable to someone's determining who you are and what you've said, but I will protect you from this possibility as much as possible by using a pseudonym for your name and for the school you attend. I will give you a hard copy of the transcript of each of your interviews. You will be able to make any changes you want. You have the right to withdraw from the study any time up until March 1, 1999. At that point, I will be in the final stages of the writing process and will not be able to remove quotations from the document.

This study will be shared with my dissertation committee and other appropriate members of the University of Massachusetts community. The dissertation that results from this work will be published in hard copy and microfiche, which will be housed at the W. E. B. DuBois Library on campus.

I appreciate your giving time to this study, which will help me learn more about the effect of participation in a GSA. If you have any questions, please feel free to call me at _____. You may also contact my committee chairperson, Professor _____ at _____.

Thank you,

Janice E. Doppler (signed)

Please sign below if you are willing to participate in the dissertation research project outlined above.

Signature _____

Print name _____

Date _____

SOURCE: Reprinted by permission of Janice Doppler.

pseudonyms will be discussed with any participant who wants her or his name to be used. Participants will be promised every reasonable attempt to maintain confidentiality with the exception of self-reports of suicidality or abuse. . . ."

Doppler also included a section entitled
Advocacy/Intervention, in which she wrote

"I anticipate that ethical considerations around advocacy/intervention may create personal dilemmas during my fieldwork. During the course of interviews, it is likely that I will hear about harassment and discrimination. My impulse may be to intervene in the situation. At this point, I believe that it will be appropriate to be sure students know what avenues they can take to deal with harassment or discrimination. When that sort of situation arises, I will continue the interview to keep the flow going, but at the end of the interview session, I can offer to discuss channels of possible support within their individual schools or provide phone numbers for supports outside their schools. . . ."

She then provided an example of her recent use of this strategy.

These excerpts from Doppler's (1998) proposal demonstrate sensitivity. She went on to show how she would manage political independence, how she would protect her ownership of the data, and why potential benefits would outweigh any risks associated with conducting the study. As she illustrates, informed consent can be a complicated process. Simplistic, trite, and unreflective verbiage will not suffice.

Review Boards

To protect human subjects from unnecessary harm, universities and professional associations have created codes of ethics and Research Review Boards. Institutional Review Boards or Internal Review Boards (IRBs) in universities and agencies receiving federal funds must review all research proposals to ensure that the research will proceed with appropriate protections against risk to humans and animals, as mandated by the National Research Act, Public Law 93–348. Standards and guidelines are most stringent in the United States and Canada, and less so in other countries. Universities and agencies vary in their interpretations of the guidelines, and sometimes board members are unfamiliar with qualitative proposals. Further, IRBs' primary purpose—to avoid biomedical and physical experimentation and to avoid manipulation of humans without their consent—is less relevant for many qualitative social science proposals. (See the overview of IRB benefits and drawbacks in Brainard, 2001).

Sometimes qualitative proposals undergo criticism and demands for revisions as IRBs expect them to conform to more conventional designs. This has recently been compounded by the National Research Council's (2002) report stipulating what should be considered scientific inquiry. In her commentary on these conservative trends in the research community, Lincoln (2005) notes that:

> Currently there appear to be four ways in which the work of qual-
> itative researchers and scholars who teach qualitative research
> philosophies and methods is constrained by the manner in which
> new paradigms encounter institutional review board regulation
> on campuses: (a) increased scrutiny surrounding research with
> human subjects (a response to failures in biomedical research), (b)
> new scrutiny of classroom research and training in qualitative
> methods involving human subjects, (c) new discourses regarding
> what constitutes "evidence-based research," and (d) the long-term
> effects of the recent National Research Council (2002) report on
> what should be considered to be scientific inquiry. (p. 166)

Nevertheless, the principles of ethical management of role, access, data collection, storage, and reporting serve as essential reminders. IRBs require answers to certain specific questions: Describe the research, sites, and subjects; how will you attain access? How will you provide for informed consent and what will your entry letter and informed consent form look like? What kinds of interactions will you have with subjects? What risks will subjects take and how will you reduce those risks? How will you guard your data and your infor-mants' privacy? (Glesne, 1999)

Cultural Challenges to Informed Consent

The Institutional Review Board, with its requirement of informed consent, is a uniquely Western practice. Informed consent is based on principles of individualism and free will——also uniquely Western cul-tural assumptions. Written informed consent forms also assume liter-acy, a skill that may not be present when doing fieldwork in countries with different cultural and legal traditions. When working in cross-cultural contexts, where cultural beliefs and values may be collectivist and hierarchical, how does the notion of informed consent play out? Putting one's name or mark on a piece of paper may seem dangerous to participants outside the United States or Europe. These issues must be engaged directly, especially as international students doing field-work in their countries of origin must complete appropriate forms and undergo the required human subjects review by the university. How do they meet the demands for the protection of human subjects required by U.S. universities and yet still respect the cultural norms operating in the settings for their research?

Formulaic completion of the required forms evades deeper issues of the cultural biases embedded in the documents and procedures. Observing the intent behind the protection of human subjects that is encoded in documents and procedures, though, means that students must address three key demands: (a) that participants understand (have explained to them) that this is a research study with specific parameters and interests; (b) that they are free to participate or not without preju- dice (but this raises its own set of issues discussed below); and (c) that their identities will be masked (protected) as much as possible.

VIGNETTE 15

Talking Through Cultural Challenges

MacJessie-Mbewe, a doctoral student from Malawi in Southern Africa, dis- cussed with Rossman at length how he would approach the participants in his study, given that Malawi is a highly collectivist and hierarchical culture. In his human subjects review forms, he wrote, "According to Malawian rural cul- ture, informed consent will be obtained orally. Getting them to sign a form will yield unpleasant reactions and many will fear to participate because of that. Permission will be taken from heads of school, district, and Ministry [of Education]. According to Malawian rules, once you take permission from the Ministry of Education and the district education manager, it is enough to use schools for research" (2004, no page).

Although this rationale passed the review process, many ethical issues arose in their discussion. For example, what does consent mean when, if a higher official has approved the study, teachers and heads of schools—as civil servants—must comply and participate? Are they freely agreeing to par- ticipate? Can they withdraw without repercussions from higher officials? Discussions with MacJessie-Mbewe and other students from Malawi cen- tered on these issues. While working on the required forms, Rossman engaged students in discussions of how culturally inappropriate a written informed consent may be and encouraged them to elaborate on the reasons why. One typical reason is that written forms, which one must sign or put one's mark on, are associated with the government, often with sinister con- notations in repressive or highly corrupt regimes. Another is that the partici- pant (subject) is not literate and hence cannot be fully informed as to what he/she is signing. A third is that, in more collectivist cultures than the United States or Europe, trust and good faith are observed through one's word rather than one's signature. Thus, asking someone to sign a form will be taken as a sign of disrespect. In the end, students agreed upon ways to discuss how they will observe the intent of the procedures: informing participants about their research; engaging their willing participation; and protecting their identities as much as feasible. So, now MacJessie-Mbewe had more guidance.

While no perfect solutions emerged in this vignette, the issues were engaged openly, using a cultural critique of Western practice for research conducted in very different cultural contexts.

Planning the Exit

The logical, but often forgotten, extension of entry, access, role, reciprocity, and ethics is the researcher's exit strategy. A plan is needed, whether it is the thank you and goodbye after a 20-minute interview or the array of separations from roles played in a one-year immersion in an organization. For all respondents, the initial negotiation of entry and access should have, at the very least, some explanation of what the final product will look like and, by implication, the stated expectation that the relationship is temporary. Still, with intense interaction, and over time, with sharing, proferring of assistance, gifts, and confessions, this exit expectation fades. Researchers must decide. Some choose to maintain some relationship in small ways, such as birthday cards, or more fully.

Whether the researcher chooses to end the relationships or to continue them in some way, being respectful of people and relationships is essential for being an ethical researcher. One does not grab the data and run. At the very least, for participants who have provided access, opened up their daily lives and their views, the researcher should plan a gradual exit, talking about the completion of the project, providing samples of how the report will look, and leaving gifts or offers of assistance as tokens that supplement words and notes of gratitude. Asking to be kept on a mailing list, taking time to send articles of interest or photos from the setting and other personal notes ease potential resentments or a sense of abandonment. Also, after intense commitments of time and focus, the researcher most likely will, on leaving the field, have strong feelings of separation, loneliness, and loss. Anticipating these feelings is especially important for researchers with very social, relationship-oriented natures. Some never get over the transition to lonelier phases of analysis and writing. Finally, researchers' plans for role management have to include self-care strategies to deal with fatigue, with "compassion stress," and other powerful emotions (Rager, 2005). Knowing how to anticipate the emotions of fieldwork is part of the research design, to be addressed in proposal sections on role, entry, and ethics.

The preceding discussions have taken the reader through the recursive process of deciding on an overall approach to the study, building a rationale around it, discussing the sites and participants, and thinking about their role, their access, their ways of reciprocating for access and help, and the ethical issues in the conduct of the study. The next chapter describes an array of primary and supplementary data collection methods—the concrete answers to the question, How will I do this study?

DIALOGUE AMONG LEARNERS

Melanie,

Thanks for the reply. I like what you said about qualitative work as hopelessly intertwined (and the image of the Gordian knot is wonderful). This brings to mind conversations I've had about the self-reflexive nature of qualitative work. Good qualitative research, it seems, is continually aware of the processes that produce and analyze the data. (Here I mean "processes" in terms of the mechanisms and artifacts involved in data collection and analysis as well as those social processes that shade our daily actions, if that makes any sense.) This self-reflexiveness allows us to trace our often messy path through the Gordian knot of our research. So, we begin the many kinds of work involved in qualitative research and then reflexively look back at that work, allowing our later endeavors to be affected by the reflexive act. If we fail to do this, it seems we could easily plunge through, gathering data and analyzing it without being attuned to the subtleties involved in qualitative work (and, oh man, are there ever so many subtleties!).

Let me know if any of this makes sense. Hope all is well,

Aaron

Aaron,

Oh, I completely agree! The self is an integral part of qualitative research—for better or worse!—and without that self-reflectivity, a piece of the research is lost. I've been struggling with this lately, however (how timely is this conversation!), because I often found myself in the participant observer role during my study. My issue at the moment isn't with my status or my engagement, though, but with my level of transparency in writing up this research. How self-reflective should I be? How much of myself do I include in this study? How do I divide "researcher self" from "former instructor self" from "friend self"—and how do I present those selves legitimately in my work?

While I can accept—and embrace—the self-reflective component of qualitative research, I find myself confused as to its parameters. Perhaps I'm suffering from long years of quantitative approaches to research? Still, where does the self begin and end in our research? Yes, technically I know we infuse our research, but our research isn't about us (unless we're purposefully taking a phenomenological approach), it's about our question, our topic, (most importantly) our people. I suppose this is another strand of the Gordian knot. I don't want to plunge right through without engaging the subtleties (as you so aptly said) but neither do I want to enmesh myself with my own reflectivity to the point of suffocation.

Now I'm rambling! This is what happens when I haven't had my dinner. Does any of this make sense?

Melanie

❖ FURTHER READING

Rationale and Evolving Design

Becker, H. S., Geer, B., Hughes, E. C., & Strauss, A. L. (1961). *Boys in white: Student culture in medical school.* Chicago: University of Chicago Press.

Brantlinger, E. A. (1993). *The politics of social class in secondary schools* (1st ed.). New York: Teachers College Press.

Campbell, A. (1991). *The girls in the gang* (2nd ed.). Cambridge: Blackwell.

Chase, S. E. (1995). *Ambiguous empowerment: The work narratives of women school superintendents.* Amherst: University of Massachusetts Press.

Janesick, V. J. (1994). The dance of qualitative research design. In N. K. Denzin & Y. S. Lincoln (Eds.), *Handbook of qualitative research* (pp. 209–219). Thousand Oaks, CA: Sage.

Lesko, N. (1988). *Symbolizing society: Stories, rites, and structure in a Catholic high school.* New York: Falmer.

Metz, M. H. (1978). *Classrooms and corridors: The crisis of authority in desegregated secondary schools.* Berkeley: University of California Press.

Olesen, V. L., & Whittaker, E. W. (1968). *The silent dialogue: A study in the social psychology of professional socialization.* San Francisco: Jossey-Bass.

Smith, L. (1971). *Anatomy of an educational innovation.* New York: John Wiley.

Valli, L. (1986). *Becoming clerical workers.* Boston: Routledge & Kegan Paul.

Whyte, W. F. (1981). *Street corner society: The social structure of an Italian slum* (3rd ed.). Chicago: University of Chicago Press.

Personal Reflections

Brizuela, B. M., Stewart, J. P., Carrillo, R. G., & Berger, J. G. (Eds.). (2000). *Acts of inquiry in qualitative research.* Cambridge, MA: Harvard Educational Review, Reprint Series No. 34.

deMarrais, K. B. (Ed.). (1998). *Inside stories: Qualitative research reflections.* Mahwah, NJ: Lawrence Erlbaum.

Eisner, E. W. (1991). *The enlightened eye: Qualitative inquiry and the enhancement of educational practice.* New York: Macmillan.

Geertz, C. (1988). *Works and lives: The anthropologist as author.* Palo Alto, CA: Stanford University Press.

Gitlin, A. (Ed.). (1994). *Power and method: Political activism and educational research.* New York: Routledge.

Glesne, C., & Peshkin, A. (1992). *Becoming qualitative researchers: An introduction.* White Plains, NY: Longman.

Golde, P. (1970). *Women in the field.* Chicago: Aldine.

Jorgensen, D. L. (1989). *Participant observation: A methodology for human studies.* Newbury Park, CA: Sage.

McLaughlin, D., & Tierney, W. G. (1993). *Naming silenced lives: Personal narratives and processes of educational change.* New York: Routledge.

Piotrkowski, C. S. (1979). *Work and the family system: A naturalistic study of working-class and lower-middle-class families.* New York: Free Press.

Van Maanen, J. (1988). *Tales of the field: On writing ethnography.* Chicago: University of Chicago Press.

Weis, L., & Fine, M. (2000). *Speed bumps: A student-friendly guide to qualitative research.* New York: Teachers College Press.

Whyte, W. F. (1984). *Learning from the field: A guide from experience.* Beverly Hills, CA: Sage.

Negotiating Entry and Access in General Texts

Bogdan, R. C., & Biklen, S. K. (1998). *Qualitative research for education: An introduction to theory and methods* (3rd ed.). Boston: Allyn & Bacon.

Eisner, E. W. (1991). *The enlightened eye: Qualitative inquiry and the enhancement of educational practice.* New York: Macmillan.

Patton, M. Q. (1990). *Qualitative research and evaluation methods* (2nd ed.). Newbury Park, CA: Sage.

Schwartz, H., & Jacobs, J. (1979). *Qualitative sociology: A method to the madness.* New York: Free Press.

Taylor, S. J., & Bogdan, R. (1984). *Introduction to qualitative research: The search for meanings* (2nd ed.). New York: John Wiley.

Personal, Political, and Ethical Dilemmas

Brainard, J. (2001). The wrong rules for social science? *Chronicle of Higher Education, 47*(26), A21–A23.

Bowen, E. S. (1964). *Return to laughter.* Garden City, NY: Doubleday.

Christians, C. G. (2000). Ethics and politics in qualitative research. In N. K. Denzin & Y. S. Lincoln (Eds.), *Handbook of qualitative research* (2nd ed., pp. 133–155). Thousand Oaks, CA: Sage.

Emerson, R. (1983). Introduction. In R. Emerson (Ed.), *Contemporary field research: A collection of readings* (pp. 255–268). Prospect Heights, IL: Waveland.

Everhart, R. B. (1977). Between stranger and friend: Some consequences of long-term fieldwork in schools. *American Educational Research Journal, 14*, 1–15.

Feldman, M. S., Bell, J., & Berger, M. T. (Eds.). (2003). *Gaining access: A practical and theoretical guide for qualitative researchers.* Walnut Creek, CA: AltaMira Press.

Fine, M. (1994). Negotiating the hyphens: Reinventing self and other in qualitative research. In N. K. Denzin & Y. S. Lincoln (Eds.), *Handbook of qualitative research* (pp. 70–82). Thousand Oaks, CA: Sage.

Galliher, J. F. (1983). Social scientists' ethical responsibilities to superordinates: Looking up meekly. In R. Emerson (Ed.), *Contemporary field research: A collection of readings* (pp. 300–311). Prospect Heights, IL: Waveland.

Glesne, C. (1989). Rapport and friendship in ethnographic research. *International Journal of Qualitative Studies in Education, 2*, 43–54.

Krieger, S. (1985). Beyond subjectivity: The use of self in social science. *Qualitative Sociology, 8*, 309–324.

Lincoln, Y. S. (1997). Self, subject, audience, text: Living at the edge, writing in the margins. In W. G. Tierney & Y. S. Lincoln (Eds.), *Representation and the text: Re-framing the narrative voice.* Albany: State University of New York Press.

Lincoln, Y. S. (2005). Institutional Review Boards and methodological conservatism: The challenge to and from phenomenological paradigms. In

N. K. Denzin & Y. S. Lincoln (Eds.), *The handbook of qualitative research* (3rd ed., pp. 165–181). Thousand Oaks, CA: Sage.

Lincoln, Y. S., & Tierney, W. G. (2004). Qualitative research and institutional review boards. *Qualitative Inquiry, 10*(2), 219–234.

Olesen, V., & Whittaker, E. (1967). Role-making in participant observation: Processes in the research-actor relationship. *Human Organization, 26,* 273–281.

Peshkin, A. (1988). In search of subjectivity: One's own. *Educational Researcher, 17,* 17–21.

Punch, M. (1986). *The politics and ethics of fieldwork.* Beverly Hills, CA: Sage.

Punch, M. (1994). Politics and ethics in qualitative research. In N. K. Denzin & Y. S. Lincoln (Eds.), *Handbook of qualitative research* (pp. 83–97). Thousand Oaks, CA: Sage.

Rist, R. (1981, April). *Is there life after research? Ethical issues in the study of schools.* Paper presented at the annual meeting of the American Educational Research Association, Los Angeles.

Smith, M. (1999). Researching social workers' experiences of fear: Piloting a course. *Social Work Education, 18*(3), 347–354.

Spradley, J. S. (1979). *The ethnographic interview.* New York: Holt, Rinehart & Winston.

Thorne, B. (1983). Political activist as participant observer: Conflicts of commitment in a study of the draft resistance movement of the 1960s. In R. Emerson (Ed.), *Contemporary field research: A collection of readings* (pp. 216–234). Prospect Heights, IL: Waveland.

Van Maanen, J. (1983). The moral fix: On the ethics of fieldwork. In R. Emerson (Ed.), *Contemporary field research: A collection of readings* (pp. 269–287). Prospect Heights, IL: Waveland.

Wax, M. L. (1983). On field-workers and those exposed to fieldwork: Federal regulations and moral issues. In R. Emerson (Ed.), *Contemporary field research: A collection of readings* (pp. 288–299). Prospect Heights, IL: Waveland.

Welland, T., & Pugsley, L. (2002). *Ethical dilemmas in qualitative research.* Hants, England: Ashgate.

Wolcott, H. F. (2002). *Sneaky kid and its aftermath: Ethics and intimacy in fieldwork.* Walnut Creek, CA: Alta Mira Press.

Role, Access, and Ethics Issues with Special Populations

Dewing, J. (2002) From ritual to relationship: A person-centred approach to consent in qualitative research with older people who have dementia. *Dementia, 1*(2), 157–171.

Holmes, R. (1998). *Fieldwork with children.* Newbury Park, CA: Sage.

4

Data Collection Methods

Qualitative researchers typically rely on four methods for gathering information: (a) participating in the setting, (b) observing directly, (c) interviewing in depth, and (d) analyzing documents and material culture. These form the core of their inquiry—the staples of the diet. Several secondary and specialized methods of data collection supplement them. This chapter provides a brief discussion of the primary and the secondary methods to be considered in designing a qualitative study. This discussion does not replace the many excellent, detailed references on data collection (we refer to several at the end of this chapter). Its purpose is to guide the proposal writer in stipulating the methods of choice for his study and in describing for the reader how the data will inform his research questions. How the researcher plans to use these methods, however, depends on several considerations.

Chapter 1 presents an introductory discussion of qualitative methodological assumptions. As the grounding for a selection of methods, we extend that discussion here, using Brantlinger's (1997) useful summary of seven categories of crucial assumptions for qualitative inquiry. The first concerns the researcher's views of the *nature of the research:* Is the inquiry technical and neutral, intending to conform to traditional research within her discipline, or is it controversial and critical, with an explicit political agenda? Second, How does she construe her location, her *positioning relative to the participants:* Does she view herself as distant and objective or intimately involved in their lives? Third, what is the *"direction of her 'gaze'"*: Is it outward, toward others—externalizing the research problem—or does it include explicit inner contemplation? Fourth, what is the *purpose of the research:* Does she assume that the primary purpose of the study is professional and essentially private (e.g., promoting her career), or is it intended to be useful and informative to the participants or the site? Related to the fourth category is the fifth: Who is the *intended audience of the study*—the scholarly community or the participants themselves? Sixth, what is the researcher's *political positioning:* Does she view the research as neutral or does she claim a politically explicit agenda? Finally, the seventh assumption has to do with how she views the *exercise of agency:* Does she see herself and the participants as essentially passive or as "engaged in local praxis"? (Brantlinger, p. 4). Assumptions made in these seven categories shape how the specific research methods are conceived and implemented throughout a study. Explicit discussion of assumptions strengthens the overall logic and integrity of the proposal.

❖ PRIMARY METHODS

Observation

Observation entails the systematic noting and recording of events, behaviors, and artifacts (objects) in the social setting chosen for study. The observational record is frequently referred to as *field notes*—detailed, nonjudgmental, concrete descriptions of what has been observed. For studies relying exclusively on observation, the researcher makes no special effort to have a particular role in the setting; to be tolerated as an unobtrusive observer is enough. Classroom studies are one example of observation, often found in education, in which the researcher documents and describes actions and interactions that are complex: what they mean can only be inferred without other sources of information. This method assumes that behavior is purposeful and expressive of deeper values and beliefs. Observation can range from a highly structured, detailed notation of behavior structured by checklists to a more holistic description of events and behavior.

In the early stages of qualitative inquiry, the researcher typically enters the setting with broad areas of interest but without predetermined categories or strict observational checklists. In this way, the researcher is able to discover the recurring patterns of behavior and relationships. After these patterns are identified and described through early analysis of field notes, checklists become more appropriate and context-sensitive. Focused observation then is used at later stages of the study, usually to see, for example, if analytic themes explain behavior and relationships over a long time or in a variety of settings.

Observation is a fundamental and highly important method in all qualitative inquiry. It is used to discover complex interactions in natural social settings. Even in studies using in-depth interviews, observation plays an important role as the researcher notes the interviewee's body language and affect in addition to her words. It is, however, a method that requires a great deal of the researcher. Discomfort, uncomfortable ethical dilemmas and even danger, the difficulty of managing a relatively unobtrusive role, and the challenge of identifying the big picture while finely observing huge amounts of fast-moving and complex behavior are just a few of the challenges.

Whether a researcher is simply observing from afar or finding a participant-observer role in the setting, some contexts may present dangers. *Street ethnography* is a term that describes research settings which can be dangerous, either physically or emotionally, such as working with the police (as Manning did, described in Chapter 3), drug users, cults, and situations in which political or social tensions may erupt into violence (Weppner, 1977).

Observations involve more than just "hanging out." Planful and self-aware observers use observation systematically (DeWalt & DeWalt, 2001). At the proposal stage, the researcher should describe the purpose of the observing, the phase of the study in which it is likely to be most fruitful, and the use of field notes to respond to the research questions.

Field notes are not scribbles. The proposal writer should have explicit note-organizing and note-management strategies. Figure 4.1 provides an example of edited and "cleaned-up" field notes for a study of kindergarten teachers. O'Hearn-Curran (1997) has formatted descriptive notes in a column on the left while reserving a second column on the right for her comments. These include her emerging analytic insights about the behavior. Observers' comments are often a quite fruitful source of analytic insights and clues that focus data collection more tightly (more on this in Chapter 5). They may also provide important questions for subsequent interviews.

Figure 4.1   Sample Field Notes

Tuesday, November 13, 1997 12:40 p.m. Observation	*Observer's comments*
There are 17 children in the room. There are 3 adults: 1 teacher, 1 classroom assistant, and 1 student teacher (the student teacher is an older woman).	
The room is in the basement of the school. The school is a brick building approximately 90 to 100 years old. The room is about 40 feet by 30 feet. The room is carpeted and is sectioned off by furniture. There is an area with big books and a chart in the left-hand back corner of the room. Next to that is a shelf with a mixture of small books, tapes, and big books in baskets. Next to that is a small area with toy kitchen furniture and dolls. There is an area with several tables in front of the kitchen area. There are many small chairs pulled up to the table. In the front of the room is an area with a sand table. There is a semicircle table in the left-hand front corner of the room. The walls are colorful with papers that have been made by the children. One wall has papers with apples on them. Another wall has pictures of children with their names on the front of the papers. There are several small windows in the room and the florescent lighting seems to be the major source of light.	*The teacher seems to have done a great job of making the room seem very inviting. The space itself is not optimal*
The children have just come into the room. They have put their coats and backpacks onto their hooks in the hall outside.	*Most of the children appear to know the routine*

Participant Observation

Developed primarily from cultural anthropology and qualitative sociology, participant observation (as this method is typically called) is both an overall approach to inquiry and a data-gathering method. To some degree, it is an essential element of all qualitative studies. As its name suggests, participant observation demands firsthand involvement in the social world chosen for study. Immersion in the setting permits the researcher to hear, to see, and to begin to experience reality as the participants do. Ideally, the researcher spends a considerable amount of time in the setting, learning about daily life there. This immersion offers the researcher the opportunity to learn directly from his own experience. Personal reflections are integral to the emerging analysis of a cultural group, because they provide the researcher with new vantage points and with opportunities to make the strange familiar and the familiar strange (Glesne, 1999).

This method for gathering data is basic to all qualitative studies and forces a consideration of the role or stance of the researcher as a participant observer—her positionality. We have explored issues of her role more fully in Chapter 3. We reiterate that, at the proposal stage, it is helpful to elaborate on the planned extent of participation: what the nature of that involvement is likely to be, how much will be revealed about the study's purpose to the people in the setting, how intensively the researcher will be present, how focused the participation will be, and how ethical dilemmas will be managed. The researcher should be specific as to how his participation will inform the research questions.

In-Depth Interviewing

Qualitative researchers rely quite extensively on in-depth interviewing. Kahn and Cannell (1957) describe interviewing as "a conversation with a purpose" (p. 149). It may be the overall strategy or only one of several methods employed. To distinguish the qualitative interview from, for example, a journalist's or television talk-show interview, we might speak of its width instead of its depth (Wengraf, 2001). Interviewing varies in terms of a priori structure and in the latitude the interviewee has in responding to questions. Patton (2002, pp. 341–347) puts interviews into three general categories: the informal, conversational interview; the general interview guide approach; and the standardized, open-ended interview.

Qualitative, in-depth interviews typically are much more like conversations than formal events with predetermined response categories. The researcher explores a few general topics to help uncover the participant's views but otherwise respects how the participant frames and structures the responses. This method, in fact, is based on an assumption fundamental to qualitative research: The participant's perspective on the phenomenon of interest should unfold as the participant views it (the emic perspective), not as the researcher views it (the etic perspective). A degree of systematization in questioning may be necessary in, for example, a multisite case study or when many participants are interviewed, or at the analysis and interpretation stage when the researcher is testing findings in more focused and structured questioning.

The most important aspect of the interviewer's approach is conveying the attitude that the participant's views are valuable and useful. The interviewer's success will depend on how well he has anticipated and practiced his role in ethical issues, as discussed in Chapter 3.

Interviews have particular strengths. An interview yields data in quantity quickly. When more than one person participates (e.g., focus group interviews, discussed later), the process takes in a wider variety of information than if there were fewer participants—the familiar trade-off between breadth and depth. Immediate follow-up and clarification are possible. Combined with observation, interviews allow the researcher to understand the meanings that everyday activities hold for people.

Interviewing has limitations and weaknesses, however. Interviews involve personal interaction; cooperation is essential. Interviewees may be unwilling or may be uncomfortable sharing all that the interviewer hopes to explore, or they may be unaware of recurring patterns in their lives. The interviewer may not ask questions that evoke long narratives from participants because of a lack of expertise or familiarity with the local language or because of a lack of skill. By the same token, she may not properly comprehend responses to the questions or various elements of the conversation. And at times, interviewees may have good reason not to be truthful (see Douglas, 1976, for a discussion).

Interviewers should have superb listening skills and be skillful at personal interaction, question framing, and gentle probing for elaboration. Volumes of data can be obtained through interviewing but are time-consuming to analyze. Finally, there is the issue of the quality of the data. When the researcher is using in-depth interviews as the sole way of gathering data, she should have demonstrated through the conceptual framework that the purpose of the study is to uncover and describe the participants' perspectives on events—that is, that the subjective view is what matters. Studies making more objectivist assumptions would triangulate interview data with data gathered through other methods. Finally, because interviews, at first glance, seem so much like natural conversations, researchers sometimes use them thoughtlessly, in an undertheorized manner, as if the respondent is surely providing "an unproblematic window on psychological or social realities" (Wengraf, 2001, p. 1).

Figure 4.2 provides elaborated notes from an interview conducted for a study of students of color in a community college. Koski (1997) was particularly interested in how these students identified and defined effective teachers. She was intrigued with the notion of culturally relevant pedagogy and conducted several in-depth interviews with teachers identified by students as especially effective. She has formatted the notes from the interview to provide space for her comments, as did O'Hearn-Curran in the field notes presented in Figure 4.1.

In addition to generic in-depth interviewing, there are several more specialized forms, including ethnographic interviewing, phenomenological interviewing, elite interviewing, focus-group interviewing, and interviewing children. We now describe each of these methods briefly.

Figure 4.2   Sample Field Notes

Interview with DC October 15,
1997 1:30-3:40

*DC is an adviser
with an academic department.
The interview was set
up by the dean.*

Setting: DC's office in the academic department. It's bright and lively—colorful tapestry on one wall, posters on the other walls. A giant poster about "I am okay." Books and papers are everywhere. On the corner of the desk are some wood games: tic-tac-toe, pyramid, and others.

DC is a small, dark-colored woman with her hair in small but longish braids all over her head. She wears large glasses and a pinkish shade of lipstick that complements her coloring. She is lively, with a ready smile and a quick laugh. She comments on her height: "I'm smaller than all my advisees, so I'm not a threat to anyone."

I explain what I'm interested in and what my project is about. I tell her that I would like three things from her: One is an idea of what she as an adviser thinks are the attributes of a good teacher and what her students of color say, which teachers might possess those attributes, and which students I might talk to for the project.

DC listens very intently here.

DC: "OK. Good. Well, ask me a question."

KK: "Tell me a little bit about what you do."

DC: "I'm an adviser here. We get them in fresh off the street. I sit down with them and make out an educational plan. I like it when they know what's expected of them."

DC: "The educational plan lists not only courses to be taken but clubs and other student activities. It lists the advising events the student will attend."

This is an awkward moment for me and for her. I wasn't sure what to do. This general question seems to surprise her.

She hands me a form that she has worked on with a student. Just then someone comes in and tells her she has an important phone call that they can't transfer. She leaves for about 10 minutes. I am able to look around.

DC returns. KK: "How many students do you have?"

DC: "About 100."

KK: "100! Are you able to have a relationship with so many?"

DC: "I feel I'm an advocate for students. I do whatever needs to be done to get them through this. I tell them not to overload, to relax about this. . . . I think being honest with students is important. If I don't know, I tell them. But we can always look it up on the Net!"

I don't remember her exact answer here. Something about keeping in touch.

Ethnographic Interviewing

Based on cognitive anthropology, ethnographic interviewing elicits the cognitive structures guiding participants' worldviews. Described as "a particular kind of speech event" (Spradley, 1979, p. 18), ethnographic questions are used by the researcher to gather cultural data. Ethnographic interviewing is not simply doing an interview. Instead, it is an elaborate system of a series of interviews structured to elicit insiders' cultural knowledge. Spradley identifies three main types of questions: descriptive, structural, and contrast. Descriptive questions allow the researcher to collect a sample of participants' language. Structural questions discover the basic units in the participants' cultural knowledge, and contrast questions provide the ethnographer with the meaning of various terms.

The value of the ethnographic interview lies in its focus on culture through the participant's perspective and through firsthand encounter. This approach is especially useful for eliciting participants' meanings for events and behaviors and for generating a typology of cultural classification schemes. It also highlights the nuances of the culture. The method is flexible in formulating working hypotheses and avoids oversimplification in description and analysis because of its rich narrative descriptions.

There are weaknesses in this method, however. The ethnographer can impose her values through the phrasing of questions or the interpretation of data (a concern with all forms of research but perhaps especially salient with qualitative methods). If the member of the cultural group chosen to participate does not represent that culture, the subsequent analysis will be impoverished. The success of this method, as in all interviewing, is highly dependent on the researcher's interpersonal skills.

Phenomenological Interviewing

Phenomenological interviewing is a specific type of in-depth interviewing grounded in a philosophical tradition. Phenomenology is the study of lived experiences and the ways we understand those experiences to develop a worldview. It rests on the assumption that there is a structure and essence to shared experiences that can be narrated. The purpose of this type of interviewing is to describe the meaning of a concept or phenomenon that several individuals share.

As developed by Seidman (1998), three in-depth interviews compose phenomenological inquiry. The first focuses on past experience with the phenomenon of interest; the second focuses on present experience; and the third joins these two narratives to describe the individual's essential experience with the phenomenon. Prior to interviewing, however, the researcher using this technique has written a full description of her own experience, thereby bracketing off her experiences from those of the interviewees. This phase of the inquiry is referred to as *epoche*. The purpose of this self-examination is to permit the researcher to gain clarity from her own preconceptions, and it is part of the "ongoing process rather than a single fixed event" (Patton, 1990, p. 408).

The next phase is called *phenomenological reduction;* here, the researcher identifies the essence of the phenomenon (Patton, 1990). The researcher then clusters the data around themes that describe the "textures of the experience" (Creswell, 1998, p. 150). The final stage, *structural synthesis,* involves the imaginative exploration of "all possible meanings and divergent perspectives" (Creswell, 1998, p. 150) and culminates in a description of the essence of the phenomenon and its deep structure.

The primary advantage of phenomenological interviewing is that it permits an explicit focus on the researcher's personal experience combined with those of the interviewees. It focuses on the deep, lived meanings that events have for individuals, assuming that these meanings guide actions and interactions. It is, however, quite labor-intensive and requires a reflective turn of mind on the part of the researcher.

Interviewing of Elites

An interview with an "elite" person is a specialized case of interviewing that focuses on a particular type of interviewee. Elite individuals are considered to be influential, prominent, and/or well-informed in an organization or community; they are selected for interviews on the basis of their expertise in areas relevant to the research.

Elite interviewing has many advantages. Valuable information can be gained from these participants because of the positions they hold in social, political, financial, or administrative realms. Elites can provide an overall view of an organization or its relationship to other organizations, albeit from their own limited and bounded perspectives. They may be quite familiar with the legal and financial structures of the organization. Elites are also able to report on an organization's policies, histories, and plans, again from a particular perspective. Interviewing religious or political leaders would be obvious examples, as is Bennis and Nanus's (2003) study of 90 corporate executives. Less obvious examples include interviews with gang leaders, union bosses, or tribal chiefs.

Elite interviewing also presents disadvantages. It is often difficult to gain access to elites because they are usually busy people operating under demanding time constraints; they are also often difficult to contact initially. (This is also a consideration when requesting interviews with, for example, rural village women who have substantial work responsibilities.) The interviewer may have to rely on sponsorship, recommendations, and introductions for assistance in making appointments with elite individuals.

Another disadvantage in interviewing elites is that the interviewer may have to adapt the planned structure of the interview, based on the wishes and predilections of the person interviewed. Although this is true with all in-depth interviewing, elite individuals who are used to being interviewed by the press and other media may well be quite sophisticated in managing the interview process. (Sophistication and political astuteness are not exclusively the domain of elites, and we do not mean to suggest that they are.) They may want an active interplay with the interviewer. Well practiced at meeting the public and being in control, an elite person may turn the interview around, thereby taking charge of it. Elites often respond well to inquiries about broad areas of content and to open-ended questions that allow them the freedom to use their knowledge and imagination.

Working with elites often places great demands on the ability of the interviewer to establish competence and credibility by displaying knowledge of the topic or, lacking such knowledge, by projecting an accurate conceptualization of the problem through thoughtful questioning. The interviewer's hard work usually pays off, however, in the quality of information obtained. Elites may contribute insight and meaning to the interview through their specific perspectives. On the other hand, elites (just like other interviewees) may well have only vague understandings of a setting that is limited by a narrow viewpoint.

Interviewing Children

Children may be the primary focus of a study or one of many groups the researcher wants to interview. Increasingly, there are calls for including children's perspectives as relevant and insightful in learning more about aspects of their worlds. This is especially true in education where all too often those most affected by educational policy and programmatic decisions—the students—are absent from inquiry. There are special considerations, however, when the qualitative researcher proposes a study that involves children.

First are age considerations. Interviewing preschoolers, for example, is quite different from interviewing early adolescents. Young children are often active; early adolescents are frequently very self-conscious. Three-year-olds, exploring their emerging language skills, can drive one to distraction with their incessant questions (often quite sophisticated ones!), whereas early adolescents may be taciturn. It is unrealistic to expect young children to sit still for long, but joining them in some activity can create a climate for focused talk. Some adolescents may feel more comfortable with their peers in a focus-group interview, whereas others may prefer the intimacy of one-to-one interviews. Decisions about how to gather data with various age groups requires sensitivity to their needs, their developmental issues, and flexibility.

Second are role considerations. Fine and Sandstrom (1988) note that the roles an adult researcher assumes when studying children vary along two dimensions: "(1) the extent of positive contact between adult and child, and (2) the extent to which the adult has direct authority over the child" (p. 14). They offer the roles of supervisor, leader, observer, and friend as appropriate. Of these, they find the role of friend the most fruitful, noting that the researcher then interacts with the children "in the most trusted way possible—without any explicit authority role" (p. 17). They caution, however, that age and power differences between adults and children are always salient.

Background and Context and Review of Documents

For every qualitative study, data on the background and historical context are gathered. This may not be a major part of data collection but at least, in proposing a particular setting, the researcher gathers demographic data and describes geographic and historical particulars. When she reviews old property transactions, skims recent newspaper editorials, or obtains information from a Web site, she is collecting data. Whether or not she counts this as data collection, she must proceed with caution.

Knowledge of the history and context surrounding a specific setting comes, in part, from reviewing documents. Researchers supplement participant observation, interviewing, and observation with gathering and analyzing documents produced in the course of everyday events or constructed specifically for the research at hand. As such, the review of documents is an unobtrusive method, rich in portraying the values and beliefs of participants in the setting. Minutes of meetings, logs, announcements, formal policy statements, letters, and so on are all useful in developing an understanding of the setting or group studied. Research journals and samples of free writing about the topic can also be quite informative.

Archival data are the routinely gathered records of a society, community, or organization and may further supplement other qualitative methods. For example, marital patterns among a group of Mexicans, discovered through fieldwork in a community, could be tested through marriage records found in the offices of the county seat or state capitol. Descriptions of articulated funding priorities by policymakers could be corroborated (or not) through an analysis of budgetary allocations. As with other methodological decisions, the decision to gather and analyze documents or archival records should be linked to the research questions developed in the conceptual framework for the study. Furthermore, documents must be viewed with the skepticism that historians apply as they search for truth in old texts.

The use of documents often entails a specialized analytic approach called content analysis. The raw material for content analysis may be any form of communication, usually written materials (textbooks, novels, newspapers, e-mail messages); other forms of communication—music, pictures, or political speeches—may also be included. Historically, content analysis was viewed as an objective and neutral way of obtaining a quantitative description of the content of various forms of communication; thus, counting the mention of specific items was important (Berelson, 1952). As it has evolved, however, it is viewed more generously as a method for describing and interpreting the artifacts of a society or social group.

Probably the greatest strength of content analysis is that it is unobtrusive and nonreactive: It can be conducted without disturbing the setting in any way. The researcher determines where the emphasis lies after the data have been gathered. Also, the procedure is relatively clear to the reader. Information can therefore be checked, as can the care with which the analysis has been applied. A potential weakness, however, is the span of inferential reasoning. That is, the analysis of the content of written materials or film, for example, entails interpretation by the researcher, just as in the analysis of interactively gathered data: Numbers do not speak for themselves. Care should be taken, therefore, in displaying the logic of interpretation used in inferring meaning from the artifacts. Later in the chapter, we provide more details on historical methods and on content analysis.

Some combination of these primary research methods is typical for in-depth qualitative inquiry. In Vignette 16, Shadduck-Hernandez (1997) articulates a complex design that incorporates several. The vignette is adapted from her proposal for research about CIRCLE (Center for Immigrant and Refugee Leadership and Empowerment), a participatory project involving newcomer undergraduate students, graduate students, and members from refugee and immigrant communities.

VIGNETTE 16

Using Multiple Methods

Imagine 12 university students, on a chilly Saturday morning, sprawled out on a classroom floor formulating their thoughts for a proposal on scattered sheets of newsprint. Laughter, silence, and intense discussion highlight the writing process of these authors who are first-generation refugee and immigrant (newcomer) students from China, Cambodia, Vietnam, Laos, and Korea participating in an undergraduate seminar on cross-cultural experiences in community development.

This dissertation research acknowledges the real tensions that exist in any qualitative research endeavor. Certain models can be rigid, one-way streets if they seduce participants into a process of inquiry in which the researcher alone is the analyzer and interpreter of data. This study consciously tried to counter such situations by applying participatory research as the guide of the inquiry (Maguire, 2000; Reardon, Welsh, Kreiswirth, & Forester, 1993). Study participants have been involved in this inquiry as researchers and valued members of a learning team in order to produce knowledge that may help stimulate social change.

Stemming from my commitment to participatory processes, the research I am conducting is collaborative in nature, emerging from the students and the communities I work with. Collaboration and participation in developing critical learning environments produce pooled resources and shared expertise leading to integrated and collective activities. Collaboration, action, and reflection enhance the legitimacy of each participant's knowledge (Brice Heath & McLaughlin, 1993) and set the stage for the sources of multilevel data collection employed in this study. These six sources of data have evolved as a complement to the development of CIRCLE courses and community outreach activities and support the concept of a pedagogy for affirmation, advocacy, and action. They include the following: (a) journal entries and self-reflection papers; (b) focus group interviews with eight undergraduate students; (c) in-depth interviews with 10 students; (d) video and photography documentation; (e) oral history interviews conducted by students and youth with each other; and (f) research field notes, reflections, and academic papers for courses and conferences over the 4 years of my involvement with and participation in the project. These latter data provide critical insights into my own theoretical development in relation to this research and my role as researcher in this study.

Shadduck-Hernandez's (1997) discussion of the various sources of qualitative data—some generated as part of the CIRCLE project, others to be generated specifically for the dissertation—is eloquently congruent with her assumptions about the nature of this work, its purpose and audience, and her political stance. Note that she plans to rely on several methods: documents in the form of journals, self-reflective writing, and papers written for courses or conferences (both her own and those of the student participants); a focus-group interview; in-depth interviews; and video and photography. Videotaping and photography are what we describe as secondary data collection methods.

With many of the primary methods, transcription and translation challenges must be addressed. Even in his own culture, a white, middle-class sociology scholar will encounter challenges in transcribing and translating, for example, in-depth interviews of adolescents' attitudes toward religion (Smith & Faris, 2002).

Issues With Transcribing and Translating

Especially in the use of interviews, transcribing and translating text have become increasingly salient issues in the discourse on qualitative research. Neither is a *merely technical task;* both entail judgment and interpretation. In some way, when data have been translated and/or transcribed, they are not raw data any more—they are "processed data" (Wengraf, 2001, p. 7). Only recently has the methodological literature offered discussions about the issues in transposing the spoken word (from a tape-recording) into a text (a transcription), or in transposing the spoken word in one language (from a tape-recording) into another language (a translation) and then into a text (a transcription). Unfortunately, the literature has not problematized the challenges in these apparently transparent acts until very recently. Moreover, our review of the literature suggests that only issues with translation are currently being addressed.

Transcribing. If the researcher is fortunate enough to have interview partners who are comfortable with tape-recordings, she leaves the research encounter with spoken words, dutifully and seemingly unproblematically recorded on tape. Those who have then sat down to transcribe the tapes, however, know well the pitfalls of assuming that the spoken word closely parallels the written one. We do not speak in paragraphs, nor do we signal punctuation as we speak. The judgments involved in placing something as simple as a period or a semicolon are complex and shape the meaning of the written word and, hence, of the interview itself. Similarly, the visual cues that we rely on to interpret another's meaning are lost when we listen to a tape; the transcriber no longer has access to those important paralinguistic clues about meaning. (See Tilley, 2003, for further discussion.)

For example, Rossman (1994) conducted interviews for an evaluation of a systemic school reform initiative. One interviewee used a discursive style that could charitably be described as complex and dense. The interviewee would begin one topic, then loop to another midsentence, then on to another, finally saying, "Where was I?" and returning to the original topic after a prompt from the interviewer. While fascinating, this style was extremely difficult to transcribe—sentences were interrupted by the speaker herself, topics were left unfinished, and overall clarity was difficult to ascertain. Rossman struggled with this transcription, finally sharing it with the interviewee to be sure that the meaning was accurately rendered in the transcribed account of her words. In Chase's (1995) study of women school superintendents, responses to questions were replete with long pauses, in which the subject was changed. These gaps were, in the end, interpreted as indicators of a strong pattern of avoiding talking about and even denying experiences of sex discrimination—a major finding in her study. What if this researcher had made the mistake of simplistic transcription? But there is a cautionary note here: The meaning of pauses in conversation is not transparent; the researcher should use caution, as did Chase, in drawing inferences and offering interpretations of these linguistic patterns.

Experiences such as this are common. The implication is that the researcher needs to discuss the problematic nature of transcribing in the proposal and provide strategies for handling the judgments and interpretations inherent in such work.

Translating. Clearly, the issues associated with translating from one language into another are much more complex than transcribing because they involve more subtle issues of connotation and meaning. As noted above, the methodological literature has recently grown to include essays discussing the difficult issues with translating (Esposito, 2001; Temple & Young, 2004). Writing in the context of the need for more sophistication in cross-language health research with refugee and immigrant populations, Esposito (2001) notes that translation is "the transfer of meaning from a source language . . . to a target language" and that the translator is "actually an interpreter who . . . processes the vocabulary and grammatical structure of the words while considering the individual situation and the overall cultural context" (p. 570). Thus the focus on generating *accurate and meaningful data* through translation processes is paramount.

In another article on translating, Temple and Young (2004) address three primary issues: (a) whether to identify the translation act in the research report; (b) whether it matters if the researcher is also the translator; and (c) whether to involve the translator in analysis. These topics help move the field forward, but Rossman's experience in her graduate teaching, working intensively with students whose first language (or even second or third) is not English, critiques their discussion as naïve. Addressing each of the issues in turn, she takes the position that none is problematic. First, she says that there is an ethical imperative to inform the reader that translation has occurred and to address how this will be (in the case of a proposal) or has been (in the case of a final research report) managed. Second, more issues of meaning and interpretation arise when *someone other than* the researcher translates spoken or written words. Third, since translation entails the construction of meaning, she believes that analysis is happening whether or not it is acknowledged.

So what are the important issues with translating the spoken or written word? Most important are the processes and procedures that the researcher/translator has used (or will use) to construct meaning through multiple transpositions of the spoken or written word from one language into another. Rossman and Rallis (2003, p. 260) identify three others:

- If you have translated from one language to another, which language constitutes the direct quotes?
- Can you use translated words as a direct quote?
- How do you signal that a translation is accurate and captures the subtle meanings of the original language?

There are no simple strategies or blueprints for addressing these and other issues associated with translation. What is simple and clear, however, is that the reader of the proposal must know that the researcher understands the issues, will take an ethical stance on translating, and will make clear in the final report just what she has done. For example, Rossman insists that her students discuss the language for interviewing (and/or document review) in the proposal, indicating whether or not the student is fluent in the language. If she is not, what strategies will she use to ensure accuracy and subtlety in translation? She also recommends that students include phrases and key words from the original language from time to time in their final narratives. Translations or interpretations of those phrases can be put into parentheses with the caveat that there is no direct translation of the phrase's meaning into English. Including phrases or words in the original language (often italicized) also serves as a reminder to the reader that the interviews were originally conducted in a language other than English. This subtle reminder helps to decenter the hegemony of an English-centered world.

For example, the doctoral student who proposed a mixed-methods study of a complex policy domain in Malawi (MacJessie-Mbewe, 2004) described how he would use the local language, Chichewa, for his interviews. Since he was fluent in this language, this posed no real problem for his dissertation committee. In his dissertation, he included several words and phrases that had evocative meaning in Chichewa but did not translate easily into English. Cohen-Mitchell (2005) studied the literacy and numeracy practices of market women in Quetzaltenango, Guatemala, for her dissertation. She was fluent in Spanish but not in Quiche, the local language of the women in her study. She had to convince her dissertation committee that she would work closely with Rosa, an educated literacy practitioner fluent in Quiche and Spanish, as a coresearcher and translator to obtain strong data from the women. Cohen-Mitchell proposed, moreover, that she would take Quiche lessons during her fieldwork to improve her limited understanding of that language. She used both Quiche and Spanish phrases and words in her dissertation.

Issues of transcribing and translating are subtle and complex; they are not merely technical tasks. The writer of a qualitative research proposal has an ethical obligation to discuss these issues and how she will approach them, especially since qualitative research generates words— the primary symbol system through which meaning is conveyed and constructed. Not all of the issues can be solved at the proposal stage; in fact, we are quite skeptical of those who write that they have them all wrapped up. Instead, the proposal should have a thoughtful discussion of the more generic issues of transcribing and translating, as well as the ones specific to the research site and participants.

❖ SECONDARY AND SPECIALIZED METHODS

In addition to the primary data-gathering methods outlined above, the researcher can choose to incorporate several secondary and supplemental methods in the design of a study, as appropriate. Each of those described below is a full and complete method in and of itself and has a methodological literature explicating its nuances and subtleties. In some instances, the same terminology is used for data collection methods and for modes of reporting or presentation. For example, some speak of "doing case studies" as a way of collecting data, but, more often, an entire report, even a book, is a case study. Ethnographers talk of "doing an ethnography" to describe their approach to data collection when, in fact, an ethnography is a written product—*ethno = culture; graphy = writing* or an inscription. *Nisa: The Life and Words of a !Kung Woman* (Shostak, 1983) is a book that is a life history of one African woman, and the data collection method is called life history, consisting of long-term participant observation and in-depth and ethnographic interviewing. Yes, this *is* confusing!

The discussions that follow are necessarily simplified and brief, as was the preceding, and the list is not exhaustive. The methods discussed below, if used, should always be used with the understanding that observation and interviewing are the primary data collection methods for discovering context-laden patterns and understandings.

Focus Groups

The method of interviewing participants in focus groups comes largely from marketing research but has been widely adapted to include social science and applied research. The groups are generally composed of 7 to 10 people (although groups range from as small as 4 to as large as 12) who are unfamiliar with one another and have been selected because they share certain characteristics relevant to the study's questions. The interviewer creates a supportive environment, asking focused questions to encourage discussion and the expression of differing opinions and points of view. These interviews may be conducted several times with different individuals so that the researcher can identify trends in the perceptions and opinions expressed, which are revealed through careful, systematic analysis (Krueger, 1988).

This method assumes that an individual's attitudes and beliefs do not form in a vacuum: People often need to listen to others' opinions and understandings to form their own. One-to-one interviews may be impoverished because the participant had not reflected on the topic and feels unprepared to respond. Often, the questions in a focus-group setting are deceptively simple; the trick is to promote the participants' expression of their views through the creation of a supportive environment.

The advantages of focus-group interviews are that this method is socially oriented, studying participants in an atmosphere more natural than artificial experimental circumstances and more relaxed than a one-to-one interview. When combined with participant observation, focus groups are especially useful for gaining access, focusing site selection and sampling, and even for checking tentative conclusions (Morgan, 1997). The format allows the facilitator the flexibility to explore unanticipated issues as they arise in the discussion. The results have high "face validity": Because the method is readily understood, the findings appear believable. Furthermore, the cost of focus groups is relatively low, they provide quick results, and they can increase the

sample size of qualitative studies by permitting more people to be interviewed at one time (Krueger, 1988). In action research and in program
design and evaluation, focus groups are especially useful. They were
useful tools, for example, in data gathering to design a program for
working on the employment issues of persons with HIV/AIDS, based
on their answers to questions about specifics needs ranging from stress
and availability of health care to family, spirituality, and hopes for the
future (O'Neill, Small, & Strachan, 1999).

There are, however, certain disadvantages to this method as well:
First and foremost is the issue of power dynamics in the focus-group setting. Should the researcher choose to use this method she should be
exquisitely aware of power dynamics and be able to facilitate well—
these are crucial skills. In addition, the interviewer often has less control
over a group interview than an individual one. Time can be lost while
dead-end or irrelevant issues are discussed; the data are difficult to analyze because context is essential to understanding the participants' comments; the method requires the use of special room arrangements and
highly trained observer moderators; the groups can vary a great deal
and can be hard to assemble; and logistical problems may arise from the
need to manage a conversation while getting good quality data.

Life Histories and Narrative Inquiry

Life histories and narrative inquiry are methods that gather, analyze, and interpret the stories people tell about their lives. They assume
that people live "storied" lives and that telling and retelling one's story
helps one understand and create a sense of self. The story is important but so is how the story is told (Hatch & Wisniewski, 1995). The
researcher, working closely with the participant, explores a story and
records it. Life histories and narrative analysis are used across the
social science disciplines and are particularly useful for giving the
reader an insider's view of a culture or era in history (Edgerton &
Langness, 1974).

Life Histories

Life histories seek to "examine and analyze the subjective experience of individuals and their constructions of the social world" (Jones,
1983, p. 147). They assume a complex interaction between the individual's understanding of his or her world and that world itself. They are,
therefore, uniquely suited to depicting and making theoretical sense
of the socialization of a person into a cultural milieu (Dollard, 1935).
Thus, one understands a culture through the history of one person's

development or life within it, a history told in ways that capture the person's feelings, views, and perspectives. The life history is often an account of how an individual enters a group and becomes socialized into it. That history includes the learning to meet the normative expectations of that society by gender, social class, or age peers. Life histories emphasize the experience of the individual—how the person copes with society rather than how society copes with the stream of individuals (Mandelbaum, 1973).

Life histories can focus on critical or fateful moments. Indecision, confusion, contradiction, and irony are captured as nuanced processes in a life (Sparks, 1994). These histories are particularly helpful in defining socialization and in studying aspects of acculturation and socialization in institutions and professions. Their value goes beyond providing specific information about events and customs of the past—as a historical account might—by showing how the individual creates meaning within the culture. Life histories are valuable in studying cultural changes that have occurred over time, in learning about cultural norms and transgressions of those norms, and in gaining an inside view of a culture. They also help capture how cultural patterns evolve and how they are linked to the life of an individual. Often, this point of view is missing from standard ethnographies (Atkinson, 1998; Edgerton & Langness, 1974).

The term *life history* is sometimes used when, in fact, in-depth interviews are more focused on respondents' evolution or development over time. These parts of larger studies are particularly useful for identifying patterns in health (e.g., Goldman, Hunt, Allen, Hauser, Emmons, & Maeda et al., 2003), in the acculturation of immigrants, and the like. Scholars may also research family histories using parallel logics and methods (Miller, 1999).

The first strength of life history methodology is that, because it pictures a substantial portion of a person's life, the reader can enter into those experiences. The second is that it provides a fertile source of testable hypotheses, useful for focusing subsequent studies. The third strength is that it depicts actions and perspectives across a social group that may be analyzed for comparative study. Life history as a methodology emphasizes the value of a person's story and provides pieces for a mosaic depicting an era or social group. This kind of research requires sensitivity, caring, and empathy by the researcher for the researched (Cole & Knowles, 2001). Life histories are often used in feminist research as a way of understanding, relatively free of androcentric bias, how women's lives and careers evolve (Lawless, 1991).

Jones (1983) offers five criteria for life histories. First, the individual should be viewed as a member of a culture; the life history "describe[s] and interpret[s] the actor's account of his or her development in the common-sense world." Second, the method should capture the significant role that others play in "transmitting socially defined stocks of knowledge." Third, the assumptions of the cultural world under study should be described and analyzed as they are revealed in rules and codes for conduct as well as in myths and rituals. Fourth, life histories should focus on the experience of an individual over time so that the "processual development of the person" can be captured (pp. 153–154). And fifth, the cultural world under study should be continuously related to the individual's unfolding life story.

The major criticisms of the life history are that it makes generalizing difficult, offers only limited principles for selecting participants, and is guided by few accepted concepts of analysis. Once the researcher acknowledges the possible weaknesses in the method, however, he can circumvent them. Official records may provide corroborating information or may illuminate aspects of a culture absent from an individual's account. The researcher can substantiate meanings presented in a history by interviewing others in a participant's life. Before publishing *The Professional Thief,* for example, Sutherland and Conwell (1983) submitted the manuscript to four professional thieves and to two police detectives to assess possible bias and to ensure that their interpretations resonated with the understandings of other professional thieves and those who come in contact with them.

A life history account can add depth and evocative illustration to any qualitative study. As with any qualitative genre, however, the abundance of data collected in a life history should be managed and reduced so that analytic headway can be made. Instead of using chronological order, the researcher can focus on (a) critical dimensions or aspects of the person's life, (b) principal turning points and the life conditions between them, and (c) the person's characteristic means of adaptation (Mandelbaum, 1973).

Narrative Inquiry

Closely related to life history is narrative inquiry, an interdisciplinary method that views lives holistically and draws from traditions in literary theory, oral history, drama, psychology, folklore, and film philosophy (Connelly & Clandinin, 1990). The method assumes that people construct their realities through narrating their stories. The researcher explores a story told by a participant and records that story.

Narrative analysis can be applied to any spoken or written account—for example, to an in-depth interview.

Narrative inquiry requires a great deal of openness and trust between participant and researcher: The inquiry should involve a mutual and sincere collaboration, a caring relationship akin to friendship that is established over time for full participation in the storytelling, retelling, and reliving of personal experiences. It demands intense and active listening and giving the narrator full voice. Because it is a collaboration, however, it permits both voices to be heard.

This method is criticized for its focus on the individual rather than on the social context. Like life histories, however, it seeks to understand sociological questions about groups, communities, and contexts through individuals' lived experiences. Like any method that relies on participants' accounts, narrative may suffer from recalling selectively, focusing on subsets of experience, filling in memory gaps through inference, and reinterpreting the past (Ross & Conway, 1986). Crites (1986) cautions against "the illusion of causality" (p. 168)—the inference that the narrator's sequencing of the story uses cause and effect accurately. Narrative inquiry is also time-consuming and laborious and requires some specialized training (Viney & Bousefield, 1991). In the past decade, researchers have articulated criteria for good narrative inquiry (see Connelly & Clandinin, 1990; Jones, 1983; Riessman, 1993).

As a qualitative research method for the social sciences and applied fields it is relatively new, but narrative inquiry has a long tradition in the humanities because of its power to elicit voice. Narrative analysis values the signs, the symbols, and the expression of feelings in language, validating how the narrator constructs meaning. It has been particularly useful in developing feminist and critical theory (Eisner, 1988; Grumet, 1988; Riessman, 1993). Narrative inquiry is especially useful when exploring issues of social change, causality, and social identity (Elliott, 2005).

Narrative inquiry may rely on journal records, photographs, letters, autobiographical writing, e-mail messages, and other data. Typically, field notes are shared with the narrator, and the written record may be constructed collaboratively. In the conduct of narrative inquiry, there is open recognition that the researcher is not just passively recording and reporting the narrator's reality. Connelly and Clandinin (1990) assert that researchers need to "be prepared to follow their nose and, after the fact, reconstruct their narrative of inquiry" (p. 7). This becomes, in effect, the recounting of methodology.

Historical Analysis

A history is an account of some event or combination of events. Historical analysis is a method of discovering what has happened using records and accounts. It is particularly useful in qualitative studies for establishing a baseline or background prior to participant observation or interviewing. Sources of historical data are classified as either primary or secondary. Oral testimony of eyewitnesses, documents, records, and relics are primary. Reports of persons who relate the accounts of eyewitnesses and summaries, as in history books and encyclopedias, are secondary.

The researcher should consider the following sources of historical data: (a) contemporary records, including instructions, stenographic records, business and legal papers, and personal notes and memos; (b) confidential reports, including military records, journals and diaries, and personal letters; (c) public reports, including newspaper reports and memoirs or autobiographies; (d) questionnaires; (e) government documents, including archives and regulations; (f) opinions, including editorials, speeches, pamphlets, letters to the editor, and public opinion polls; (g) fiction, songs, and poetry; and (h) folklore.

Historical analysis is particularly useful in obtaining knowledge of unexamined areas and in reexamining questions for which answers are not as definite as desired. It allows for systematic and direct classification of data. Historical research traditions demand procedures to verify the accuracy of statements about the past, to establish relationships, and to determine the direction of cause-and-effect relationships. Many research studies have a historical base or context, so systematic historical analysis enhances the trustworthiness and credibility of a study.

There is a dialectical tension in this kind of analysis between contemporary and historical interpretations of events, even though texts representing either perspective are influenced by the social contexts in which they are produced. Historical analysis cannot use direct observation, and there is no way to test a historical hypothesis. There are also weaknesses in the classification of historical data. One must remember that documents may be falsified deliberately or may have been interpreted incorrectly by the recorder. Words and phrases used in old records may now have different meanings. The meanings of artifacts are perceived and interpreted by the investigator. Errors in recording, as well as frauds, hoaxes, and forgeries, pose problems in dealing with the past. The researcher should retain a modest skepticism about such data.

Films, Videos, and Photography

Films and photography have a long history in anthropology. Called *visual anthropology* or *film ethnography*, this tradition relies on visual representations of the daily life of the group under study. Films are records of natural events and may be used as permanent resources. The concept and method of the research film have emerged and are now compatible with a variety of research methods to describe how people navigate in public places (Ryave & Schenkein, 1974) and how they use space (Whyte, 1980), to present findings (Jackson, 1978), and to empower participants (Ziller & Lewis, 1981). The various forms of photography can be used for data collection and for organizing, interpreting, and validating qualitative inquiry (Szto, Furman, & Langer, 2005). As Banks (2001) illustrates, films of marriage ceremonies in different social strata in contemporary India, coupled with historical photos and documents, raised key questions in his search for cultural understanding of the interconnections between economics and tradition in handicrafts, dowries, and trousseaux.

Film has the unique ability to capture visible phenomena seemingly objectively—yet always from the perspective of the filmmaker, just as with other forms of observation. The filmmaker, the observer, must decide what to focus on while recording and then how to interpret the data in that recording (whether on film or in field notes). Research film methodology requires the documentation of the time, place, and subject of the filming, as well as the photographer's intent and interests. There is a great wealth of visual information in all natural events: To attempt a complete record of even a small event would be fruitless.

There are three kinds of sampling in films: opportunity, programmed, and digressive (Sorenson, 1968). Opportunity sampling documents unanticipated or poorly understood phenomena as they occur. Programmed sampling involves filming according to a predetermined plan—deciding in advance what, where, and when to film. Grounded in the research proposal's conceptual framework, programmed sampling stipulates which events are likely to be significant. It is guided by the research design rather than by intuition, as in opportunity sampling. Digressive sampling is deliberate searching beyond the obvious to the novel, to the places and events beyond typical public recognition.

Researchers choose to use ethnographic film for its obvious strengths. Visual samples enhance the value of any record. Film documents life crises and ceremonies, transmits cultural events to successive generations, and documents social conflicts (court proceedings, public speakers, Senate sessions, and so on). The film researcher is limited by what the mind can imagine and the camera can record—significant limitations because they involve ideology and other forms of cultural bias. But, of course, events can be documented in their natural setting.

Film is especially valuable for discovery and validation. It documents nonverbal behavior and communication such as facial expressions, gestures, and emotions. Film preserves activity and change in its original form. It can be used in the future to take advantage of new methods of seeing, analyzing, and understanding the process of change. Film is an aid to the researcher when the nature of what is sought is known but the elements of it cannot be discovered because of the limitations of the human eye. It allows for the preservation and study of data from nonrecurring, disappearing, or rare events. Interpretation of information can be validated by another researcher or by participants. The researcher can obtain feedback on the authenticity of interpretation, and the film can be reshot to be more authentic. Two excellent examples of ethnographic film are *Educating Peter* (Home Box Office Project Knowledge, 1992), the story of the experiences of a boy with severe cognitive challenges in a regular classroom, and *High School*, a depiction of life in a comprehensive high school in the early 1970s (Wiseman, 1969).

Film has certain weaknesses and limitations. There are always fundamental questions—What is the nature of truth? Does the film manipulate reality?—and concerns about professional bias and the interests of the filmmaker. Film is expensive, and most research budgets are minimal. Production can be problematic. The researcher needs technical expertise. And filming can be very intrusive, affecting settings and events. Film cannot be included in a book, journal, or dissertation. Finally, serious consideration must be given to the ethics of ethnographic filming.

Interaction Analysis

There are times when—since much is already known either because of much participant observation or good previous research—very focused data collection techniques can be deployed. At those times, researchers wanting finely focused data on verbal and nonverbal communication can use forms of interaction analysis to quantify patterns of interaction. An observer uses a predetermined coding scheme, often called a protocol, to produce a listing of the likely interactions. Then she samples duration at predetermined intervals. For example, the observer might sample blind-date eye contact for 5 seconds every 5 minutes or teachers' responses to student questions in a 30-minute lesson. First used as a method for studying small groups in organizations in the 1920s, interaction analysis gained prominence as a method for observing classrooms and for aiding teacher training (Flanders, 1970; Freiberg, 1981). Now it is being used in research on couples to develop coding systems that can powerfully analyze an ongoing stream of dyadic behaviors (Baucom & Kerig, 2004).

One strength of this approach is that systematic, quantified data are obtained. It is particularly useful for verifying patterns that emerged in early observations and interviews. Systems for assessing inter-rater reliability can also be constructed. Large amounts of focused data can be collected in a variety of settings, making statistical analyses useful.

Clearly, interaction analysis is only as good as the categories used to focus observations. When they are culturally biased, too reflective of the researcher's prejudgments, or not well designed for the setting, these categories are not particularly fruitful. Two well-developed types of this method—kinesics and proxemics—offer examples of finely focused analyses.

 Kinesics. Learning about society can be enhanced if we study not only what people say but also what their body movements reveal. Kinesics is the study of body motion and its communicative messages. Motion is analyzed systematically so that researchers can see and measure significant patterns in the communications process.

Birdwhistell (1970) asserts that nonverbal body behaviors function like significant sounds that combine like words into single or relatively complex units. Body movements ranging from a single nod of the head to a series of hand and leg gestures can attach additional meaning to spoken words. (Remember these gestures when transcribing an interview, as discussed above.) All kinesics research rests on the assumption that individuals are unaware of being engaged constantly in adjustments to the presence and activities of other persons. People modify their behavior and react verbally and nonverbally. Their nonverbal behavior is influenced by culture, gender, age, and other factors associated with psychological and social development.

Birdwhistell labels four channels in the communicative process: vocal, visual, olfactory, and tactile. It is important that the researcher be aware of these channels because the verbal interaction between researcher and subject consists of a steady flow of nonverbal clues. Behind the words are messages both parties are communicating. Educated by this knowledge of nonverbal clues, the researcher can monitor subjects' behaviors, discovering their attitudes and giving their actions additional meaning. Body language can express unconscious thoughts that may be essential for observers to decode if they are to analyze situations accurately.

In the interpretation of body language lies one of the weaknesses of kinesics. Novice body readers who have a "pop-psych" understanding of the science of kinesics may make incorrect, perhaps damaging, interpretations of behavior. Related closely to this possibility of misinterpretation is that body language as an analytic tool can be trivialized. For example, many studies focus on frequency counts of isolated units of behavior that convey little meaning by themselves. The fact that a person blinked 100 times during a 15-minute interview is not significant unless the context of the situation is also apparent.

The strengths of kinesic analysis are that it provides a view into unconscious thoughts and a means for the triangulation of verbal data. A researcher can be more confident about the accuracy of information provided by a participant if the speaker's body language is congruent with his words. Also, the researcher can monitor her own nonverbal behavior to clarify messages sent to the subject and to stay in touch with her own feelings during data collection.

Kinesic analysis is limited because body language is not universal; researchers must be aware of cultural differences. Many gestures signal different meanings in different cultures. In some countries, moving the head up and down signifies no and moving it from side to side means yes. Body movements must be interpreted in context, and only experts can make fine-tuned kinesic interpretations. Pupil dilation or movements of tiny jaw or neck muscles should be interpreted cautiously.

Proxemics. This is the study of people's use of space in relation to culture. The term was coined by Hall (1966), although he did not perform the original work in this area. Many studies have been conducted on human activities in bars, airports, subways, and other public places where individuals have to deal with one another in a limited space. Using proxemics, the researcher focuses on space, from interpersonal distance to the arrangement of furniture and architecture. Anthropologists, for example, have used proxemics to determine the territorial customs of cultures. Proxemics has been useful in the study of the behavior of students in the classroom and of marital partners undergoing counseling.

There are several advantages to the use of proxemics. It is unobtrusive, and usually it is difficult for a subject to mislead the observer deliberately. Because it is concerned with nonverbal behavior, subjects would have to be skillful to "lie" about their feelings. Proxemics is useful for studying the way individuals react to the invasion of their territory. Likewise, proxemics can be used in cross-cultural studies because people's use of personal space varies greatly from one culture to the next. Finally, proxemic analysis is useful for studies in areas such as the effect of seating arrangements on student behavior or the effect of crowding on workplace productivity.

The greatest disadvantage of proxemics as a data collection method is that the researcher must be skilled in the interpretation of the observed behaviors. If the researcher is observing a conference or a business meeting, the manner in which the subjects take their seats can be of vital importance, but the data must be interpreted carefully. Exclusive reliance on proxemics could be misleading because relationships that do not exist might be suggested. Because proxemics is relatively new as a data collection method, few instruments to measure space in research are available, further limiting its diverse use. The use of proxemics is increasing throughout research arenas, however. It provides a revealing and interesting method of gathering information about individual social behavior.

Unobtrusive Measures

Unobtrusive measures are ways of collecting data that do not require the cooperation of the subjects and, in fact, may be invisible to them. Webb, Campbell, Schwartz, and Sechrest (1966) describe these measures as "nonreactive research" because the researcher is expected to observe or gather data without interfering in the ongoing flow of everyday events. Data collected in this manner are categorized as documents, archival records, and physical evidence. Of these three, documents and archival records are the most frequently used in qualitative studies and were discussed earlier.

Physical evidence not produced specifically for the purpose of research often constitutes data. During the 1960s, the floor tile around the chick-hatching exhibit at the Museum of Science and Industry in Chicago had to be replaced every 6 weeks. Tile in other parts of the museum did not require replacement for years. The selective erosion of the tiles, indexed by the replacement rate, provided a measure of the relative popularity of exhibits (Webb et al., 1966).

Unobtrusive measures are particularly useful for triangulation. As a supplement to interviews, nonreactive research provides another perspective on a phenomenon, elaborating its complexity. These methods can be used without arousing subjects' notice and data collection is relatively easy because it often involves using data already collected by someone else (e.g., bills, archival records, sales records).

When used in isolation, however, unobtrusive measures may distort the picture. Erosion and survival may be affected by activities unknown to the researcher. For example, tiles near the chick-hatching exhibit may have worn out because it is close to the candy machine, not because of the exhibit's popularity. Some researchers consider the use of unobtrusive methods (e.g., monitoring exchanges on newsgroups or searching through garbage) to be unethical: They feel that those studied should be informed of the nature of the research.

When the researcher needs information for measures of frequency or attendance or when direct observation would be impossible or would bias the data, however, this method permits her to be quite creative. Unobtrusive data collection is often aided by hardware, such as audiotapes, hidden cameras, one-way mirrors, gauges, and infrared photos. Clearly, though, ethical issues abound in surreptitious observation.

Questionnaires and Surveys

Researchers administer questionnaires to some samples of a population to learn about the distribution of characteristics, attitudes, or beliefs. In deciding to survey a group of people, researchers make one critical assumption—that a characteristic or belief can be described or measured accurately through self-reporting. In using questionnaires, researchers rely totally on the honesty and accuracy of participants' responses. Although this limits the usefulness of questionnaires for delving into tacit beliefs and deeply held values, there are still many occasions when surveying can be useful.

Questionnaires typically entail several questions that have structured response categories; some open-ended questions may also be included. The questions are examined (sometimes quite vigorously) for bias, sequence, clarity, and face-validity. Questionnaires are usually tested on small groups to determine their usefulness and, perhaps, reliability.

In sample surveys, data are collected in a standardized format, usually from a probability sample of the population. The survey is the preferred method if the researcher wishes to obtain a small amount of information from a large number of subjects.

Survey research is the appropriate mode of inquiry for making inferences about a large group of people based on data drawn from a relatively small number of individuals in that group. Its basic aim is to describe and explain statistically the variability of certain features in a population. The general logic of survey research gives a distinctive style to the research process; the type of survey instrument is determined by the information needed. Surveys are conducted in three ways: by mail, telephone, and personal interview. Any method of data collection, however, from observation to content analysis, can be and has been used in survey research.

Most survey studies involve cross-sectional measurements made at a single point in time or longitudinal measurements taken at several different times. Other forms of survey research include trend studies that examine a population by studying separate samples at different points in time, cohort studies of a bounded population, and panel studies of a single sample of individuals at several points in time. Analysis of survey data takes the form of quantitative analysis that relies mainly on either descriptive or inferential statistics.

The relative advantages and disadvantages of survey research are weighed according to the following criteria: (a) appropriateness of the method to the problem studied, (b) accuracy of measurement, (c) generalizability of the findings, (d) administrative convenience, and (e) avoidance of ethical or political difficulties in the research process.

Surveys have definite advantages when the goals of research require obtaining quantitative data on a certain problem or population. They facilitate research in politically or ethically sensitive areas. They are used in programs for public welfare or economic development. Large surveys often focus on sensitive or controversial topics within the public domain.

The strengths of surveys include their accuracy, generalizability, and convenience. Accuracy in measurement is enhanced by quantification, replicability, and control over observer effects. Results can be generalized to a larger population within known limits of error. Surveys are amenable to rapid statistical analysis and are comparatively easy to administer and manage.

Surveys have weaknesses, however. They are of little value for examining complex social relationships or intricate patterns of interaction. Their strengths can also be weaknesses. Although controlling accuracy, a survey cannot assure without further evidence that the sample represents a broader universe. Thus, the method of drawing the sample and the sample size are critical to the accuracy of the study and its potential for generalizability. Also, even though surveys are convenient, they are generally a relatively expensive method of data collection. Finally, surveys may result in an invasion of privacy or produce questionable effects in the respondent or the community. Some research projects relying on these methods may enhance the position or resources of a particular group, and conflicts may arise between sponsors and research teams concerning how problems are defined. This problem is not specific to surveys and questionnaires, however.

Projective Techniques and Psychological Testing

Some types of interpretive psychological strategies were developed many years ago by clinical psychologists to obtain personality data. These strategies have been used fairly extensively in comparative studies about culture and for analysis of personality dynamics. Based on an internal, perceptual frame of reference, the techniques assume that one can get a valid picture of a person by assessing the way the individual projects his personality onto some standard, ambiguous stimuli.

Standardization and ambiguity are common elements in tests of this nature, although so-called clinical judgments form the primary interpretation bases of responses to these stimuli. Results are typically expressed in the form of a verbal report assessing the subject's dominant needs and ambitions, tolerance of frustrations, attitudes toward authority, major internal conflicts, and so on. The reputation and qualifications of the tester sometimes play a role in how the report is received and how much credibility is attached to the interpretation.

Two of the most well-known and frequently used psychological strategies of this notion are the Rorschach inkblot test and the Thematic Apperception Test (TAT). The original idea behind both includes the assumption that the stimuli are ambiguous so the subject has to be imaginative and projective in response. The Rorschach test uses pictures (symmetrical inkblots), usually presented in a predetermined order; the subject reports what each picture resembles or suggests. The number, quality, and variety of the subject's responses are compared with specific personality types and with the responses of other people to the same stimuli. In the TAT, the subject is asked to tell stories about a set of picture scenes. Test results are used to assess personality traits such as aggressiveness, dependence, and sexual conflicts.

Although projective instruments have been the object of considerable criticism for many years, they are still commonly employed in clinical contexts by psychologists. Questions remain as to their validity and reliability; environmental and cultural factors may also affect results. Today, concern focuses on the more concrete aspects of personality traits, such as self-esteem and styles of interpersonal behavior, rather than on the vague generalizations that characterized earlier interpretive schemes.

A number of other psychological tests and measurements have been developed for use in qualitative and anthropological research.

Examples include the study of (a) the perception of illusions, in which optical and auditory illusions are examined for differences in perception related to differences in types of environments; (b) judgments of aesthetic qualities, in which pictures of art objects or musical stimuli are used to elicit opinions concerning aesthetic excellence; (c) psychomotor skills, in which physical activity measures indicate personality qualities, such as introversion and extroversion; (d) games people engage in, to provide significant information about community and social behavior; and (e) games as a laboratory device, in which a specific game involving family members is used to determine a relationship between communication patterns and socioeconomic differences. Attitude scales can be used in qualitative inquiry, as supplementary measures, and for triangulation (see more on triangulation in Chapter 5). Other qualitative methods have been devised for studying entire communities, group living patterns, and the social integration of individuals in different residential contexts; these are referenced at the end of this chapter.

Dilemma Analysis

Dilemma analysis brings into focus respondents' reactions to situations that have no right answers: that is, dilemmas. The approach can be used as a focused part of interviewing, particularly to get at the core of the respondent's processes of thinking, assessing, valuing, and judging. It has been developed primarily in developmental psychology. However, it can be adapted wherever the research probes at moral issues and practical decision-making processes. We describe two common types.

The first, the *hypothetical, researcher-generated dilemma,* is the most common. Many respondents are given a standardized dilemma and asked about what they would do and what would guide their decision making. The famous example devised by Kohlberg elicits respondents' moral reasoning about the so-called Heinz dilemma. Heinz's wife has a terminal illness and the only way to obtain a life-saving drug is to break a Biblical commandment: violate someone's property, commit a crime, or steal it. Kohlberg used this method to generate theory on moral development. Later, Carol Gilligan (1982) critiqued Kohlberg's theory and methodology, arguing that the theory was gender-biased because his samples were college-aged men. She devised data collection strategies that were more contextualized and more attuned to real lives, as well as ones which focused on women. As a result, she developed very different conclusions about moral development. The real-life, researcher-generated dilemma uses a real crisis—from history, from typical workplace or family life situations—and asks for respondents' choices and the thoughts and feelings surrounding those choices.

The second, the *real-life, respondent-generated dilemma*, encourages respondents to describe the most difficult or heart-wrenching choices they have made, for example, while growing up, at work or in their families. Thus, the situations are generated in a more naturalistic fashion. While focused, they are closer to a straightforward interview, allowing respondents, at least to some extent, to choose what to focus on. For example, Marshall (1992, 1993, 1996) asked assistant principals to describe a situation that, in the last two years, had created ethical dilemmas for them in their workplaces. She guided them through standard questions to probe the parameters affecting the choices they made. In the interviews, telling the stories, in depth, to a sympathetic, nonjudgmental ear seemed cathartic. The rich data included stories of denying services to students because of policy, firing teachers, turning down promotions to avoid upsetting their family stability, and so on. While the interviews were wonderfully rich with personal context, pulling them together in data analysis and reporting was no easy task.

Dilemma analysis can be fun. Commonly focusing on one respondent at a time, it produces a thematic coherence that does not depend upon academic theories or hunches of the researcher (Winter, 1982). It opens doors to innermost thoughts and can be designed to collect standardized data. Real-life, researcher-generated dilemmas, if well constructed using insights from previous research, can be very useful, especially for focusing and standardizing data collection, when that is appropriate. Gathering data through real-life dilemmas is often enjoyable. People like to recount poignant, heroic, angst-provoking situations— when they are in the past and when they believe they created an adequate resolution. However, analysis of these data needs to stipulate clearly that these are recollections and, perhaps, represent the 20/20 vision of hindsight.

Dilemma analysis can be dilemma-laden, too. As in the Heinz example, people may not take the situation seriously, and the data may well reflect this. Also, the choice of a dilemma and the interview questions may be skewed to shape the choices, producing "interesting" data. In addition, the very personalized data elicited from real-life, but respondent-generated dilemmas may be difficult to interpret and to compare with other data. Finally, directing people to recall all the agonies associated with a dilemma that may still be unresolved can be problematic ethically.

Using Computer and Internet Technologies

There is no question that the Internet and its associated hardware (desktop computers, most commonly) have changed the methodologies of social science research. Searching the Internet for resources (now called Googling), using software to manage citations and some aspects of data analysis, interviewing by means of e-mail or in dedicated chat rooms, and using dialogues and interactions online as sites for study are all now part and parcel of much scholarship in the social sciences and applied fields. One way to track the changes over the past decade is to examine the chapters in the *Handbook of Qualitative Research* (Denzin & Lincoln, 2005, 2000, 1994) dedicated to some discussion of the use of computers in qualitative research. Between the second and third editions, there is a major shift.

The first edition (1994) included a chapter titled "Using computers in qualitative research" (Richards & Richards) in which the authors described various software programs designed to assist in qualitative data management and analysis. The second edition contained a similar chapter, "Software and qualitative research" (Weitzman, 2000). Shorthand in this developing field is the acronym QDA, for *qualitative data analysis.*

The software for qualitative data analysis raised both hopes and fears among qualitative researchers. In the second edition of the *Handbook,* Weitzman notes that computers can assist the analysis phase because they facilitate making and writing observational notes, editing, coding, storing, searching and retrieval, linking data, writing memos, analyzing content, displaying data, drawing and verifying conclusion, building theory, mapping graphics, and writing reports. He goes on to note, however, that "software . . . cannot do the analysis for you, not in the same sense in which a statistical package like SPRR or SAS can do, say, multiple regression" (pp. 805–806). Our experience is that novice qualitative researchers hope that software will do the hard work of analysis for them, somewhat magically. We caution that software is only a tool to help with some of the mechanical and management aspects of analysis.

The third edition of the *Handbook* (2005) includes no chapter on QDA. Instead, Markham focuses on what is called *Internet ethnography,* illustrating the growing focus on the Internet itself as a site for identity representation and construction. Scholars from communications and cultural studies have contributed fascinating studies of the Internet and its wealth of opportunities to reflect changing social identities, communities, and cultures (see, e.g., Baym, 2000; Kendall, 2002; Hine,

2001; Miller & Slater, 2000). Their fascination emerges in part from the postmodern turn that has examined and problematized the embodied construction of identity. The Internet provides a disembodied site where social identities (gender, social class, sexual orientation, and so on) are hidden. Thus emerges the possibility of studying the construction of identity solely through text. As Markham (2005) notes, "Although we recognize that reality is socially negotiated through discursive practice, the dialogic nature of identity and culture is thrown into high relief in computer-mediated environments" (p. 795). Studies of online culture include *Tune In, Log On* (Baym, 2000), *The Internet: An Ethnographic Approach* (Miller & Slater, 2000), and *Hanging Out at the Virtual Pub* (Kendall, 2002).

Using computers for data collection presents challenges and questions: Are data collected from an internet discussion board more or less authentic than data from, for example, interviews or focus groups? How can you guard the anonymity of sources if you collect data online? How do you manage the fact that your data come only from persons who are computer-savvy, comfortable with computers, and have computer access? Despite these challenges, computer-mediated data gathering may offer an alternative to face-to-face interviewing and be most appropriate for certain research projects. One major advantage is that one's sample can quite literally be a global one. Computers also provide access to populations uncomfortable with or unwilling to engage in face-to-face interactions.

❖ COMBINING DATA COLLECTION METHODS

Many qualitative studies combine several data collection methods over the course of the study, as seen in Shadduck-Hernandez's (1997) proposal discussed in Vignette 21 (see page 167). The researcher can assess the strengths and limitations of each method, then decide if that method will work with the questions and in the setting for a given study. Tables 4.1 and 4.2 display the strengths and limitations of each method, based on how it is generally used in qualitative studies. The tables should help researchers select the best combination of methods: Limitations in one method can be compensated for by the strengths of a complementary one.

In drafting a proposal, the researcher should consider whether the method will provide adequate information and be cost-effective and feasible in terms of the subtleties of the setting and the resources available for the study. The relative emphasis on participation in many qualitative studies, for example, suggests certain methods over others. Lutz and Iannaccone (1969) provide guidelines for method selection based on role, as shown in Table 4.3. These choices should be logically linked to the conceptual framework and research questions, the overall strategy of the study, and early decisions about role.

Vignette 17 describes how a researcher selected data collection methods in a study about a long-term health care facility.

VIGNETTE 17

Choosing Data Collection Methods

How might one's view of life be shaped by residence in a long-term health care facility? A doctoral student in health care management (Kalnins, 1986) wanted to examine—in depth and in detail—the contexts, processes, and interactions that shaped patients' perspectives. She reasoned that a qualitative approach would be most fruitful in picking up everyday actions and interactions about complex social structures.

From the variety of data collection strategies, she proposed a combination of direct observation, participant observation, and semistructured interviewing. Her beginning point would be direct observation of residents and staff in various areas of the facility, "witnessing events which particularly preoccupied the hosts, or indicated special symbolic importance to them" (Schatzman & Strauss, 1973, p. 59). This would allow her to get a holistic view and to gather data that would inform the interview process.

Kalnins's plan as a participant observer would be to observe the residents and staff in the natural setting of the long-term health care facility, requiring her "commitment to adopt the perspective of those studied by sharing in their day-to-day experiences" (Denzin, 1970, p. 185). In her proposal, Kalnins anticipated that participant observation and interviewing would run concurrently, allowing data from each to be used to substantiate events, explore emerging hypotheses, and make further decisions about the conduct of the research. Her role as participant observer would mean that Kalnins would become immersed in the lives and activities of those she was studying. She understood the interactive-adaptive nature of participant observation, reflecting the complex relationship between field observation and emerging theory, and the impact of this relationship on decisions about further data collection. Her decisions about the data to be collected and methods for collecting those data would be guided by Wilson's (1977) list of five relevant types of data employed to get at meaning structures: (a) the form and content of verbal interaction between participants, (b) the form and content of their verbal interaction with researcher, (c) nonverbal behavior, (d) patterns of actions and nonaction, and (e) traces, archival records, artifacts, and documents (p. 255).

Table 4.1   Strengths of Data Collection Methods

	PO	O	I	FG	DR	N	HA	F	IA	UM	Q	PT	DA	C
Fosters face-to-face interactions with participants	x	x	x	x		x						D		
Useful for uncovering participants' perspectives	x	x	x	x		x						D	D	
Data collected in natural setting	x	x	x	x	D	x		x	x	x				
Facilitates immediate follow-up for clarification	x	x	x	x		x		x	D					x
Good for documenting major events, crises, conflicts	x	x		x	x	x	x	x					x	
Collects data on unconscious thoughts and actions	x				D	D		x	x	x		x		
Useful for describing complex interactions	x	x	x	x		x	x	x	x		x	D		
Good for obtaining data on nonverbal behavior and communication	x	x	D	D	D	D		x	x	x		D		
Facilitates discovery of nuances in culture	x	x	x	x	D	x	x	x	x	x				
Provides for flexibility in formulating hypotheses	x	x	x	x	D	x	x	x	x	x			D	
Provides context information	x	x	x	x	x		x	x					D	
Facilitates analysis, validity checks, and triangulation	x	x	x	x	x			x	x	x	x	x	x	
Facilitates cooperation	x	D	D	x	x	x			x	x	x	x		x
Data easy to manipulate and categorize for analysis					x				x	D	x			x
Obtains large amounts of data quickly		x		x			x	x				x		
Allows wide range of types of data and participants	x			D	D				D	x		x		x
Easy and efficient to administer and manage					x		x		x	x	x			
Easily quantifiable and amenable to statistical analysis					x				x	x	x	x	x	x
Easy to establish generalizability					D		D		x	x	x	x		
May draw on established instruments					x				x	x	x	x	x	x
Expands access to distant participants				x	x					x	x	x	x	x

NOTE: x = strength exists; D = depends on use; PO = participant observation; O = observation; I = interview; FG = focus-group interviewing; DR = document review; N = narratives and life histories; HA = historical analysis; F = film; IA = interaction analysis; UM = unobtrusive measures; Q = questionnaires and surveys; PT = psychological techniques; DA = dilemma analysis; C = internet.

Table 4.2 Weaknesses of Data Collection Methods

	PO	O	I	FG	DR	N	HA	F	IA	UM	Q	PT	DA	C
Leads researcher to fixate on details	x	x		D	x	x		x	x	x	x	x		x
Possible misinterpretations due to cultural differences	x	x	x	x	x	x	x	x	x	x	x	x	x	
Requires technical training								x	x		x	x		
Dependent on cooperation of key individuals	x	x	x			x		x		D		x		
Readily open to ethical dilemmas	x	x	x	x		x	D	x				x	x	x
Difficult to replicate	x	x	x	x		x		x				x		
Data more affected by research presence	x	x	X	x	D	D		D	D			D	x	
Expensive materials and equipment								x		x				
Can cause discomfort or even danger to researcher	x											x		
Too dependent on participant openness/honesty	x		x			x		x					x	x
Too artistic an interpretation undermines research	x	x	x	x		x	x	x				x		
Dependent on "goodness" of initial research question		x		x	D		x		x		x		x	x
Dependent on the researcher's interpersonal skills	x	x	x	x	x	x	x					x		

NOTE: x = weakness exists; D = depends on use; PO = participant observation; O = observation; I = interview; FG = focus-group interviewing; DR = document review; N = narratives and life histories; HA = historical analysis; F = film; IA = interaction analysis; UM = unobtrusive measures; Q = questionnaires and surveys; PT = psychological techniques; DA = dilemma analysis; C = internet.

Table 4.3   Data Collection Methods Related to Observation Role

Method	Role			Comment
	I—Participant as observer	II—Observer as participant	III—Observer as nonparticipant	
Observation and recording of descriptive data	+	+	+	Particularly useful to Role I in areas of guarded interaction and sentiment
Recording direct quotations of sentiment	+	+	+	Same as above
Unstructured interview	+	+	*	If the researcher is skillful, a structure emerges
Structured interview guides	–	*	+	Most useful in survey work (e.g., census)
Detailed interaction guides	–	–	*	Most useful in small-group work
Interaction frequency tallies	+	+	+	Meaning in leadership studies
Paper-and-pencil tests				Very helpful in certain circumstances for certain purposes
Questionnaires	–	–	+	
Scales	–	–	+	
Achievement or ability	–	–	*	
Written records				Very important to Role I in checking reliability of observed data
Newspaper	+	+	*	
Official minutes	+	+	*	
Letters	+	+	*	
Speeches	+	+	*	
Radio and television reports	+	+		Same as above

SOURCE: Lutz and Iannaccone (1969, p. 113). Reprinted with permission.
NOTE: + = likely to be used; * = may occasionally be used; – = difficult or impossible to use.

135

To generate facts, opinions, and insights (Yin, 1984), Kalnins planned for open-ended structured interviews (using questionnaires) that would enable the exploration of many topics but that could focus on cultural nuances, first-hand encounters, and the perceptions, meanings, and interpretations of others. Information would also be gathered from various documents and archives, lending a historical perspective to the study.

Vignette 17 illustrates how a researcher chose an array of data collection methods, knowing that each method had particular strengths and that each would help elicit certain desired information. It shows that data collection strategies and methods cannot be chosen in a vacuum. Intensively examining the possible methods, trying them out, examining their potentials, and fitting them to the research question, site, and sample are important design considerations. In addition, researchers must consider their *own* personal abilities in carrying out any particular overall approach or method.

❖ GENERAL PRINCIPLES FOR DESIGNING DATA COLLECTION STRATEGIES

In the proposal, the methods planned for data collection should be related to the type of information sought. Zelditch's (1962) chart, reproduced in Table 4.4, provides guidelines for three large categories of methods: enumerating, participant observation, and in-depth interviewing. Each broad category best yields a particular type of information. In determining which method to use, the researcher should carefully examine the questions guiding the study. Many *how* questions are really *how many* questions. For example, interviewing people in a program would not adequately answer the question of how many people drop out of the program.

The researcher should determine the most practical, efficient, feasible, and ethical methods for collecting data as the research progresses. He should also consider whether he can fashion and manage a role that works with the chosen data collection strategies. He might need to consider whether, in seeking approval or funding for the research, his chosen strategies will be seen as legitimate. He might start with participant observation as he seeks to identify questions, patterns, and domains. This strategy might change as the research becomes more focused and progresses toward more specific questions and

Table 4.4   Information Types and Methods of Obtaining Information

| Information type | Method of obtaining information | | |
	Enumerations and samples	Participant observation	Interviewing informants
Frequency distributions	Prototype and best form	Usually inadequate and inefficient	Often, but not always, adequate; if adequate, efficient
Incidents, histories	Not adequate by itself; not efficient	Prototype and best form	Adequate, with precautions, and efficient
Institutionalized norms and statuses	Adequate but inefficient	Adequate but inefficient, except for unverbalized norms	Most efficient and hence best form

SOURCE: Zelditch (1962, p. 575). Reprinted by permission.

clearer concepts that suggest the use of representative samples. Then the researcher could develop surveys and enumerate the findings. On the other hand, the findings might be descriptions, not numbers. If the research goal is a description of processes, concepts, categories, and typologies, then sampling and counting are merely tools of analysis, not necessarily part of the research findings. The proposal should demonstrate that the researcher is capable of designing and selecting data collection methods that are appropriate, well-thought-out, and thorough. Because the research question may change as the research progresses, the methods may change and the researcher must ensure this flexibility. Vignette 18 provides an example.

VIGNETTE 18

Design Flexibility[1]

A graduate student wanted to explore the implementation of a state mandate for local school councils. Rodriguez first proposed participant observation of meetings and in-depth interviews with board members. The data collection plan showed a schedule for observing the meetings, goals for interviewing, and a time allowance for analysis of data and for follow-up data collection. But in the process of initial data collection and preliminary analysis, he discovered that teacher resentment of the councils was creating a pattern of unintended negative consequences. This discovery could have important implications for policy development. Did Rodriguez have to stay with the original question and data collection plan? Wouldn't a design alteration offer important insights?

Rodriguez reasoned that if he could describe the processes whereby well-intended policy is thwarted, policymakers could gain insight that might help them make timely alterations in policy development or implementation. Given this possible benefit to the study, he could choose to focus subsequent data collection on the conflicts between teacher needs and the mandate to school boards that they implement councils. This would require him to turn to additional literatures on, for example, teacher needs, teacher participation in decision making, or teacher unions. He might also need to employ additional data collection methods (such as surveying teacher needs, observing teacher union meetings, and doing historical research on the reactions of teacher lobbies to mandates for school councils), or he might need to sample additional settings or people. As the research question became more focused, his initial research design and data collection strategy would most likely undergo some changes.

————————— |||| —————————

In the example in Vignette 18, the research proposal probably did not include a plan for analysis of lobbying efforts or observation of collective bargaining sessions. It would, however, be entirely appropriate— indeed, recommended—for the researcher to modify the research proposal if an exciting and significant focus emerges from early data collection. In fact, the primary strength of the qualitative approach is this very flexibility, which allows, even encourages, exploration, discovery, and creativity.

Along with choosing appropriate strategies for data collection, the researcher must address the complex processes of managing, recording, and analyzing data. Rather than discrete, sequential events, these processes occur dialectically throughout the conduct of a qualitative study: Analysis occurs as themes are identified, as the deeper structures of the social setting become clear, and as consequent modifications are made in the initial design. At the proposal stage, however, the researcher should present some initial ideas about how the data will be managed and stored and provide some preliminary discussion of the processes for analyzing those data. We discuss these issues in the next chapter.

DIALOGUE BETWEEN LEARNERS

Melanie,

I really feel and appreciate your questions about the many selves that are infused within our research. I'm a former writing instructor so I have a tendency to believe in writing through these types of difficulties. I wonder what would happen if you did a bit of writing on the same topic from your different perspectives: your self as researcher, former instructor, and friend. Would they each look differently at the same topic? Where would they overlap? What I'm getting at is if you were to consciously take on the persona of one of your selves and then took on an issue from three perspectives you might get some wonderful insights into how your unique position creates an interpretation. Does that make any sense? My guess is that you'll find more points of overlap than not. It might, however, allow you to examine and honestly address your role in your research.

You've no doubt noted the number of different approaches in Chapter 4 of Catherine and Gretchen's book—it's a bit overwhelming to say the least! Sometimes it's a bit hard to not get caught up in the specifics of one particular approach, to not feel as though there were only one right way to complete an ethnographic interview or narrative analysis. I have a tendency to read up on different approaches and run the risk of losing sight of what I bring to the project—that there is perhaps a bit of a dialectical relationship between what I bring to the project and the effect the project has on me.

While I agree that, ultimately, our research might not be about us, I can't deny that it does, in no small way, reflect us and our experiences. We might say that our research is, in a very real sense, autobiographical. No doubt you selected your area of research because in some way you connect with it. Imagine working so hard on something that you were distinctly separate from and neutral toward!

But there is something so very disconcerting or indulgent about ongoing navel-gazing. Like you, I hedge at focusing too much on myself (or, my self). There are the voices and selves of the students you work with and study. Hmmm . . . I suppose this is where we look to our mentors to read our work and say,

"Hey, this is not all about you" or ask, "Where do you fall in all of this?" I suppose we can also turn to other graduate students! I get a lot out of our conversations; it's nice to have someone to chat with about these issues and writing it down in an e-mail seems to help.

Hope all is well.

Aaron

Hi Aaron,

You make some good points, especially that our research does, in some way, revolve around us; otherwise, it wouldn't be **our** research. Thanks for the suggestions, too; I like the idea of writing from my different selves. (I'm a former English teacher—bring on the pen!) I think it's quite easy to get stuck at approaching our research in one specific way; remembering the flexibility in technique and presentation really opens up our options.

I really like thinking through these topics, too. Working through the tangles with a fellow grad student gives one the license to be ignorant! Even though we know so much about so many different things, we're still making sense in personal, practical ways. Conversations among grad students are more of a meaning-making experience, working together to create an understanding that applies to our personal situations. I get a lot out of seeing other grad students tackle different techniques, too. A few of my friends here are dedicated to life history and film ethnography. I'm more of an in-depth interview, computer-interaction type of researcher. Even if I don't see myself taking on those specific types of techniques (yet!), I learn from seeing their use of different approaches. We might gain info like this faster by asking a professor or reading an article, but we don't absorb it or apply it the same way.

So, what else is on your mind?

Melanie

❖ NOTE

1. This vignette is fictitious.

❖ FURTHER READING

Participant Observation

Bogdan, R. C., & Biklen, S. K. (2003). *Qualitative research in education: An introduction to theory and methods* (4th ed.). Boston: Allyn & Bacon.

Brock, K., & McGee, R. (2002). *Knowing poverty: Critical reflections on participatory research and policy*. Sterling, VA: Earthscan Publications.

Delamont, S. (2001). *Fieldwork in educational settings: Methods, pitfalls, and perspectives* (2nd ed.). London: RoutledgeFalmer.

Jorgensen, D. L. (1989). *Participant observation: A methodology for human studies*. Newbury Park, CA: Sage.

Lee, R. M. (1995). *Dangerous fieldwork*. Thousand Oaks, CA: Sage.

Nordstrom, C., & Robben, A. (1995). *Fieldwork under fire: Contemporary studies of violence and survival*. Berkeley: University of California Press.

Pelto, P., & Pelto, G. H. (1978). *Anthropological research: The structure of inquiry* (2nd ed.). New York: Cambridge University Press.

Spradley, J. S. (1980). *Participant observation*. New York: Holt, Rinehart & Winston.

Wolcott, H. F. (2005). *The art of fieldwork* (2nd ed.). Walnut Creek, CA: AltaMira.

Observation

Adler, P. A., & Adler, P. (1994). Observational techniques. In N. K. Denzin & Y. S. Lincoln (Eds.), *Handbook of qualitative research* (pp. 377–392). Thousand Oaks, CA: Sage.

DeWalt, K. M., & De Walt, B. R. (2001). *Participant observation: A guide for fieldworkers*. Walnut Creek, CA: AltaMira Press.

Lofland, J., & Lofland, L. H. (1995). *Analyzing social settings: A guide to qualitative observation and analysis* (3rd ed.). Belmont, CA: Wadsworth.

Smith, C. D., & Kornblum, W. (Eds.). (1996). *In the field: Readings on the field research experience*. Westport, CT: Praeger.

Generic In-Depth Interviewing

Gubrium, J. F., & Holstein, J. A. (Eds). (2002). *Handbook of interview research*. Thousand Oaks, CA: Sage.

Holstein, J. A., & Gubrium, J. F. (1995). *The active interview*. Thousand Oaks, CA: Sage.

Holstein, J. A., & Gubrium, J. F. (1997). Active interviewing. In D. Silverman (Ed.), *Qualitative research: Theory, method, and practice* (pp. 113–129). London: Sage.

McCracken, G. (1988). *The long interview.* Newbury Park, CA: Sage.

Patton, M. Q. (2002). *Qualitative research and evaluation methods* (3rd ed.). Thousand Oaks, CA: Sage.

Peace, S. D., & Sprinthall, N. A. (1998). Training school counselors to supervise beginning counselors: Theory, research, and practice. *Professional School Counseling, 1*(5), 2–9.

Riessman, C. K. (2002). Analysis of personal narratives. In J. F Gubrium & J. A. Holstein (Eds.), *Handbook of interview research* (pp. 695–710). Thousand Oaks, CA: Sage.

Rubin, H. J., & Rubin, I. S. (2005). *Qualitative interviewing: The art of hearing data* (2nd ed.). Thousand Oaks, CA: Sage.

Weiss, R. S. (1994). *Learning from strangers: The art and method of qualitative interview studies.* New York: Free Press.

Wengraf, T. (2001). *Qualitative research interviewing: Biographic narrative and semi-structured methods.* London: Sage.

Ethnographic Interviewing

Bateman, B. E. (2002). Promoting openness toward culture learning: Ethnographic interviews for students of Spanish. *Modern Language Journal, 86*(3), 318–331.

Crivos, M. (2002). Narrative and experience: Illness in the context of an ethnographic interview. *Oral History Review, 29*(2), 13–15.

Edmondson, R. (2005). Wisdom in later life: Ethnographic approaches. *Ageing and Society, 25*(3), 339–356.

Montgomery, L. (2004). "It's just what I like": Explaining persistent patterns of gender stratification in the life choices of college students. *International Journal of Qualitative Studies in Education, 17*(6), 785–802.

Spradley, J. S. (1979). *The ethnographic interview.* New York: Holt, Rinehart & Winston.

Turner, W. L., Wallace, B. R., Anderson, J. R., & Bird, C. (2004). The last mile of the way: Understanding caregiving in African American families at the end-of-life. *Journal of Marital & Family Therapy, 30*(4), 427–488.

Wolcott, H. F. (1985). On ethnographic intent. *Educational Administration Quarterly, 3*, 187–203.

Phenomenological Interviewing

Collins, M., Shattell, M., & Thomas, S. P. (2005). Problematic interviewee behaviors in qualitative research. *Western Journal of Nursing Research, 27*(2), 188–199.

Holstein, J. A., & Gubrium, J. F. (1995). *The active interview.* Thousand Oaks, CA: Sage.

Hood, Jr., R. W. (2000). A phenomenological analysis of the anointing among religious serpent handlers. *International Journal for the Psychology of Religion, 10*(4), 221–240.

Kvale, S. (1996). *InterViews: An introduction to qualitative research interviewing.* Thousand Oaks, CA: Sage.

Lackey, N. R., Gates, M. F., & Brown, G. (2001). African American women's experiences with the initial discovery, diagnosis, and treatment of breast cancer. *Oncology Nursing Forum, 28*(3), 519–517.

Seidman, I. E. (1998). *Interviewing as qualitative research: A guide for researchers in education and the social sciences* (2nd ed.). New York: Teachers College Press.

Van Manen, M. (1990). *Researching lived experience: Human science for an action sensitive pedagogy.* Buffalo: State University of New York Press.

Interviewing Elites

Aberbach, J. D., & Rockman, B. A. (2002). Conducting and coding elite interviews. *PS: Political Science & Politics, 35*(4), 673–676.

Becker, T. M., & Meyers, P. R. (1974–1975). Empathy and bravado: Interviewing reluctant bureaucrats. *Public Opinion Quarterly, 38*, 605–613.

Bennis, W., & Nanus, B. (1985). *Leaders: The strategies for taking charge.* New York: Harper & Row.

Hertz, R., & Imber, J. B. (1995). *Studying elites using qualitative methods.* Thousand Oaks, CA: Sage.

Marshall, C. (1984). Elites, bureaucrats, ostriches, and pussycats: Managing research in policy settings. *Anthropology and Education Quarterly, 15*, 235–251.

Odendahl, T., & Shaw, A. M. (2002). Interviewing elites. In J. F Gubrium & J. A. Holstein (Eds.), *Handbook of interview research* (pp. 299–316). Thousand Oaks, CA: Sage.

Platt, J. (1981). On interviewing one's peers. *British Journal of Sociology, 32*, 75–85.

Thomas, R. (1993). Interviewing important people in big companies. *Journal of Contemporary Ethnography, 22*(1), 80–96.

Zuckerman, H. (1972). Interviewing an ultra-elite. *Public Opinion Quarterly, 36*(5), 159–175.

Focus-Group Interviewing

Botherson, M. J. (1994). Interactive focus group interviewing: A qualitative research method in early intervention. *Topics in Early Childhood Special Education, 14*(1), 101–118.

Krueger, R. A., & Casey, M. A (2000). *Focus groups: A practical guide for applied research* (3rd ed). Thousand Oaks, CA: Sage.

Linhorst, D. M. (2002). A review of the use and potential of focus groups in social work research. *Qualitative Social Work, 1*(2), 208–228.

Morgan, D. L. (1997). *Focus groups as qualitative research* (2nd ed.). Thousand Oaks, CA: Sage.

Stewart, D. W., & Shamdasani, P. N. (1990). *Focus groups: Theory and practice.* Newbury Park, CA: Sage.

Studying Children

Cappello, M. (2005). Photo interviews: Eliciting data through conversations with children. *Field Methods, 17*(2), 170–184.

Daniels, D. H., Beaumont, L. J., & Doolin, C. A. (2002). *Understanding children: An interview and observation guide for educators.* Boston: McGraw-Hill Higher Education.

Faller, K. C. (2003). Research and practice in child interviewing. *Journal of Interpersonal Violence, 18*(4), 377–389.

Fine, G. A., & Sandstrom, K. L. (1988). *Knowing children: Participant observation with minors.* Newbury Park, CA: Sage.

Kortesluoma, R. L., Hentinen, M., & Nikkonen, M. (2003). Conducting a qualitative child interview: Methodological considerations. *Journal of Advanced Nursing, 42*(5), 434–441.

Lewis, A., & Porter, J. (2004). Interviewing children and young people with learning disabilities. *British Journal of Learning Disabilities, 32*(4), 191–197.

Smith, A. B., Taylor, N. J., & Gollop, M. M. (Eds.). (2000). *Children's voices: Research, policy and practice.* Auckland, NZ: Pearson Education.

Wilson, J. C., & Powell, M. (2001). *A guide to interviewing children: Essential skills for counsellors, police, lawyers and social workers.* New York: Routledge.

Unobtrusive Measures

Dilevko, J. (2000). *Unobtrusive evaluation of reference service and individual responsibility: The Canadian experience.* Westport, CT: Ablex.

Jensen, B. (2004). The case for non-intrusive research: A virtual reference librarian's perspective. *Reference Librarian, 85,* 139–149.

Lee, R. M. (2000). *Unobtrusive methods in social research.* Philadelphia: Open University.

Moss, G., & McDonald, J. W. (2004). The borrowers: Library records as unobtrusive measures of children's readings preferences. *Journal of Research in Readings, 27*(4), 401–412.

Page, S. (2000). Community research: The lost art of unobtrusive methods. *Journal of Applied Social Psychology, 30*(10), 2126–2136.

Rodler, C., Kirchler, E., & Holzl, E. (2001). Gender stereotypes of leaders: An analysis of the contents of obituaries from 1974 to 1998. *Sex Roles, 45*(11/12), 827–844.

Sechrest, L. (Ed.). (1979). *Unobtrusive measurement today.* San Francisco: Jossey-Bass.

Webb, E., Campbell, D. T., Schwartz, R. D., & Sechrest, L. (2000). *Unobtrusive measures: Nonreactive research in the social sciences* (Rev. ed.). Chicago: Rand McNally.

Survey Methods

Cox, J. (1996). *Your opinion, please: How to build the best questionnaires in the field of education.* Thousand Oaks, CA: Corwin.

Czaja, R., & Blair, J. (2005). *Designing surveys: A guide to decisions and procedures* (2nd ed.). Thousand Oaks, CA: Pine Forge.

Jick, T. D. (1979). Mixing qualitative and quantitative methods: Triangulation in action. *Administrative Science Quarterly, 24,* 602–661.

Mertens, D. M. (2005). *Research and evaluation in education and psychology: Integrating diversity with quantitative, qualitative, and mixed methods.* Thousand Oaks, CA: Sage.

Projective Techniques and Psychological Testing

Coles, R. (1971). *Children of crisis: Migrants, sharecroppers, mountaineers.* Boston: Little, Brown.

Coles, R. (1977). *Privileged ones: The well-off and the rich in America.* Boston: Little, Brown.

Edgerton, R. B. (1973). Method in psychological anthropology. In R. Naroll & R. Cohen (Eds.), *A handbook of method in cultural anthropology* (2nd ed., pp. 338–353). New York: Columbia University Press.

Groth-Marnat, G. (2003). *Handbook of psychology assessment* (4th ed.). Hoboken, NJ: John Wiley.

Mental measurements yearbook (16th ed.). (2005). Highland Park, NJ: Gryphon Press.

Rizzuto, A. (1979). *The birth of a living God: A psychoanalytic study.* Chicago: University of Chicago Press.

Life Histories and Narrative Inquiry

Atkinson, R. (1998). *The life story interview.* Thousand Oaks, CA: Sage.

Chessman, C. (1954). *Cell 2455 death row.* Englewood Cliffs, NJ: Prentice Hall.

Clandinin, D. J., & Connelly, F. M. (2000). *Narrative inquiry: Experience and story in qualitative research.* San Francisco: Jossey-Bass.

Conle, C. (2000). Narrative inquiry: Research tool and medium for professional development. *European Journal of Teacher Education, 23*(1), 49–54.

Conle, C. (2001). The rationality of narrative inquiry in research and professional development. *European Journal of Teacher Education, 24*(1), 21–33.

Etter-Lewis, G., & Foster, M. (1996). *Unrelated kin: Race and gender in women's personal narratives.* New York: Routledge.

Gluck, S. B., & Patai, P. (Eds.). (1991). *Women's words: The feminist practice of oral history*. New York: Routledge.

Josselson, R. (Ed.). (1996). *Ethics and process in the narrative study of lives*. Thousand Oaks, CA: Sage.

Josselson, R., & Lieblich, A. (Eds.). (1993). *The narrative study of lives*. Newbury Park, CA: Sage.

Lieblich, A., Tuval-Mashiach, R., & Zilber, T. (1998). *Narrative research: Reading, analysis, and interpretation*. Thousand Oaks, CA: Sage.

Mandelbaum, D. G. (1973). The study of life history: Gandhi. *Current Anthropology, 14,* 177–207.

Martin, R. R. (1995). *Oral history in social work: Research, assessment, and intervention*. Thousand Oaks, CA: Sage.

Miller, R. L. (1999). *Researching life stories and family histories*. Thousand Oaks, CA: Sage.

Mitchell, W. J. (Ed.). (1981). *On narrative*. Chicago: University of Chicago Press.

Riessman, C. K. (1993). *Narrative analysis*. Newbury Park, CA: Sage.

Riessman, C. K. (2002). Analysis of personal narratives. In J. F. Gubrium & J. A. Holstein (Eds.), *Handbook of interview research* (pp. 695–710). Thousand Oaks, CA: Sage.

Slim, H., & Thompson, P. (1995). *Listening for a change: Oral testimony and community development*. Philadelphia: New Society Publishers.

Thompson, P. R. (2000). *The voice of the past: Oral history* (3rd ed.). Oxford, UK: Oxford University Press.

Yow, V. R. (1994). *Recording oral history: A practical guide for social scientists*. Thousand Oaks, CA: Sage.

Historical Analysis

Barzun, J., & Graff, H. F. (2004). *The modern researcher* (6th ed.). Belmont, CA: Thomson/Wadsworth.

Berg, B. L. (2004). *Qualitative research methods for the social sciences* (5th ed). Boston: Pearson/Allyn & Bacon.

Brooks, P. C. (1969). *The use of unpublished primary sources*. Chicago: University of Chicago Press.

Edson, C. H. (1998). Our past and present: Historical inquiry in education. In R. R. Sherman & R. B. Webb (Eds.), *Qualitative research in education: Focus and methods* (pp. 44–57). New York: Falmer.

Gottschalk, L. A. (1969). *Understanding history*. New York: Knopf.

Hodder, I. (2000). The interpretation of documents and material culture. In N. K. Denzin & Y. S. Lincoln (Eds.), *Handbook of qualitative research* (2nd ed., pp. 703–716). Thousand Oaks, CA: Sage.

Schutt, R. K. (2001). *Investigating the social world: The process and practice of research*. Thousand Oaks, CA: Pine Forge.

Storey, W. K. (2004). *Writing history: A guide for students*. New York: Oxford University Press.

Tuchman, G. (1994). Historical social science. In N. K. Denzin & Y. S. Lincoln (Eds.), *Handbook of qualitative research* (pp. 306–323). Thousand Oaks, CA: Sage.

Film, Video, and Photography

Asch, T. (Producer). (1970). *The feast* [Motion picture]. Washington, DC: U.S. National Audiovisual Center.

Collier, J., & Collier, M. (1986). *Visual anthropology: Photography as a research method*. Albuquerque: University of New Mexico Press.

Gardner, R. (1974). *Rivers of sand* [Motion picture]. New York: Phoenix Films.

Harper, D. (1994). On the authority of the image. In N. K. Denzin & Y. S. Lincoln (Eds.), *Handbook of qualitative research* (pp. 403–412). Thousand Oaks, CA: Sage.

Hockings, P. (Ed.). (1995). *Principles of visual anthropology.* New York: Mouton de Gruyter.

Kopal, M., & Suzuki, L.A. (Eds.) (1999) *Using qualitative methods in psychology.* Thousand Oaks, CA: Sage.

McLarty, M. M., & Gibson, J. W. (2000). Using video technology in emancipatory research. *European Journal of Special Needs Education, 15*(2), 138–139.

Noyes, A. (2004). Video diary: A method for exploring learning dispositions. *Cambridge Journal of Education, 34*(2), 193–209.

Pepler, D. J., & Craig, W. M. (1995). A peek behind the fence: Naturalistic observations of aggressive children with remote audiovisual recording. *Developmental Psychology, 31*(4), 548–553.

Pink, S. (2001). More visualizing, more methodologies: On video, reflexivity and qualitative research. *Sociological Review, 49*(4), 586–599.

Prosser, J. (1998). *Image-based research: A sourcebook for qualitative researchers.* London: Falmer.

Raingruber, B. (2003). Video-cued narrative reflection: A research approach for articulating tacit, relational and embodied understandings. *Qualitative Health Research, 13*(8), 1155–1169.

Rollwagen, J. (Ed.). (1988). *Anthropological filmmaking.* New York: Harwood Academic.

Wiseman, F. (Director). (1969). *High school* [Motion picture]. Boston: Zippora Films.

Interaction Analysis (aka Proxemics and Kinesics)

Birdwhistell, R. L. (1970). *Kinesics and context: Essays on body motion communication.* Philadelphia: University of Pennsylvania Press.

Bull, P. (1983). *Body movement and interpersonal communication*. New York: John Wiley.

Edgerton, R. B. (1979). *Alone together: Social order on an urban beach*. Berkeley: University of California Press.

Flanders, N. A. (1970). *Analyzing teaching behavior*. Reading, MA: Addison-Wesley.

Freedman, J. (1975). *Crowding and behavior*. New York: Viking.

Freiberg, H. J. (1981). Three decades of the Flanders Interaction Analysis System. *Journal of Classroom Interaction, 16*(2), 1–7.

Guerrero, L. K., DeVito, J. A., & Hecht, M. L. (Eds.). (1999). *The nonverbal communication reader: Classic and contemporary readings* (2nd ed.). Prospect Heights, IL: Waveland.

Hall, E. T. (1966). *The hidden dimension*. Garden City, NY: Doubleday.

Hall, E. T., & Hall, M. R. (1977). Nonverbal communication for educators. *Theory Into Practice, 16*, 141–144.

Kering, P. K., & Baucom, D. H. (Eds.). (2004). *Couple observational coding systems*. Mahwah, NJ: Lawrence Erlbaum.

Rutter, D. R. (1984). *Aspects of nonverbal communication*. Amsterdam: Swets & Zeitlinger.

Scherer, K. R., & Ekman, R. (Eds.). (1982). *Handbook of methods in nonverbal behavior research*. New York: Cambridge University Press.

Siegman, A. W., & Feldstein, S. (Eds.). (1987). *Nonverbal behavior and communication* (2nd ed.). Hillsdale, NJ: Lawrence Erlbaum.

Dilemma Analysis

Baron, R. S., & Kerr, N. L. (2003). Social dilemmas. In R. S. Baron & N. L. Kerr, *Group process, group decision, group action* (2nd ed. pp. 139–154). Philadelphia: Open University Press.

Eek, D. (n.d.). *To work or not to work? A social dilemma analysis of health insurance*. Retrieved June 29, 2005, from http://www.psy.gu.se/download/gpr983.pdf

McCrea, H. (1993). Valuing the midwife's role in the midwife/client relationship. *Journal of Clinical Nursing, 2*(1), 47–52.

Simpson, B. (2003). Sex, fear, and greed: A social dilemma analysis of gender and cooperation. *Social Forces, 82*(1), 35–52.

Van Lange, P. A. M., Van Vugt, M., Meertens, R. M., & Ruiter, R. A. C. (1998). A social dilemma analysis of commuting preferences: The roles of social value orientation and trust. *Journal of Applied Social Psychology, 28*(9), 796–820.

Van Vugt, M. (1997). Concerns about the privatization of public goods: A social dilemma analysis. *Social Psychology Quarterly, 60*(4), 355–367.

Webb, J., & Foddy, M. (2004). Vested interests in the decision to resolve social dilemma conflicts. *Small Group Research, 35*(6), 666–697.

Computers and E-data

Anderson, T., & Kanuka, H. (2003). *E-research: Methods, strategies, and issues.* Boston: Allyn & Bacon.

Basit, T. N. (2003). Manual or electronic? The role of coding in qualitative data analysis. *Educational Research, 45*(2), 143–154.

Baym, N. K. (2000). *Tune in, log on* Thousand Oaks, CA: Sage.

Best, S. J., & Krueger, B. S. (2004). *Internet data collection.* Thousand Oaks, CA: Sage.

Buchanan, E. A. (Ed.). (2004). *Readings in virtual research ethics: Issues and controversies.* Hershey, PA: Information Science Publication.

Chen, S., Hall, G. J., & Johns, M. D. (Eds.). (2003) *Online social research: Methods, issues & ethics.* New York: Peter Lang.

Delamont, S. (2001). *Fieldwork in educational settings: Methods, pitfalls, and perspectives* (2nd ed.). London: RoutledgeFalmer.

Esposito, N. (2001). From meaning to meaning: The influence of translation techniques on non-English focus group research. *Qualitative Health Research, 11*(4), 568–579.

Gough, S., & Scott, W. (2000). Exploring the purposes of qualitative data coding in educational enquiry: Insights from recent research. *Educational Studies, 26,* 339–354.

Hewson, C., Yule, P., Laurent, D., & Vogel, C. (2003). *Internet research methods: A practical guide for the social and behavioral sciences.* Thousand Oaks, CA: Sage.

Hine, C. (2001). *Virtual ethnography.* Thousand Oaks, CA: Sage.

Kendall, L. (2002). *Hanging out in the virtual pub: Masculinities and relationships online.* Berkeley: University of California Press.

Leedy, P. D. (Ed.). (1997). *Practical research: Planning and design* (6th ed.). Upper Saddle River, NJ: Merrill.

Mann, C., & Stewart, F. (2000). *Internet communication and qualitative research: A handbook for researching online.* London: Sage.

Markham, A. N. (2004). Internet communication as a tool for qualitative research. In D. Silverman (Ed.), *Qualitative research: Theory, method and practice* (pp. 95–124). Thousand Oaks: Sage.

Markham, A. N. (2005). The methods, politics, and ethics of representation in online ethnography. In N. K. Denzin & Y. S. Lincoln (Eds.), *Handbook of qualitatative research* (3rd ed., pp. 793-820). Thousand Oaks, CA: Sage.

Maynard-Tucker, G. (2000). Conducting focus groups in developing countries: Skill training for local bilingual facilitators. *Qualitative Health Research, 10*(3), 396–410.

Miller, D., & Slater, D. (2000). *The internet: An ethnographic approach.* New York: Berg.

Selwyn, N. (2002). Telling tales on technology: The ethical dilemmas of critically researching educational computing. In T. Welland & L. Pugsley (Eds.), *Ethical dilemmas in qualitative research* (pp. 42–56). Hants, England: Ashgate.

Seymour, W. S. (2001). In the flesh or online? Exploring qualitative research methodologies. *Qualitative Research, 1*(2), 147–168.

Sixsmith, J., & Murray, C. D. (2001). Ethical issues in the documentary data analysis of internet posts and archives. *Qualitative Health Research, 11*(3), 423–432.

Temple, B., & Young, A. (2004). Qualitative research and translation dilemmas. *Qualitative Research, 4*(2), 161–178.

Tesch, R. (1990). *Qualitative research: Analysis types and software tools.* New York: Falmer.

Tilley, S. A. (2003). "Challenging" research practices: Turning a critical lens on the work of transcription. *Qualitative Inquiry, 9*(5), 750–773.

5

Managing, Analyzing, and Interpreting Data

❖   ❖   ❖

Once the researcher has settled on a strategy, chosen a site, selected a sample, and determined a method of collecting data, she should discuss how she will record, manage, analyze, and interpret the data. She should also put forward preliminary ideas for writing up the analysis or representing it in some other format. At the proposal stage, this discussion can be brief, but it should provide the reader with a sense that the data will be recorded efficiently and managed in ways that allow for easy retrieval. In addition, the proposal should present initial strategies for analysis and interpretation. The writer should be prepared to provide examples of how the methods of data collection and analysis might proceed; pilot studies or previous research are excellent sources for such examples.

❖   RECORDING AND MANAGING DATA

The section of the proposal on research design should include plans for recording data in a systematic manner that is appropriate for the setting, the participants, or both and that will facilitate analysis. The researcher should demonstrate an awareness that the techniques for recording observations, interactions, and interviews will not intrude excessively on the flow of daily events. In some situations, even taking notes interferes with, inhibits, or in some way acts on the setting and the participants. In the proposal, she should delineate plans to use tape recorders, cameras, and other mechanical devices and demonstrate that she will use data-recording strategies that fit the setting and the participants' sensitivities but only with participants' consent.

In participatory and action research, the researcher's intrusiveness in the setting is not an issue. Because these approaches are fundamentally interactive and include participants quite fully in framing questions and gathering data, the researcher's presence is considered an integral part of the setting. Whatever the qualitative approach, however, researchers should practice and build habits for labeling audiotapes, carrying extra batteries, and finding quiet places for taking notes. Such practices will pay off with data that are intact, complete, organized, and accessible.

In addition, the researcher should plan a system that eases retrieval for analysis. In more objectivist proposals, researchers may have lists of predetermined categories for data coding. Relying on such categories does facilitate retrieval and analysis, but to remain true to qualitative research assumptions, the researcher should plan decision rules for altering those categories during focused analysis. Furthermore, planning for the color coding of notes to keep track of dates, names, titles, attendance at events, chronologies, descriptions of settings, maps, sociograms, and so on is invaluable. In piecing together patterns, defining categories for data analysis, planning further data collection, and especially for writing the final product of the research, color coding is a useful tool. Vignette 19 provides descriptive detail of one such effort.

VIGNETTE 19

Data Management

In her dissertation research on women's socialization in school administration, Marshall (1979) developed a process by which data transcription, organization, and analysis were combined in a single operation. Her entry into the field and interviewing were directed by a conceptual framework and a set of guiding hypotheses.

She conducted data analysis by trying out conceptual levers such as Goode's (1960) role strain theory, identified in the course of the literature review. Goode's theory guided the analysis of data pertaining to conflicts experienced by women entering male sex-typed careers while continuing to live with the stereotypical expectations of mother, wife, and community member. Building on Goode's work, Marshall devised a career-role strain theory that included feminine identity and sexuality crises prompted by the demands of working in a male-normed profession.

Employing constant comparative data analysis, she developed a grounded theory of women's socialization in male sex-typed careers that explained the socialization period of transition. During this period, women resist the pull of aspiration, resent the exclusion, get angry about the double demands, and yet simultaneously create new ways to fill the roles. Observational notes and pre-fieldwork mapping of sites or subjects were recorded on hardback legal pads that could be held in the lap or used on the run. Following each interview, Marshall partially transcribed field notes of audiotaped conversations, selecting conceptually intriguing phrases that either connected with previous literature or suggested patterns emerging from the analysis of previous data.

Preserving the data and meanings on tape and combining transcription with preliminary analysis greatly increased the efficiency of data analysis. The researcher's transcription, done with the literature review, previous data, and earlier analytic memos in mind, became a useful part of data analysis and not mere clerical duty.

This is not to suggest a reprieve from transfering data to index cards, or coding data, from sorting cards to identify overlapping categories, from organizing codes into more inclusive and abstract domains, or from keeping methodological notes, analytic memos, theoretical notes, case summaries, charts, and dummy tables, all of which are steps in analysis. Combining the initial transcription with analysis, however, moved the study forward efficiently and without threat to the exploratory value of qualitative research or to data quality.

Vignette 19 describes one researcher's way of managing thick, complex data. Over the years, researchers have developed a variety of data management strategies, ranging from color and number codings on index cards to computer programs. These techniques are often shared as part of the folklore of fieldwork. Whatever method is devised, it must enable the researcher to organize and make data easily retrievable and manipulable. Most general, introductory texts on qualitative methods provide extended discussions of processes of analyzing data, and we reference several at the end of this chapter. Below we suggest a process of generic data analysis.

❖ GENERIC DATA ANALYSIS STRATEGIES

The process of bringing order, structure, and interpretation to a mass of collected data is messy, ambiguous, time-consuming, creative, and fascinating. It does not proceed in a linear fashion; it is not neat. Qualitative data analysis is a search for general statements about relationships and underlying themes; it builds grounded theory (Strauss & Corbin, 1997). As described by Wolcott (1994), description, analysis, and interpretation, three somewhat distinct activities, are often bundled into the generic term *analysis*. He notes:

> By no means do I suggest that the three categories—description, analysis, and interpretation—are mutually exclusive. Nor are lines clearly drawn where description ends and analysis begins, or where analysis becomes interpretation. . . . I do suggest that identifying and distinguishing among the three may serve a useful purpose, especially if the categories can be regarded as varying emphases that qualitative researchers employ to organize and present data. (p. 11)

This section of the research proposal should describe initial decisions about data analysis and should convince the reader that the researcher's knowledge of qualitative analysis encompasses data organization, theme development and interpretation, and report writing. Although none of these can be given exhaustive consideration in the proposal, the researcher should convince the reader that thought and awareness have gone into planning the analysis phase of the study. What follows is a discussion of some considerations the researcher should bring to this section.

Whether the researcher prefigures the analysis before collecting data, begins analyzing while collecting, or collects first and analyzes later depends on the qualitative genre and assumptions of the study. Generating categories of data to collect, like cells in a matrix, can be an important focusing activity for the study. Tightly structured, highly organized data-gathering and data-analyzing schemes, however, often filter out the unusual and the serendipitous—the puzzle that if attended to and pursued would require a recasting of the entire research endeavor. Thus, a balance must be struck between efficiency and design flexibility.

Figure 5.1   A Continuum of Analysis Strategies

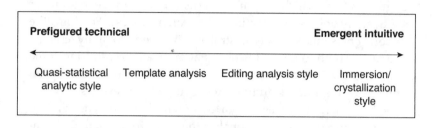

SOURCE: Adapted from Crabtree and Miller (1992, pp. 17–20).

Crabtree and Miller (1992) propose a continuum of ideal-type analysis strategies (see Figure 5.1), although they note that "nearly as many analysis strategies exist as qualitative researchers." At the extreme objectivist end of their continuum are technical, scientific, and standardized strategies in which the researcher has assumed an objectivist stance relative to the inquiry and has stipulated the categories in advance. At the other end are the "immersion strategies," in which categories are not prefigured and which rely heavily on the researcher's intuitive and interpretive capacities. What they call "template" and "editing" analysis strategies stand along the continuum, with the template process more prefigured and stipulative than the editing processes (Crabtree & Miller, pp. 17–18). Template strategies apply sets of codes to the data that may undergo revision as the analysis proceeds. Editing strategies are less prefigured. "The interpreter engages the text naively, without a template" (p. 20), searching for segments of text to generate and illustrate categories of meaning. This method is closely allied with recent writing on grounded theory (Charmaz, 2005, 2000; Harry, Sturges, & Klingner, 2005; Strauss & Corbin, 1997).

In qualitative studies, data collection and analysis typically go hand in hand to build a coherent interpretation. The researcher is guided by initial concepts and developing understandings that she shifts or modifies as she collects and analyzes the data. Her overall strategy is closer to the interpretive/subjectivist end of the continuum than the technical/objectivist end. In their classical work, still very useful, Schatzman and Strauss (1973) succinctly portray the process of qualitative data collection and analysis:

Qualitative data are exceedingly complex and not readily convertible into standard measurable units of objects seen and heard; they vary in level of abstraction, in frequency of occurrence, in relevance to central questions in the research. Also, they vary in the source or ground from which they are experienced. Our model researcher starts analyzing very early in the research process. For him, the option represents an *analytic* strategy: he needs to analyze as he goes along both to adjust his observation strategies, shifting some emphasis towards those experiences which bear upon the development of his understanding, and generally, to exercise control over his emerging ideas by virtually simultaneous checking or testing of these ideas. . . . Probably the most fundamental operation in the analysis of qualitative data is that of discovering significant *classes* of things, persons and events and the *properties* which characterize them. In this process, which continues throughout the research, the analyst gradually comes to reveal his own "is's" and "because's": he names classes and links one with another, at first with "simple" statements (propositions) that express the linkages, and continues this process until his propositions fall into *sets*, in an ever-increasing density of linkages. (pp. 108–110)

The researcher should use preliminary research questions and the related literature developed earlier in the proposal as guidelines for data analysis. This earlier grounding and planning can be used to suggest several categories by which the data initially could be coded for subsequent analysis.

As a coherent interpretation with related concepts and themes emerges from analysis, troublesome or incomplete data will lead to new collecting and analysis that serve to strengthen the interpretation. Interpretation takes shape as major modifications become rare and concepts fall into established categories and themes. Analysis will be sufficient when critical categories are defined, relationships between them are established, and they are integrated into an elegant, credible interpretation.

❖ ANALYTIC PROCEDURES

Typical analytic procedures fall into seven phases: (a) organizing the data; (b) immersion in the data; (c) generating categories and themes; (d) coding the data; (e) offering interpretations through analytic memos; (f) searching for alternative understandings; and (g) writing the report or other format for presenting the study. Each phase of data analysis entails data reduction, as the reams of collected data are brought into manageable chunks, and interpretation, as the researcher brings meaning and insight to the words and acts of the participants in the study. At the proposal stage, the researcher should project what this process will entail, in preliminary ways. The procedures to be followed, initial guides for categories, and potential coding schemes all indicate to the reader that this crucial phase of the research will be managed competently.

The interpretive act remains mysterious in both qualitative and quantitative data analysis. It is a process of bringing meaning to raw, inexpressive data that is necessary whether the researcher's language is standard deviations and means or rich description of ordinary events. Raw data have no inherent meaning; the interpretive act brings meaning to those data and displays that meaning to the reader through the written report. As Patton notes (2002, p. 432), "Qualitative analysis transforms data into findings. No formula exists for that transformation. Guidance, yes. But no recipe. . . . [T]he final destination remains unique for each inquirer, known only when—and if—arrived at." With this caution in mind, we offer some general stages to guide the analysis section of the proposal.

Organizing the Data

When beginning the more focused stage of analysis, it is important that the researcher should again spend some time organizing the data. While this should be done all along, revisiting the "huge piles" of data at this stage is very important. The researcher can list on note cards the data that have been gathered, perform the minor editing necessary to make field notes retrievable, and generally clean up what seems overwhelming and unmanageable. The researcher should also log the types of data according to dates, names, times, and places where, when, and with whom they were gathered. An example is provided below in Table 5.1:

Table 5.1   Log of Data-Gathering Activities

Date	Place	Activity	Who	What
3/21/05	Fort River School	Focus group	3 teachers – Joe, Maria, Marcella	Strategies for including students
3/25/05	Fort River School	Observation	Maria's classroom – Amy	Seeing how Amy does math
3/25/05	Amy's home	Interview	Amy's parents	Challenges, supports

At this time, the researcher could also enter the data into one of several software programs designed for the management or the analysis of qualitative data (Richards & Richards, 1994; Tesch, 1990; Weitzman, 2000; Weitzman & Miles, 1995).

Immersion in the Data

Reading, rereading, and reading through the data once more forces the researcher to become intimately familiar with those data. People, events, and quotations sift constantly through the researcher's mind. As Patton (2002) notes,

> The data generated by qualitative methods are voluminous. I have found no way of preparing students for the sheer mass of information they will find themselves confronted with when data collection has ended. Sitting down to make sense out of pages of interviews and whole files of field notes can be overwhelming. Organizing and analyzing a mountain of narrative can seem like an impossible task. (p. 440)

He then underscores how much of qualitative reporting consists of descriptive data, the purpose of which is to display the daily events of the phenomenon under study. Careful attention to how data are being reduced is necessary throughout the research endeavor. In some instances, direct transfer onto predeveloped data recording charts is appropriate, as with the template strategies. Miles and Huberman (1994) suggest several schemas for recording qualitative data. Such techniques streamline data management, help ensure reliability across the efforts of several researchers, and are highly recommended for large, complex studies such as multisite case studies (Yin, 2003). In using graphics and schemas, however, the researcher should guard against losing the serendipitous finding.

Generating Categories and Themes

For researchers relying on editing or immersion strategies, this phase of data analysis is the most difficult, complex, ambiguous, creative, and fun. Although there are few descriptions of this process in the literature, it remains the most amenable to display through example. The analytic process demands a heightened awareness of the data, a focused attention to those data, and an openness to the subtle, tacit undercurrents of social life. Identifying salient themes, recurring ideas or language, and patterns of belief that link people and settings together is the most intellectually challenging phase of data analysis, and one that can integrate the entire endeavor. Through questioning the data and reflecting on the conceptual framework, the researcher engages the ideas and the data in significant intellectual work. For editing and immersion strategies, he generates the categories through prolonged engagement with the data—the text. These categories then become buckets or baskets into which segments of text are placed.

The process of category generation involves noting patterns evident in the setting and expressed by participants. As categories of meaning emerge, the researcher searches for those that have internal convergence and external divergence (Guba, 1978). That is, the categories should be internally consistent but distinct from one another. Here, the researcher does not search for the exhaustive and mutually exclusive categories of the statistician but, instead, identifies the salient, grounded categories of meaning held by participants in the setting.

Patton (2002) describes the processes of inductive analysis as "*discovering* patterns, themes, and categories in one's data", in contrast with deductive analysis where the analytic categories are stipulated beforehand, "according to an existing framework" (p. 453). The researcher may generate "indigenous typologies" (p. 457) or "analyst-constructed typologies" (p. 458) to reflect the understandings expressed by the participants. Indigenous typologies are those created and expressed by participants and are generated through analyses of the local use of language.

Analyst-constructed typologies are those created by the researcher that are grounded in the data but not necessarily used explicitly by participants. In this case, the researcher applies a typology to the data. As with all analysis, this process entails uncovering patterns, themes, and categories but may well run the risk of imposing "a world of meaning on the participants that better reflects the observer's world than the world under study" (Patton, 2002, p. 459–460). In a related strategy, through logical reasoning, classification schemes are crossed with one another to generate new insights or typologies for further exploration in the data. Usually presented in matrix format, these cross-classifications suggest holes in the already-analyzed data, suggesting areas where data might be *logically* uncovered. Patton, however, cautions the researcher not to allow these matrices to lead the analysis but instead to generate sensitizing concepts to guide further explorations: "It is easy for a matrix to begin to manipulate the data as the analyst is tempted to force data into categories created by the cross-classification to fill out the matrix and make it work" (pp. 469–470). An example of a logically constructed matrix is presented in Figure 5.2.

Figure 5.2   An Empirical Typology of Teacher Roles in Dealing With High
School Dropouts

		Behaviors towards dropouts	
		Taking responsibility	Shfting responsibility to others
Teachers' beliefs about how to intervene with dropouts	Rehabilitation	Counselor/friend: help kids directly	Referral agent; refer them to other helping agencies
	Maintenance (caretaking)	Traffic cop: just keep them moving through the system	Ostrich: ignore the situation and hope someone else does something
	Punishment	Old-fashioned school master: make them feel the consequences	Complainer: somebody should remove the problem kids

SOURCE: Patton (1990, p. 413). Reprinted by permission.

Coding the Data

Coding data is the formal representation of analytic thinking. The tough intellectual work of analysis is generating categories and themes. The researcher then applies some coding scheme to those categories and themes and diligently and thoroughly marks passages in the data using the codes. Codes may take several forms: abbreviations of key words, colored dots, numbers—the choice is up to the researcher. Software programs for data analysis typically rely on abbreviations of key words. For example, in a dissertation proposal, Tucker (1996) discussed how she might use the following codes for her data:

TCARE.LIS: Teacher's caring as demonstrated through listening

TCARE.Q'S: Teacher's caring as demonstrated through honoring questions

TDIS.RACISMO: Teacher's disrespect as demonstrated through overt racism

Were she not using software, she might have planned to use differently colored dots to place on the interview transcripts and field notes or to underline passages with differently colored highlighting pens. Whatever system the researcher plans to use, she should know that the scheme will undergo changes—*coding is not a merely technical task*. As the researcher codes the data, new understandings may well emerge, necessitating changes in the original plan.

Writing Analytic Memos

Throughout the analytic process—the transformational process, according to Wolcott (1994)—we strongly encourage the researcher to write. Writing notes, reflective memos, thoughts, and insights is invaluable for generating the unusual insights that move the analysis from the mundane and obvious to the creative. Several recent scholars underscore the value of writing early and often throughout the research process but especially during more focused analysis. For example, in *Small-Scale Research,* Knight (2002) begins with a chapter not on designing small-scale research, nor with an overview of research methods, but one on writing. He notes that this chapter is about "the interplay of writing and thinking *from the beginning* of the small-scale inquiry . . . writing as a part of the research process" (p. 1). Richardson and St. Pierre (2005) and Richardson (2000) also emphasize the importance of writing—private writing (Knight, 2002) and more public writing—to foster creativity and push one's thinking. As Richardson and St. Pierre (p. 961) note, "Language is a constitutive force, creating a particular view of reality and of the Self."

Other authors have described a specific form of analytic writing—analytic memos. Schatzman and Strauss's (1973) classic suggestions on observational notes, methodological notes, theoretical notes, and analytic memos are quite useful, as is Maxwell's (1996) discussion of analytic memos. Rossman and Rallis (2003) discuss methodological memos, thematic memos, and theoretical memos (pp. 291–292).

Offering Interpretations

As categories and themes are developed and coding is well under way, the researcher begins the process whereby she offers integrative interpretations of what she has learned. Often referred to as "telling the story," interpretation brings meaning and coherence to the themes, patterns, categories, developing linkages and a story line that makes sense and is engaging to read. As Patton notes (2002, p. 480), "Interpretation means attaching significance to what was found, making sense of the findings, offering explanations, drawing conclusions, extrapolating lessons, making inferences, considering meanings, and otherwise imposing order." Part of this phase is evaluating the data for their usefulness and centrality. The researcher should determine how useful the data segments drawn on to support the emerging story are in illuminating the questions being explored and how they are central to the story that is unfolding about the social phenomenon.

Searching for Alternative Understandings

After the researcher develops categories and themes, his use of coding is well under way, and he has written several analytic memos that summarize key "chunks" of the findings, he begins the process of evaluating the plausibility of his developing understandings and of exploring them through the data. This entails a search through the data during which the researcher challenges the very understanding he is putting forward, searches for negative instances of the patterns, and incorporates these into larger constructs, as necessary.

As the researcher discovers categories and patterns in the data, she should engage in critically challenging the very patterns that seem so apparent. She should search for other plausible explanations for these data and the linkages among them. Alternative explanations *always* exist, and the researcher must identify and describe them, and then demonstrate how the explanation she offers is the most plausible. This recalls the discussion in Chapter 1 concerning *the proposal as an argument* that offers assertions about the data, provides substantial evidence for those assertions, builds a logical interrelationship among them, and presents a summation of how the assertions relate to previous and future research.

Writing the Report or Representing the Inquiry

Writing about qualitative data cannot be separated from the analytic process, as noted above in the section on writing analytic memos. In fact, it is central to that process, for in choosing words to summarize and reflect the complexity of the data, the researcher is engaging in the interpretive act, lending shape and form—meaning—to mountains of raw data. We suggest that the researcher consider at the proposal stage what modalities she will use for the final reporting. For dissertations, this is typically done by outlining the chapters to be included in the final document. For funded research proposals, reporting may entail periodic written reports as well as conferences, newsletters, documentary films, or exhibitions. Researchers working in the genres of performance ethnography and autoethnography often present alternative, experimental formats for presenting and re-presenting their findings. Thus, theater skits, poetry, and multimedia presentations could all form the "final product" of work in these genres. Despite interest in alternative dissemination strategies and reporting formats, however, the written report remains the primary mode for reporting the results of research.

There are several models for report writing. Wolcott (1994) describes various ways of balancing description, analysis, and interpretation. Patton (2002) discusses balancing description and interpretation, noting that "Endless description becomes its own muddle. . . . Description provides the skeleton frame for analysis that leads to interpretation" (p. 503).

Taylor and Bogdan (1984, Chapters 8–12) suggest five different approaches. First, in the purely descriptive life history, the author presents one person's account of his or her life, framing that description with an analysis of the social significance of that life. Second is the presentation of data gathered through in-depth interviews and participant observation, where the participants' perspectives are presented and their worldviews structure the report. The third approach attempts to relate practice (the reality of social phenomena) to theory. Descriptive data are summarized, then linked to more general theoretical constructs. Taylor and Bogdan's fourth approach is the most theoretical. To illustrate it, they refer to a study of institutions for individuals with severe cognitive challenges. The report addresses the sociological theory on institutionalization and the symbolic management of conditions in total institutions. Their final approach tries to build theory with data from several types of institutions gathered under a variety of research conditions. They cite a report that addresses issues of the presentation of self under various difficult circumstances and attempts to draw theoretical conclusions across types of institutions, persons, and circumstances.

In his well-known work, *Tales of the Field*, Van Maanen (1988) identifies three different genres in qualitative writing. *Realist tales*, the most easily recognized, display a realistic account of a culture and are published in journals or as scholarly monographs in a third-person voice with a clear separation between researcher and the researched. Established by the grandparents of ethnography—Margaret Mead, William Foote Whyte, Howard Becker, and Branislaw Malinowski—this tradition set the standards and criteria for credibility, quality, and respectability in qualitative work. Van Maanen views these as frequently "flat, dry and sometimes unbearably dull" (p. 48).

Confessional tales are highly personalized accounts with "minimelodramas of hardships endured in fieldwork" (Van Maanen, 1988,

p. 73). This genre aims to display the author's powers of observation and the discipline of good field habits to call attention to the ways in which building cultural description is part of social science. Powdermaker (1966) is a classic example of this genre.

In *impressionist tales,* the field-worker displays her own experiences as a sort of autoethnography. Bowen's work (1964) provides a classic example; more current ones include Krieger (1985) and Thorne (1983). The separation of the researcher from the researched is blurred in this genre, and the tale is told through the chronology of fieldwork events, drawing attention to the culture under study but also to the experiences that were integral to the cultural description and interpretation.

Considerations of one's positionality, ethics, and political stance affect report writing. One may choose to present many truths or multiple perspectives or claim to identify a single truth. Choosing to say "I interpreted this event" rather than "the data revealed" must be a clear decision. Postmodern and feminist discussions help researchers clarify such decisions. Writing *your* truth about others' lives is an assertion of power and can violate earlier assertions about working ethically and sensitively with participants (Tierney & Lincoln, 1997; Lather, 1991).

Four genres of qualitative research and their attendant reporting are worthy of special mention—case studies, action research, performance ethnography, and autoethnography. All begin with the assumption that research must begin in natural settings and incorporate sociopolitical contexts; they may use the full array of data collection strategies; and their typical reporting formats are quite different.

Case Study Reports

Reports of research on a specific organization, program, or process (or some set of these) are often called case studies (Yin, 2003). Case studies rely on historical and document analysis, interviewing, and typically, some forms of observation for data collection. A rich tradition of community studies, organizational research, and program evaluations documents the illustrative power of research that focuses in depth and in detail on specific instances of a phenomenon. Case studies take the reader into the setting with a vividness and detail not typically present in more analytic reporting formats.

Action Research Reporting

Research with practitioners, and often *by* practitioners, who want to improve their own situation and that of others and to discover and solve problems is called action research. Research questions are defined collaboratively with participants; the researcher's role is often that of a facilitator who expands the questions through consultation, problem posing, and knowledge of existing literature. Although action research follows traditions of systematic inquiry, innovative and evolving data collection strategies may shift as the inquiry proceeds (Selener, 1997; Stringer, 1999). Reporting from action research may take several forms. A written report may be collaboratively produced, depending on the interests and needs of participants. Frequently, short oral reports or displays of lessons learned in photo montages, exhibitions, or documentary films are preferred.

Because action research is fundamentally determined by participants—for their own uses—rather than by the scholarly needs of the researcher, the reporting should be true to that guiding principle. Reporting, whatever form it takes, has built-in relevance. Usefulness to participants may be more important than methodological rigor (Argyris & Schön, 1991). The researcher, as participant, may become a trusted insider with access seldom possible in more traditional observer roles (Cole, 1991). Often, action researchers take an activist, critical, and emancipatory stance, using the research process as an empowering process in an organization or a community (Cancian & Armstead, 1992; Fals-Borda & Rahman, 1991; Freire, 1970; Kemmis & McTaggart, 2005; Reason, 1994).

Researchers hope their reports will contribute to societal improvement, either directly in action and participatory approaches or indirectly by enhancing policy or programmatic decisions. (See the discussion of a study's potential significance in Chapter 2.) Choosing participatory action research, however, can be an ideological stance, a determination to try to change the world in direct ways, as Vignette 20 illustrates.

VIGNETTE 20

Planning Reporting for Qualitative Participatory Evaluation

Research design and data collection strategies can be structured to facilitate the active participation of the individuals being researched. An example of this is the work of Paul Castelloe, a graduate student in social work who designed a participatory evaluation study of the Learning Together program in North Carolina (Castelloe & Legerton, 1998). The program is designed to serve two purposes: (a) increase the school preparation of children, ages 3 to 5, with no other preschool experience, and (b) strengthen their caregivers' capacity to provide education and development support.

Drawing on the work of Fraser (1997) as well as Mouffe and LeClau (1985), Castelloe designed his research project with a radical democratic philosophy to create an evaluation process committed to sharing power with research participants. Although traditional research designs place the researcher(s) in the sole position of determining research design and creating research questions, participatory action research brings the individuals being studied into the research process. With his interest in grassroots change and democratic processes, Castelloe democratically structured his study to collect data in a way that would include participants. This approach led to data collection techniques designed to include individuals at all levels (including those traditionally silenced in a study—the individuals that a policy is supposed to help— caregivers and students).

Castelloe designed his study to teach the program staff and community members the skills required to conduct an evaluation. In this role, he decided to serve as facilitator and "colaborer" in the collaborative evaluation process. The direction, plan, questions, and goals of the evaluation were designed to be done collaboratively by Castelloe and the program staff, program participants, and the community in which the program is located.

The primary data collection techniques selected were in-depth interviews, observational methods, and focus-group interviews. He created several strategies to include participants in the research decision-making process. For example, he developed interview questions in collaboration with program administrators, program staff, and community members and asked them to provide feedback on data transcripts.

His philosophy and rationale concerning democratic process served to guide his overall approach to include participants in the research process and examine whether the Learning Together program was democratic, participatory, and inclusive. Collectively, Castelloe and the participants determined how and when reporting would take place. These deliberations strengthened the democratic principles of their work together.

Performance Ethnography Representation

Performance ethnography is the "staged re-enactment of ethnographically derived notes" (Alexander, 2005, p. 411) in which culture is represented in performed, embodied ways, rather than exclusively textual ones. The notion of performance comes from the idea that cultural materials and understandings can be presented as drama, with the attendant scripts, props, sets, costumes, and movement (McCall, 2000).

Thus, representation in performance ethnography is not only a text (the ethnography, the script) but also an embodied, transient depiction of cultural knowledge (a staged production). Recent writing about performance ethnography, however, asserts its critical, liberatory potential. As Alexander notes, some, but not all, of the work in this genre is politically and practically allied with the principles of critical pedagogy (2005, p. 424).

The Autoethnography

Autoethnography takes up some of the challenges offered by performance ethnography to disturb and challenge traditional notions of representation in qualitative research. Holman Jones (2005), who expresses her work and politics primarily through poetry, writes that autoethnography "overlaps with, and is indebted to, research and writing practices in anthropology, sociology, psychology, literary criticism, journalism, and communication . . . to say nothing of our favorite storytellers, poets, and musicians" (p. 765). Representation in autoethnography may take a traditional form such as text, often closely resembling a research report in which the author and her voice are central to the narrative. Other forms may be poetry or a theatrical performance or musical production. Representation in autoethnography is presenting one's own story with the implied or explicit assertion that the personal narrative instructs, disrupts, incites to action, and calls into question politics, culture, and identity.

Vignette 21 is taken directly from an autoethnography written by Tassaporn (Pan) Sariyant (2002). Her literature review is extraordinarily creative and theoretically interesting. While "performed" differently from most literature reviews, it holds true to the precepts of autoethnography and is engaging to read.

VIGNETTE 21

Pan in (Academic) Wonderland: Discourse Review

Knowing requires a knower. Enter any great library and one is surrounded by so much waste paper until the texts collected there are decoded. The "knowledge" of the library collection is underwritten by bodies of knowers, those who can interpret, evaluate, or, in a word, read (MacIntyre, 1981, quoted in Steedman, 1991: 53).

I don't know how long I have been sitting here. I must have dozed off on that chair for a long time. My back aches. My eyes are burning. When I look around, I notice that the few people who sat reading not far from me are not there anymore. The early afternoon sunlight that was shining through the window near the table where I sat reading is already gone. The atmosphere of the room at this moment gives me a creepy, uneasy feeling. The room looks quite dim. Rows and rows of gigantic bookshelves look spooky, like walls of a mysterious dungeon. It makes me think that some unexpected things might be lurking behind any of them. However, I don't want to leave this library room before I finish reading a couple of more books that I had taken from the shelves when I came in. I quickly brush those silly images out of my head.

After standing and stretching my weary body for a moment, I walk toward the light switch that I remember seeing on a wall at the opposite corner. As I walk toward the wall, out of the corner of my eye I suddenly notice several silhouette figures sitting quietly around a table in that very corner. Who are these people? Why do they sit talking in the dark? Ghosts of the library? A sudden cold fear runs down my spine. Goose bumps cover my whole body. I cannot decide whether I should run out of that room or go to the light switch and turn it on as quick as possible. Before I can do anything, I hear a gentle voice from the table calling, "Are you coming to join us?" I stand frozen. Another figure waves a hand, beckoning me to the table and saying, "Please turn the light on and come to join us here." Although I am horrified with the thought that those figures will vanish as soon as the light is on, I quickly flick the light on.

To my relief, they do not disappear. Under the soft fluorescent light from the ceiling above them, those silhouette figures turn out to be seven scholarly looking women and men—precisely five women and two men—who sit smiling at me. They are not ghosts as I initially thought. Although their faces look familiar, I cannot recall where I have seen them. . . . A Caucasian man, sitting on the right of a white-bearded old man, urges me, "Come and join the dialogue with us." Dialogue with these people? Oh, my word! They look so scholarly, so knowledgeable. What am I going to say or discuss with them? "Come, sit next to me. There is a chair here." A kind, motherly woman, who sits on the left of the white-bearded old man, points at an empty chair beside her. . . .

I quickly introduce myself as I sit down. "My name is Pan, a Thai doctoral student at the Center for International Education. I am at the stage of writing my dissertation. I work in the Department of Nonformal Education in Thailand. Generally, my work revolves around education for community development. I am interested in exploring the relationships among discourses on development, nonformal education, and pedagogy for empowerment, especially for rural Thai women, and I want to—"

"Wait." Before I finish my sentence, the white-bearded old man interrupts. "You are not going to do your dissertation research on all those subjects, are you?" I shake my head and say no. The short-haired woman asks the question that I am afraid to face. "What is really your focus?" I drop my eyes to the table and admit with a great shame, "I am not quite sure yet." When I look up, I see sympathetic looks on every face. I hear a quickly whispered phrase, "rookie academician," which makes my ears turn red with embarrassment. Before I can think of how to defend myself, the woman with dark hair on my right suggests, "Why don't we begin by asking her why she wants to know about those subjects, what she wants to get from those discourses, and how those discourses have anything to do with her dissertation topic. Then we can give her some suggestions later." She turns to me and says, "Could you elaborate on that for us?" My face suddenly turns pale with intimidation as every pair of questioning eyes fixes on me.

In a somewhat more traditional vein, the following two vignettes depict challenges and considerations that researchers brought to writing up their reports. Vignette 22 shows how analysis and writing are interwoven throughout a study, and Vignette 23 comes from a study of incest in which the challenges of writing were substantial.

VIGNETTE 22

Interspersing Reporting and Analysis

Often, data analysis and writing up the research are thought of and portrayed as two discrete processes. Increasingly, however, researchers are using the writing up of research as an opportunity to display, in the body of the report, how data analysis evolved. Gerstl-Pepin (1998) accomplished this quite elegantly in her study of educational reform.

Gerstl-Pepin constructed a theoretical framework to critically examine whether an arts-based educational reform movement in North Carolina functioned as a counterpublic sphere (Fraser, 1997) and led to democratically structured educational policy and reform. Although interested in examining theoretical issues concerning the prospects for democratically structured reform, she was also interested in telling the story of the reform movement.

To balance these two interests, Gerstl-Pepin decided to take an approach similar to that of Lather and Smithies (1997) and weave her shifts in thinking about research questions into the body of the text. Her interest in including the researcher's evolving thought processes arose out of an awareness of shifting research paradigms that highlight the subjectivity of the researcher. While analyzing the data, Gerstl-Pepin encountered teachable moments in the research process in which her conceptualization and understanding of the research developed and shifted. She included these pieces within the narrative story about the reform movement as separate boxes of text and titled these pieces "Interludes: Reflections on the Research." They were included at various points in the narrative, depicting shifts in her thinking process and research focus. These pieces served as stories within the story and were intended to allow the reader to participate not only in the story of the reform process but also in the discovery process for the researcher.

Philosophical inquiry and shifting paradigms highlight the subjectivity of the researcher and her relationship to the research process. Placing analytic memos, methodological notes, or interludes in the report makes these processes transparent. Our last vignette for this chapter, Vignette 23, presents the ethical dilemmas of reporting about taboo topics.

VIGNETTE 23

Talking Taboo: Continuing the Research Relationship

During analysis and reporting data, Kiegelmann (1997) was inventive with methods to protect her research participants. This is always important, but for her research on brother-sister incest she was particularly attuned to how participants had trusted her with emotion-laden and highly sensitive aspects of their lives. One had even shared her childhood journal in which she wrote just minutes after the incest occurred. Kiegelmann and the participants had become a support group, continuing to meet after the research was finished.

As data analysis proceeded, Kiegelmann identified themes and noted the range of nuances in the study participants' talk. Previous literatures guided her, especially writings about girls' views of femininity, of "good girls," and girls' ways of knowing. Three voice clusters emerged: silent voices, embodied voices, and naming voices. Anticipating the need to report, to have validity checks, and to regain permission for using their words, Kiegelmann created biographies of each woman and sent them to the women, inviting their comments. She received feedback and commentary from them, which she incorporated into her writing. As she neared completion, she sent a draft of the full study to all of them. Each participant used this opportunity to offer more details but not to change the interpretations. Furthermore, she invited the participants to write statements directly to the readers of the research, giving the women the final word. Thus, the trusting relationships were maintained beyond the time of the study, the study's truthfulness was increased, and she avoided taking away power and control over the representation of their lives from the participants.

This vignette reveals a highly ethical sensitivity to the participants in the study. Kiegelmann honored their life stories and voices throughout the process. This involved several iterations: writing biographies, sending them to the participants for commentary, incorporating their feedback, sending the full draft for further commentary, and incorporating the women's final comments in the final document. Although this process was time-consuming, it expressed Kiegelmann's deep commitment to the women and to the ethical conduct of her study.

Into the various phases of data analysis and report writing are woven considerations of the soundness, usefulness, and ethical conduct of the qualitative research study. Some consideration should be given to issues of the value, truthfulness, and soundness of the study throughout the design of the proposal. Considerations of role, for example, should address the personal biography of the researcher and how that might shape events and meanings. In what ways is the research, whether participatory or more objectivist, altering the flow of daily life? Selection of the setting and sampling of people and behaviors within that setting should consider the soundness of those decisions and present a clear rationale that has guided those choices. Chapter 7 continues this discussion of considerations of the soundness and ethical conduct of the study.

* * * * *

Chapters 3, 4, and 5 have brought the reader through the complex, sometimes tedious process of building a design and choosing research methods for the research study. This section of the proposal should demonstrate that the researcher is competent to conduct the research; knowledgeable about the issues, dilemmas, choices, and decisions to be made in the design and conduct of the research; and immersed in the literature that provides guidance for the qualitative researcher. The research design should be well written and should reveal a sensitivity to various issues, the capacity to be reflective about the nature of inquiry and the substantive questions at hand, and a willingness to tolerate some ambiguity during the conduct of the study. These qualities will stand the researcher in good stead over the course of the research. In addition, however, the researcher should demonstrate some knowledge of the management of resources in the design of a qualitative study. This is the focus of the next chapter.

DIALOGUE BETWEEN LEARNERS

Melanie,

OK, on to the next topic! Gretchen and I were talking yesterday about the "everdayness" of qualitative research practices. That is, those practices that some would find the most laborious and tedious (i.e., making sure you have fresh batteries in your recorder, the right notebook for note-taking, ink in your pen, etc.). If I'm obsessive about anything, I suppose it's these little things. My worst fear is sitting in an interview or focus group and my recorder runs out of batteries, or that I reach the place where the interview is to occur 20 minutes late (or on the wrong day). As a result, I have a drawer full of half-used batteries because I replace them so often and I often arrive at my interview sites incredibly early. I suppose I just want to be able to focus on the task at hand when I'm interviewing, etc. I mentioned to Gretchen that it was like going on a trip with the gas tank 3/4 empty. I start out on the road and inevitably my eye begins to fixate a bit on the gas gauge as I look for signs of it moving toward the red line. I begin to wonder when I should stop, how much farther can I make it? Meanwhile, I miss all of the sights and sounds that are the trip.

OK, admittedly, this might just be me and my strange fear of running out of gas/batteries. However, I do think that sometimes we talk so earnestly about the philosophy or theory behind qualitative work that we forget that there are these everyday events that actually make up the research project. For example, I have terrible handwriting. Yet, when I'm taking field notes or conducting interviews I have a tendency to speed up my writing, to scribble. Not a good thing. There's nothing worse than returning to your field notes a few hours later and having to undergo a lengthy translation of your own handwriting. I try to get around this by being very thorough in my preparations, yet there is always something that comes up.

The latest chapter I've read, Chapter 5, deals quite a bit with writing up the report (whether it be a dissertation proposal or otherwise). Of course, in order to write the report, you have to know when you've finished collecting and analyzing your data. This is a problem for me. There's no final answer in qualitative research, it seems like you can keep going back for more. When do you know you're done? Sometimes I worry that my fear of actually writing the report will keep me in the data collection/analysis stage forever! I suppose I'll need to jump off that bridge when I come to it . . .

Hope things are well with you. Enjoy the weekend,

Aaron

Hi Aaron,

So, back after a weekend reprieve. I can't argue with much that you said in your last e-mail. There are so many little tasks to take into account before an interview, for example, that the tasks overwhelm the actual purpose of the interview! My handwriting falls apart during an interview, too—thank goodness for my little digital recorder.

To me, the everydayness is the result of detail-oriented work. I double-check my supplies before I go teach a class; I scribble illegible notes while I'm skimming journal articles; I obsess about asking worthless questions before a job interview. Attention to detail has to play a part in the research process or we would miss much of the research we're trying to collect! There's a fine line, as you point out, between obsession and natural cautiousness—the battery-thing does hinge on obsession :)—but that obsessive tendency may save us later down the road when we come up against questions in the analysis and can actually refer to our notes or our carefully transcribed interview to find the answer.

As for knowing we're finished, I think you have to put your best effort forward but recognize that it's always a process. One of my professors really helped me with this when he reminded me that the data is always mine, and I can always return to it with a fresh approach, a new idea, a different lens. One of the reasons I'm drawn to qualitative research is the ability to present **an** answer instead of **the one** answer–so that gives me permission to move on, knowing that my research isn't a one-way trip.

Thanks bunches —must plan my lesson for tomorrow!

Melanie

❖ FURTHER READING

On Data Analysis

Atkinson, P., & Delamont, S. (2005). Analytic perspectives. In N. K. Denzin & Y. S. Lincoln (Eds.), *The SAGE handbook of qualitative research* (3rd ed., pp. 821–840). Thousand Oaks, CA: Sage.

Charmaz, K. (2001). Grounded theory. In R. M. Emerson (Ed.), *Contemporary field research* (2nd ed., pp. 335–352). Prospect Heights, IL: Waveland.

Emerson, R. M., Fretz, R. I., & Shaw, L. L. (1995). *Writing ethnographic fieldnotes.* Chicago: University of Chicago Press.

Harry, B., Sturges, K. M., & Klingner, J. K. (2005). Mapping the process: An exemplar of process and challenge in grounded theory analysis. *Educational Researcher, 34*(2), 3–13.

Katz, J. (2001). Analytic induction revisited. In R. M. Emerson (Ed.), *Contemporary field research* (2nd ed., pp. 331–334). Prospect Heights, IL: Waveland.

Madison, D. S. (2005). *Critical ethnography: Method, ethics, and performance.* Thousand Oaks, CA: Sage.

Miles, M. B., & Huberman, A. M. (1994). *Qualitative data analysis: An expanded sourcebook* (2nd ed.). Thousand Oaks, CA: Sage.

Mills, G. E. (1993). Levels of abstraction in a case study of educational change. In D. J. Flinders & G. E. Mills (Eds.), *Theory and concepts in qualitative research: Perspectives from the field* (pp. 103–116). New York: Teachers College Press.

Patton, M. Q. (2002). *Qualitative research and evaluation methods* (3rd ed.). Thousand Oaks, CA: Sage.

Richards, L. (2005). *Handling qualitative data: A practical guide.* Thousand Oaks, CA: Sage.

Ryan, G. W., & Bernard, H. R. (2000). Data management and analysis methods. In N. K. Denzin & Y. S. Lincoln (Eds.), *Handbook of qualitative research* (2nd ed., pp. 769–802). Thousand Oaks, CA: Sage.

Sanjek, R. (1990). On ethnographic validity. In R. Sanjek (Ed.), *Fieldnotes: The makings of anthropology* (pp. 385–418). Ithaca, NY: Cornell University Press.

Silverman, D. (1993). *Interpreting qualitative data: Methods for analyzing talk, text and interaction*. London: Sage.
Silverman, D. (2000). Analyzing talk and text. In N. K. Denzin & Y. S. Lincoln (Eds.), *Handbook of qualitative research* (2nd ed., pp. 821–834). Thousand Oaks, CA: Sage.
Silverman, D. (2005). *Doing qualitative research* (2nd ed.). Thousand Oaks, CA: Sage.
Tanaka, G. (1997). Pico College. In W. G. Tierney & Y. S. Lincoln (Eds.), *Representation and the text: Re-framing the narrative voice* (pp. 259–304). Albany: State University of New York Press.
Thornton, S. J. (1993). The quest for emergent meaning: A personal account. In D. J. Flinders & G. E. Mills (Eds.), *Theory and concepts in qualitative research: Perspectives from the field* (pp. 68–82). New York: Teachers College Press.
Wolcott, H. F. (1994). *Transforming qualitative data: Description, analysis, and interpretation*. Thousand Oaks, CA: Sage.

On Analysis Using Computer Software

Kelle, E. (Ed.). (1995). *Computer-aided qualitative data analysis*. Thousand Oaks, CA: Sage.
Morse, J. M., & Richards, L. (2002). *Read me first for a user's guide to qualitative methods*. Thousand Oaks, CA: Sage.
Richards, T. J., & Richards, L. (1994). Using computers in qualitative research. In N. K. Denzin & Y. S. Lincoln (Eds.), *Handbook of qualitative research* (pp. 445–462). Thousand Oaks, CA: Sage.
Tesch, R. (1990). *Qualitative research: Analysis types and software tools*. New York: Falmer.
Weitzman, E. A. (2000). Software and qualitative research. In N. K. Denzin & Y. S. Lincoln (Eds.), *Handbook of qualitative research* (2nd ed., pp. 803–820). Thousand Oaks, CA: Sage.
Weitzman, E. A., & Miles, M. B. (1995). *Computer programs for qualitative data analysis*. Thousand Oaks, CA: Sage.

On Writing

Ellis, C., & Bochner, A. P. (Eds.). (1996). *Composing ethnography: Alternative forms of qualitative writing*. Walnut Creek, CA: AltaMira.
Gitlin, A. (Ed.). (1994). *Power and method: Political activism and educational research*. New York: Routledge.
Meloy, J. M. (1994). *Writing the qualitative dissertation: Understanding by doing*. Hillsdale, NJ: Lawrence Erlbaum.
Richardson, L. (1990). *Writing strategies: Reaching diverse audiences*. Newbury Park, CA: Sage.
Richardson, L. (1994). Writing: A method of inquiry. In N. K. Denzin & Y. S. Lincoln (Eds.), *Handbook of qualitative research* (pp. 516–529). Thousand Oaks, CA: Sage.

Richardson, L., & St. Pierre, E. A. (2005). Writing: A method of inquiry. In N. K. Denzin & Y. S. Lincoln (Eds.), *The SAGE handbook of qualitative research* (3rd ed., pp. 959–978). Thousand Oaks, CA: Sage.

Stake, R. (1995). *The art of case study research.* Thousand Oaks, CA: Sage.

Tierney, W. G., & Lincoln, Y. S. (Eds.). (1997). *Representation and the text: Re-framing the narrative voice.* Albany: State University New York Press.

Van Maanen, J. (1988). *Tales of the field: On writing ethnography.* Chicago: University of Chicago Press.

Van Maanen, J. (Ed.). (1995). *Representation in ethnography.* Thousand Oaks, CA: Sage.

Wolcott, H. F. (2001). *Writing up qualitative research.* Thousand Oaks, CA: Sage.

Zinsser, W. (1990). *On writing well: An informal guide to writing nonfiction* (4th ed.). New York: Harper.

6

Planning Time
and Resources

The process of planning and projecting the resource needs for a qualitative study is an integral aspect of proposal development. The resources most critical to the successful completion of the study are time, personnel, and financial support. The last of these is not always readily available, especially in dissertation research; serious consideration, however, must be given to time and personnel. Many hidden costs associated with qualitative research may become apparent only after the researcher has carefully analyzed and reflected on the study's demands. Convincing potential funding agencies that the expenses are worthwhile may also be a challenge.

This chapter provides the researcher with detailed analyses and projections of the resource demands of qualitative research. Using three vignettes as illustrations, we provide general guidelines for consideration in the development and projection of resource needs. Vignette 24 shows the process of planning resource needs for a multiresearcher, multisite study developed with ample financial resources and a long time frame for completion of the project. In contrast, Vignette 25 reveals the planning process of a solo doctoral student proposing a study with few financial supports to back it up. The contrast between Vignettes 24 and 25 is intended to display how each proposal must address difficult resource questions. Finally, Vignette 26 demonstrates the need to teach reviewers about the labor intensity of qualitative analysis. Careful, detailed consideration of the resource demands of a study is critical in demonstrating that the researcher is knowledgeable about qualitative research, understands that its inherent flexibility will create resource difficulties at some point, has thought-through the resource issues, and recognizes the demands that will be made.

Many resource decisions cannot be made until basic design decisions are in place. The researcher, however, should consider resources as she struggles with the conceptual framework and design issues. For example, a researcher cannot decide to conduct a multisite, multiperson project unless she has some prospect of financial resources in sight, nor can she prudently plan to conduct a long-term, intensive, participant-observation study when she knows she must continue to work full time and cannot possibly devote the necessary time to the study. Thus, general decisions about resources and design are made in parallel and are major criteria for the do-ability of the study.

In the narrative structure of the proposal, after discussing the design of the study, the researcher should address resource needs specifically. These include time demands and management, personnel needs and staffing, and financial support for the entire endeavor. The two vignettes presented below are followed by a discussion of the major resource needs of each. The vignettes are intended to display the strategies for resource allocation in two quite different studies.

❖ PLANNING RESOURCES FOR A LARGE STUDY

Although the resource needs for a long-term, complex study are substantially more elaborate than those for dissertation research, the processes of projecting those resources remain very similar. Careful and explicit plans regarding resource allocation need to flow from the overall design of the study. The challenges are exacerbated in multisite comparative research conducted over several years. Sometimes these are collaborations among researchers in several institutions or with practitioners. The larger the scope, the more resources are demanded, so that resources are adequate and available in terms of time (sufficient to describe and analyze practices in detail), personnel (capable of thoroughly and efficiently gathering the needed data), and financial support for personnel, travel, data analysis, and report writing.

The first task in projecting resource needs for a larger scale study is to organize its activities into manageable tasks. These consist of (a) planning, (b) meetings of research team, (c) meetings among principal investigators, (d) advisory committee meetings, (e) site visits in the field for data gathering, (f) data analysis, (g) report writing, (h) conference attendance for dissemination, and (i) preparation for and management of a final policy forum or other means to give the findings real-world implications. A research team can refine its initial projections of time, as it is able to make associated cost projections. That is, the team can first plan an ideal study, one in which resources are virtually infinite. Creative insights often emerge through imagining such an ideal study before tempering these with the realism associated with assessments of feasibility, the do-ability criterion discussed in Chapter 1. Often such ideal plans call for immersion in the setting, with many site visits. Refinements must be made when realistic costs in terms of time, personnel, and travel are estimated.

Vignette 24 details how resource decisions were made in planning for a two-state qualitative study of successful leadership in multicultural schools. It paraphrases the research proposal and details the final allocation of resources to each research task.

VIGNETTE 24

Projecting Resources for a Large-Scale Study

"Leading Dynamic Schools for Newcomer Students: Studies of Successful Cross-Cultural Interaction" (Rossman & Rallis, 2001) proposed a collaborative research project between the Center for International Education at the University of Massachusetts and the Neag School of Education of the University of Connecticut. The purpose of the study was to create grounded depictions of how leadership is enacted in multicultural schools. The principal investigators wanted to learn how successful school principals—and leadership more broadly—interact across cultural differences with empathy and respect. They posed the following broad research questions:

- In what ways are school leaders savvy and attuned to the multiple cross-cultural dynamics in schools that serve migrant, refugee, and immigrant children particularly well?
- How do they mediate the cultural differences that can be confusing, emotional, humorous, hurtful, and inspirational?

In designing a proposal to respond to the call for field-initiated research from the Office of Educational Research and Improvement of the U.S. Department of Education, Rossman and Rallis had to make a series of decisions to support their multisite, multiresearcher, multiyear case studies of leadership practices in 12 schools in Connecticut and Massachusetts. As the principal investigators (PIs) identified important aspects of the study that would require time and effort (i.e., more data), the study grew and grew. But ideal projections then had to be grounded in real considerations of the total budget allocated for the study. Using the study's conceptual framework and the requirements of the RFP, the researchers ensured sound adherence to the initial research questions. Table 6.1 shows the final allocation of staff days to tasks.

In the text of the proposal, Rossman and Rallis explained that the project would: (a) identify leadership strategies used successfully in dynamic schools that serve large populations of newcomer students (migrants, immigrants, and refugees); (b) analyze and synthesize the research to develop prototype strategies that can be used in professional development; and (c) disseminate these prototypes to practitioners (administrators, teacher groups, administrator preparation programs, and community groups), policymakers, and the scholarly community.

They then proposed using a multisite case study design to describe and analyze the leadership in 12 such schools in Massachusetts and Connecticut that serve newcomer students particularly well. The findings of the research project would be disseminated to practitioners, policymakers, and the scholarly community through a project Web site, presentations at conferences, articles in journals, and two policy forums. Further, the project would articulate them with the National Institute for the Education of At-Risk Students and the National Institute on Educational Governance, Finance, Policymaking, and Management.

The research design section proposed a multisite case study. The PIs explained, "The local school and the community it serves will be the unit for analysis. . . . Case studies, in-depth explorations of a single phenomenon, seek to understand that larger phenomenon through close examination of a specific instance. . . .The case studies in this project will generate grounded depictions of leadership. Observations and interviews will yield rich descriptions that illustrate the complexities of the settings: their structures, politics, cultures, and moral principles. Six sites will be selected in each state, yielding a total of 12 schools. Yearlong fieldwork will be conducted at each site, generating qualitative data descriptive of leadership in context. Cross-case analysis to generate prototype leadership strategies will be performed in year two of the project. The key activities for each year, focusing on data gathering, data analysis, Site Researcher responsibilities, and Advisory Committee roles are described below."

To justify the resource requests, the proposal provided details for data gathering: "We envision yearlong fieldwork in the 12 schools for the first year of the project. The design will deploy the Site Researchers to the schools for one day per week per school. Thus, each Site Researcher will focus on two schools, providing the depth of knowledge necessary for constructing prototypes of leadership. Typical fieldwork strategies will be employed: informal and formal observations coupled with conversations (both informal and structured interviews) and the review of key documents. Observations of interactions between the principal and other key leaders in the school and community members will occur. Interviews with these key individuals will be scheduled. In addition, focus group interviews with community members and teachers will be conducted." Activities for the project are summarized in Table 6.1.

The proposal also explained the resources allocated for data analysis: "Preliminary data analysis will be ongoing, as the Site Researchers gather information, conduct initial analyses of it, and share those analyses in analytic memos and in the Research Team meetings. During year 2, the Site Researchers, supervised by the Project Director and Codirector, will engage in detailed data analysis to build the prototypes of leadership in the 12 dynamic schools. During this process, they will return to the sites on a twice-monthly basis to share emergent conclusions with principals and other participants and gather additional data as needed. This will ensure that the conclusions and prototypes are grounded in the realities of the schools and the perspectives of participants."

Next, the proposal explained the duties of site researchers who would conduct the yearlong fieldwork for the project and be actively involved in data analysis and the development of products during the second year. The proposal then presented the makeup and duties of the advisory committee, meeting semi-annually to provide feedback to the project and to ensure that the emerging results are incorporated into policy and practitioner dialogues.

The explanation of products and dissemination called for a Web site devoted to the project to share emergent findings and relevant literature. The Web site would link to the Institute for the Education of At-Risk Students. Dissemination strategies also included two policy forums, presentations to scholarly audiences at national conferences, articles submitted to research journals, and dissertations by the site researchers.

Next, the proposal attempted to justify the time and resources of personnel. It requested salary support for the directors, the principal investigators, the community liaisons, a fiscal administrator, six full-time site researchers (research associates) and four half-time research assistants. Time allocations of 20% for the directors, who were responsible for the management of the project, were justified for production of reports and supervision of staff and finances. The principal investigators would devote 10% of their time to provide management support and supervision of the site researchers. The community liaisons would devote 15% of their time and the fiscal administrator would work half time on the project. Responsibilities of the six research associates, three in each university, were to conduct the field research; the four half-time research assistants would develop and maintain the Web page and support software for advanced data analysis. Table 6.2 summarizes the key budget features of the proposal.

Table 6.1   Schedule of Work

Year 1: August 2001—July 2002
Planning and Site Research

Year 1	Aug	Sept	Oct	Nov	Dec	Jan	Feb	Mar	April	May	June	July
Planning	⇑	⇑										
University-based research team meetings	T	T	T	T	T	T	T	T	T	T	T	T
Full research-group meetings	T		T	T	T	T	T	T	T	T	T	
Director & codirector meetings		T		T	T	T	T	T	T	T		T
Advisory committee meetings			T						T			
Data gathering in schools		⇑	⇑	⇑	⇑	⇑	⇑	⇑	⇑			
Data gathering in communities	⇑		⇑					⇑		⇑		
Preparation for/attendance at conference						⇑	⇑	T				
Planning for/conduct of policy forum						⇑	⇑	⇑	T			
Deliverables					®						©	

® Report of planning and implementation in 12 school sites.

© Report of preliminary data gathering.

(Continued)

Table 6.1 (Continued)

Year 1: August 2002—July 2003
Data Analysis & Product Develpment

Year 2	Aug	Sept	Oct	Nov	Dec	Jan	Feb	Mar	April	May	June	July
Planning	⇑	⇑										
University-based research team meetings	T	T	T	T	T			T	T	T	T	T
Full research-team meetings	T		T		T			T		T		T
Director & codirector meetings		T		T		T		T		T		T
Advisory committee meetings			T						T			
Site visits for verification	⇑	⇑	⇑	⇑	⇑	⇑						
Summarizing interviews	⇑	⇑	⇑		⇑		⇑					
Summarizing field observations	⇑	⇑	⇑		⇑		⇑					
Writing analytic memos			⇑	⇑		⇑	⇑					
Writing interim summaries	⇑	⇑	⇑									
Preparation for/attendance at conferences	⇑	⇑	T			⇑	⇑	T				
Preparation for/conduct of policy forum						⇑	⇑	⇑	⇑	T		
Writing final report						⇑	⇑	⇑	⇑	⇑	⇑	⇑
Deliverables			®									©

® Report of feedback from schools on preliminary analysis.

© Final report.

SOURCE: Rossman, G. B., & Rallis, S. F. (2001). *Leading Dynamic Schools for Newcomer Students.* Proposal submitted to the U.S. Department of Education, Office of Educational Research and Improvement. Adapted by permission.

Table 6.2   Budget Summary

| | Year 1 | | |
Budget item	Requested from ED	In-kind support	Total
Direct costs			
1. Salaries	134,201	3,343	137,544
2. Employee benefits	15, 678	40,740	56,418
3. Employee travel	12, 340		12,340
4. Equipment	11, 590		11,590
5. Materials & supplies	1,250		1,250
6. Consultants and contracts	318,629		318,629
7. Other	13,550		13,550
Total Direct Costs	507,238	44,083	551,321
Indirect costs	**124,981**		**124,981**
Total	**632,219**	**44,083**	**676,302**

| | Year 2 | | |
Budget item	Requested from ED	In-kind support	Total
Direct costs			
1. Salaries	101,672	3,444	105,116
2. Employee benefits	19,571	40,740	60,311
3. Employee travel	15,940		15,940
4. Equipment	-0-		- 0 –
5. Materials & supplies	850		850
6. Consultants and contracts	325,087		325,087
7. Other	13,550		13,550
Total Direct Costs	476,670	44,184	520,854
Indirect costs	**109,436**		**109,436**
Total	**586,106**	**44,184**	**630,290**
Total budget request			**$1,306,592**

SOURCE: Rossman, G. B., & Rallis, S. F. (2001). *Leading Dynamic Schools for Newcomer Students.* Proposal submitted to the U.S. Department of Education, Office of Educational Research and Improvement. Adapted by permission.

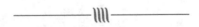

Once Rossman and Rallis had determined the scope of the study, they were able to plan its implementation, presented in Table 6.1. This, in turn, had implications for staffing the research (discussed above in the vignette) which, in turn, had a direct effect on the overall budget. The final decisions that are represented in Tables 6.1 and 6.2 are the end result of many iterations in projections about the scope of the study, the personnel needed, and the costs of personnel, travel, data analysis.

Time

As Vignette 24 illustrates, projecting sufficient time to undertake a richly detailed study that also remains doable is a difficult task but one that can be rewarding. Thinking through the time necessary for various research activities can be sobering even for experienced researchers; the novice learns a great deal from this discipline. For example, each of the research tasks described in this vignette required a certain number of days for its successful completion. The first step was to determine the optimal number of days for each site visit. Although this depended on the year of the study, the research team was able to estimate days by deciding on the number of interviews possible in each school, the hours to allocate for observations as well as the amount of time necessary to talk with community members and to gather documents and other archival data.

In qualitative proposals, the number of days allocated to data gathering becomes a metric for estimating the time required for other tasks, such as data management, analysis, and report writing. That is, the amount of data gathered dictates the amount of time needed to manage and analyze it. Once the researcher has projected time for fieldwork, a management plan can be developed. The projections developed for Table 6.1 helped construct a framework for estimating costs, discussed below.

The researcher should also use this kind of framework to address practical concerns. A time management chart, research agenda, calendar of research events, description of research phases, or some other concrete plan shows a funding agency or dissertation committee that the researcher has thought-through the feasibility of involving specific people, settings, events, and data in the research. This demonstrates that the research is feasible. But the researcher should remind the reader that this plan is a guide; it is a tentative road map that will most likely undergo some modifications as data are collected and analyzed and as new patterns for more focused data collection become apparent. The chart serves as a guide for initial contacts and reminds the reader of the inherently flexible nature of qualitative research. It also serves as an important reminder—sometimes an anchor—for the researcher herself once she becomes immersed in the study.

Personnel

The allocation of time to tasks also shapes decisions about personnel needs. In Vignette 24, as the scope of the study developed (number of school sites, single- or multiple-person research teams), personnel decisions could be made. Principal investigators with university contracts can allocate the equivalent of the summer months and one day per week to the effort. Their time can be supplemented by a cadre of graduate students who can be awarded research assistantships to work on the project for limited hours per week for the academic year, with additional summer funding budgeted into the proposal. These kinds of "person loadings" are illustrated in the budget summarized in Table 6.2.

Financial Resources

For dissertation research or sole-investigator studies, analyzing tasks can help the researcher decide to purchase certain services; for example, audiotape transcription or data processing. This analysis can also introduce the novice to the variety of tasks associated with the project. Determining the resources necessary for the study must often wait until fundamental design decisions have been made. Those design choices, however, must be made with some knowledge of the finances available. In the preceding vignette, the evaluators knew that they were constrained by a total budget of approximately $1 million for the two-year study.

Although this sum may seem considerable to the novice proposal writer, planning a multisite, multiyear study with intensive data gathering as a primary design goal became quite difficult within this budget. Travel and personnel costs increased with inflation and rising salaries, and they represented a substantial proportion of the total budget.

The other major costs associated with the evaluation activities included (a) local travel; (b) equipment (computers, fax machine); (c) office supplies, telephones, and postage; (d) books and subscriptions; (e) printing and duplicating; and (f) contracted services (tape transcription, data analysis, consultants). Because the costs of data analysis specialists vary considerably, the proposal writer would consult local costs and time allocations in developing that portion of a qualitative proposal. The time required for thorough transcription also varies. Each hour of tape requires from 3 or 4 to 7 or 8 hours for transcription. Thus, transcription costs, which are always high, could vary enormously.

❖ PLANNING DISSERTATION RESEARCH

Many of the same issues confronted in the large-scale evaluation project are apparent in Vignette 25, a proposal for dissertation research. Although the scope is considerably smaller, similar resource challenges emerged in planning the study.

VIGNETTE 25

Feasibility and Planning for Dissertation Research

"Should I do a study that is clean, relatively quick, limited, and do-able so as to finish and get on with my professional life, or should I do something I really want to do that may be messy and unclear but would be challenging and new enough to sustain my interest?" (Hammonds-White, personal communication, August 5, 1987)

A doctoral student, finding any number of stumbling blocks standing between her and the completion of her dissertation project, was asked to reflect on the process through which the research plan had been developed. Her response indicated that, as with any kind of major investment, a preliminary notion of how to proceed should be tempered by a comparison of anticipated costs and available resources. In this student's case, she had to weigh energy (her physical and emotional stamina), time, and finances.

The demands of the student's chosen research methods were many. Seeking to explore a process, she chose naturalistic inquiry, which would encourage her to search for multiple views of reality and the ways such views were constructed. Her training, experience, and interest in counseling psychology, coupled with a positive assessment of her knowledge and competence in this field, constituted excellent sources of personal energy. This was an area of particular interest (the want-to-do-ability); methods were elegantly suited to that substantive focus. The researcher realized, however, that personal energy and a deep commitment to the topic were not going to be sufficient.

She looked to the university for two types of support that she described as "risk-taking support" and "learning support." The first would encourage someone attempting to go beyond the conventional in his or her research. The second was offered by faculty members who possessed the interests and the skills necessary to advise her.

In addition to personal energy and commitment and faculty support, a third source of energy was a support group made up of others who were engaged in dissertation research. Of that group she wrote, "We meet every other week, set short-term goals for ourselves, and help each other with the emotional highs and lows of the process."

The commitment in time required of an individual doing qualitative research is substantial. This particular researcher was quick to advise that those following similar research plans would do well to build into their proposals more time than they thought would be required to make allowances for the unexpected. In her case, a change in her family situation necessitated a return to full-time employment, thus suspending her research when it was only two-thirds complete.

Financial resources need to be equal to the financial demands of a study. When it appeared unlikely that grant monies would be available, the student opted for a smaller-scale study that she could finance personally.

Vignette 25 illustrates the importance of being practical and realistic. Although it is impossible to anticipate all the potential stumbling blocks, a thoughtful and thorough research proposal will address the issue of feasibility by making an honest assessment of available energy, time, and financial resources and requirements.

While the researcher was planning for and conducting the above study, several resource issues became apparent. First, the commitment to a graduate student's dissertation research differs from that required of the researchers in Vignette 24. A dissertation, often one's first major, independent, scholarly work, carries more professional and personal significance than subsequent research projects. Furthermore, the project described in Vignette 24 had built-in supports for the researchers. As a team project funded by an external agent, commitments to colleagues and professional responsibilities to the funding agent were adequate to rebuild interest when it began to wane. A dissertation demands different kinds of supports; the most important are those of mentors and peers.

Mentors and Peers

In planning qualitative dissertation research, the judgments of university faculty about the adequacy of the proposal are crucial. At least one committee member, preferably the chair, should have had experience conducting qualitative studies. Such experience enables the faculty to help in making decisions about how to allocate time realistically to various tasks, given that all-important idea that qualitative research often takes much more time than one might predict. The support and encouragement of faculty are critical for developing research proposals that are substantial, elegant, and doable, and for advocating in the larger university community the legitimacy of a particular study and of qualitative research generally.

The experiences of our graduate students suggest that the support of peers is also crucial for the personal and emotional sustenance that students find so valuable in negotiating among faculty whose requests and demands may be in conflict with one another. Graduate seminars or advanced courses in qualitative methods provide excellent structures for formal discussions as students deal with issues arising from role management to building grounded theory in their dissertations. Student support groups also build in a commitment to others not unlike that found in the team project described in Vignette 24. By establishing deadlines and commitments to one another, students become more efficient and productive. These groups bridge the existential aloneness of dissertation research. Finally, rereading literature on qualitative inquiry is both a support and a reminder of the traditions and challenges faced by all of us. It helps to know that William Foote Whyte managed ethical dilemmas in the field, too.

Time on a Small Scale

Developing a qualitative dissertation proposal demands sensitivity to the time necessary for the thorough completion of the project. This is where the experience of mentors on the university faculty becomes crucial. As noted in Chapter 3, complying with institutional review board requirements for proceeding ethically takes time. Gaining access to a setting can take 6 months or more and may require the skills of a diplomat. As in Vignette 25, personal circumstances may intervene to alter dramatically the student's available time and energy to conduct the study. Thus, even though not all critical events can be anticipated, planning for more time than initially appears necessary is prudent. As Locke, Spirduso, and Silverman note (2000, p. 44, emphasis added), "Relatively few research studies finish on schedule, and *time requirements invariably are underestimated*. Frequent setbacks are almost inevitable." We have both had the experience of advanced doctoral students needing to find jobs. The economic necessity often has to take priority over completing their degrees, at least in a timely manner. This most often delays completion and, in a few cases, means that students don't finish at all. While unfortunate, this is the reality of doctoral-level work.

Financing

In some fields (notably, mental health, urban planning, anthropology, and international education), financial support for dissertation research may be available through federal agencies or private foundations. Unfortunately, this is not typically the case in most social science fields, in education, or in other applied fields. Opportunities do sometimes become available, however, to work on a university professor's funded grant as a research assistant. This was the case in Vignette 24. Several graduate students would have been supported annually, and several of them could have dovetailed their research interests with those of the project.

Much more common, especially in education, is the case in Vignette 25. The student had to modify the proposed research to conform to the personal financial resources she was able to devote to the project. Recall that the proposal for funded research described in Vignette 24 suffered the same fate. The researchers planned an ideal study based on design considerations and the purposes of the study and then had to modify that ideal design based on the real budgetary constraints imposed by the funding agency.

For dissertation research, many costs, some obvious and some hidden, will arise over the course of the study. Planning ahead for these makes them a bit more manageable. These costs are clustered into three categories: materials, services, and personal costs.

Materials. The materials necessary for the completion of a dissertation may include word-processing equipment and materials, computer software for data analysis, computer disks, note cards and filing systems, tape recorders and tapes, video equipment and cameras, books, articles, and copies of completed dissertations. The student should project the costs in each category, being sure to include the costs of photocopying journal articles, drafts of the work as it proceeds, and copies of the final document.

Services. The services necessary for the completion of the dissertation vary depending on the skills of the student. Typical services, however, might include tape transcribing, word processing, statistical data analysis consulting, and professional proofreading and editing. The student often wants to have copies of the work professionally bound; this is an additional service that might be important for the student to consider as well.

Personal costs. Personal costs are the most difficult to specify but may also be the most important in terms of perceived costs to the individual student. Dissertation work is unlike any scholarly work the student has ever undertaken (and, most likely, any the student will do in the future). It is not like a large course or like reading for exams. It is of a quite different magnitude than those. The sustained effort necessary to complete the project takes time away from all the other commitments in the student's life, whether these are work, family, friends, or professional associations and volunteer groups. Students who are the most successful in moving through the phases of the dissertation build support networks for themselves within their families or through friends and colleagues. Dissertation proposal sections discussing researcher role (see Chapter 3) should include assessments of the researcher's ability to manage the personal costs. Even though not all the costs associated with personal sacrifice can be anticipated, knowledge that the undertaking is not trivial and will require sacrifices on the part of the student can make the entire process more manageable.

Sometimes, researchers seek new funds to continue a project that uncovered interesting data. It is difficult to convince funding agency reviewers that a reworking of data analysis is a worthwhile venture. Vignette 26 describes a researcher trying to convince funding agency reviewers that a secondary analysis of qualitative data was worthy of financial support.

VIGNETTE 26

Walking the Reviewers Through Qualitative Analysis

The data collected were voluminous, comparative, qualitative and quantitative from key state education policy makers in six states. From a study funded by the National Institute of Education, Mitchell, Wirt, and Marshall (1986) developed a taxonomy of state mechanisms for influencing school programs and practices and showed the effect of political culture and the relative power of policy makers to affect the choices made in state capitals about education. Captivated by the richness of the interview data, Marshall began to develop a grounded theory of assumptive worlds—the understandings that policy makers have about the way things are done, as demonstrated in their stories. Although this theory had been published (Marshall, Mitchell, & Wirt, 1985, 1986), the next step required funds. Her proposal to the National Science Foundation's political science program promised a secondary analysis of the interview data from six states, assisted by a computer program for data analysis to elaborate the theory. The funding could be minimal because no new data collection was required.

Months later, the reviewers came back. One of them wrote, "This proposal breaks fresh and important ground in the political field." Another noted that "using qualitative data in a systematic way and employing computers in data management are innovative techniques well worth development." A third, however, objected: "The proposal is to apply qualitative analysis to the interview materials. Perhaps that term has some [other] understood connotation in other research traditions, but so far as I could fathom what it means is the investigator would read/listen to interview materials and file them on a micro computer." The proposal was rejected.

Overcoming frustration, Marshall revised and resubmitted her proposal with important changes. First, for the theoretical framework, related literature, and significance, she created a chart, tracing the precise place where assumptive worlds fit with other political science and education policy theory and literature. Second, after explaining the traditions of qualitative research, she cited political scientists' calls for more theory building with comparable case studies and calls to get behind the scenes to find how values of the policy culture affect policy outcomes. Third, with Table 6.3, she demonstrated the promise of the theory. Narratively, she described its significance for understanding the policy culture. Finally, and perhaps most important, following a section on the philosophy of qualitative methodology and a section on the use of microcomputers with qualitative data, she wrote the following step-by-step description:

Qualitative data analysis seems to be mystical processes to those accustomed to statistical analysis. However, the goal of both methodologies is the same: to identify clear and consistent patterns of phenomena by a systematic process. I will follow the following steps:

1. Transcribe data in Ethnograph files, using categories from preliminary analysis. Analyze field notes and taped interviews from Wisconsin, Illinois, Arizona, and California.
2. Expand assumptive world rules by examining all computer files with relevant descriptors. For example, when identifying patterns of behavior in legislative–state board relations, call up all files under the descriptor "state board" or, when identifying constraints on legislative staffers, call up all field notes and quotations under that label.
3. Content analysis of all six states' data to (a) identify any additional patterns of behavior or belief, and (b) redefine domains and operational principles.
4. Reanalyze the file data using the alterations of assumptive world domains and operational principles.
5. Reorder the six states' files until clear, mutually exclusive, and exhaustive categories of behavior and belief systems are identified that organize the data descriptions of the policy environment.

6. Identify assumptive world effects on policy outcomes from field notes and interview data based on analytic notes regarding assumptive worlds (already started with West Virginia and Pennsylvania data).

Table 6.3   Functions of the Operative Principles of Assumptive Worlds

Action guide domains and operational principles	Maintain power and predictability	Promote cohesion
Who has the right and responsibility to initiate?		
The prescription for the CSSO role	x	
The prescription for the SDE role	x	
Legislative-SDE role	x	
Variations in initiative in legislature	x	
What policy ideas are deemed unacceptable?		
Policies that trample on powerful interests		x
Policies that lead to open defiance		x
Policies that defy tradition and dominant interests		x
Policy debates that diverge from the prevailing value		x
Untested, unworkable policy		x
What uses of power in policy-making activities are appropriate?		
Know your place and cooperate with the powerful	x	
Something for everyone	x	
Touch all the bases	x	
Bet on the winner	x	
Limits on social relationships	x	
Constraints on staffers	x	
Work with constraints and tricks	x	
Policy actors' sponsorship of policy issue network		x
Uses of interstate comparison		x
What are the special state conditions affecting policy?		
Cultural characteristics		x
Geographic, demographic characteristics		x

SOURCE: C. Marshall, grant proposal to National Science Foundation, 1988.

NOTE: CSSO = Chief State School Officer; SDE = State Department of Education.

Vignette 26 demonstrates the tasks involved in convincing funding agencies of the labor intensiveness of qualitative data analysis. It requires time and money and is not as simple as sitting in a comfy chair and reading over interview data. Those more attuned to traditional research, however, may need explicit details before they will provide support for that labor. Charts, diagrams, time lines, examples of precedents from highly regarded publications, and explicit delineation of the procedures will be convincing when tied to text. Funding agencies, pressed by the needs of many eager researchers and guided by the peer review process, will not provide resources unless everyone involved can see clearly how the money will be converted into knowledge. Even small requests for a graduate assistant or a computer program will be denied if the research sounds like a mystical process or if it sounds like simple filing. Anyone who has ever done qualitative data analysis knows better, but those with the funds need explicit guidance so they can see how the expenditure is justified. Vignette 26 shows the need to fit explanations to the knowledge bases and predilections of reviewers by walking them through the steps to be followed and thereby providing assurances that the researcher can produce something meaningful on their terms.

* * * * *

This chapter has displayed the recursive processes of planning sufficient resources to support the conduct of a qualitative research project. Vignette 24 could aptly be retitled "Planning in a Context of Largesse" because the study was proposed to a funding agency with substantial financial resources. The major problem for that study was paring down the ideal design to conform to those budget parameters.

Vignette 25 portrays some of the unique problems associated with planning dissertation research, in which financial resources are largely unavailable and where time and personal support systems become critical. Each type of project has unique challenges when the researcher is designing the proposal. Consideration of these issues strengthens the proposal by demonstrating that the researcher is aware of and sensitive to the many challenges that may arise during the conduct of the study. Finally, Vignette 26 reminds us that even low-budget studies will be criticized if they cannot lead the reviewers to an understanding of the resources needed for qualitative analysis. Attention to these considerations helps strengthen the overall proposal and makes its positive evaluation more likely.

Throughout this book, we have presented considerations for building clear, thorough, and thoughtful proposals for qualitative research. In the final chapter, we make these considerations more explicit by describing them as a set of criteria.

DIALOGUE BETWEEN LEARNERS

Hi Aaron,

Okay, my next topic of choice is (drumroll, please) time. How do you maximize your research time, especially for analysis and writing? Do you set aside a few hours each day, a specific day a week, work only on the weekends, grab chunks of time as they come? In the past, when I was working on a lengthy paper, I set aside whole afternoons and evenings, even several days in a row, and just pounded out the work. That isn't possible with qualitative research: there are too many tasks and too many levels of complexity. I question working in small segments of time. Can you immerse yourself deeply enough to produce anything of quality in short amounts of time? Don't you need lengthy involvement to appreciate the subtleties found in your data? When I'm truly interested in something, it's easy for me to push aside other demands and concentrate on that particular issue. While that may benefit the task I'm working on, other things fall by the wayside. Suddenly, my time has become a resource I have to allocate, just like the gas in my car! Anyway, I'm curious as to how you approach this particular part of the research process.

One question I haven't asked you: How did you narrow your study down to a manageable question?! My questions always begin so broadly, and I really struggle to narrow my interests down to functional bits. I didn't expect the research question to be one of the hardest parts of the research process. After all, you have a question, you answer the question. How naive! Crafting a good research question is very difficult but just narrowing down the general to the specific is a sweat-inducing task for me. And it takes so much time! What techniques do you use to help in the process? Are you working with one encompassing question or several more focused ones? Do you also struggle with this?!

Hope things are going well in Amherst! I have to hit the pile of papers now. . . .

Melanie

Hi Melanie,

In terms of your questions about time—I try to break my day into chunks for reading and chunks for writing. I'm the type that would be quite happy strolling around the library (material or virtual) for the rest of my life. I find that I have to be very disciplined about setting aside my reading and actually putting pen to paper. So, I tend to get up early in the morning and read and/or make notes about what I'm reading. I love mornings so this seems like a satisfying way to begin my day. At night I try to write (if I read I fall asleep). Keeping this schedule also has a tendency to keep me on task. I've found that writing small bits of analysis (almost like little letters to myself) throughout the process of data collection and analysis helps quite a bit. There's no pressure to perform when writing these short bits, there's just a sense of trying to get an early read on what I've encountered. If nothing else, it can, at times, make me feel as though I've produced something.

I don't want to be a student forever (no matter what the perks!), so the issue of the time it takes to adequately take on qualitative research is pretty big for me. Time is a resource that I don't want to take for granted. I know that dissertations can sometimes take years to finish; however, I've also been told that "the best dissertation is a done dissertation." Knowing my tendency to dig deeper and deeper into the papers I write, I worry a bit about how long it will take me to produce the dissertation. From defining the research question to entering the field, collecting data, analysis, and writing the actual dissertation, I can easily understand why people are perpetually ABD.

You've asked about how to narrow down the research questions and my friends here would laugh, as I'm the last person they would ask. I, like you, also begin with a very broad question and then try and try to get it more and more specific. My writing teachers used to tell me to write the introductions to my papers last, after the paper has been written. This way you get a sense of what the introduction will actually be introducing. Often, I find that the research question doesn't come to me until I'm out there in the field and have interactions with a variety of people. Not that it's inspired stuff, mind you, just that it sort of evolves into a more specific question as time wears on. I've become OK with that practice and I'm lucky to have an adviser who is very patient and quite kind to humor me along the way. Yes, concision and precision are issues that I need to work on. However, at some point I need to trust that I will figure it out. After all, someone let me into this program; they must have felt that I could pull something off. . . .

Hope all is well. We're hoping for a break in the weather here. I'm tired of sweating while brushing my teeth.

Take care,

Aaron

❖ FURTHER READING

Cheek, J. (2000). An untold story? Doing funded qualitative research. In N. K. Denzin & Y. S. Lincoln (Eds.), *Handbook of qualitative research* (2nd ed., pp. 401–420). Thousand Oaks, CA: Sage.

Coley, S. M., & Scheinberg, C. A. (2000). *Proposal writing* (2nd ed.). Thousand Oaks, CA: Sage. (See Appendix A on estimating time.)

Locke, L. F., Spirduso, W. W., & Silverman, S. J. (2000). *Proposals that work: A guide for planning dissertations and grant proposals* (4th ed.). Thousand Oaks, CA: Sage. (See Chapters 9 and 10.)

Morse, J. M. (1994). Designing funded qualitative research. In N. K. Denzin & Y. S. Lincoln (Eds.), *Handbook of qualitative research* (pp. 220–235). Thousand Oaks, CA: Sage.

Tripp-Riemer, T., & Cohen, M. Z. (1991). Funding strategies for qualitative research. In J. M. Morse (Ed.), *Qualitative nursing research: A contemporary dialogue* (pp. 243–256). Newbury Park, CA: Sage.

7

Articulating Value
and Logic

M any social sciences have put aside the old doubts and mistrusts of qualitative inquiry. Arguments and concerns about quantitative versus qualitative can now be recast. The research community now generally recognizes that the rationales and the supporting criteria for various inquiries will differ.

[Writers of any research proposal must develop a sound rationale for the choice of methodology. The credibility and the usefulness of the study will hinge upon this presentation. In qualitative proposals, the crucial task is developing the logic and argument for the interpretive paradigm, the idea of conducting research in a natural setting with the researcher as the primary means for gathering and interpreting data. Qualitative research involves a series of choices: "These choices and the theoretical reasons for them need to be presented explicity" (Sanjek, 1990, p 395).

The contested nature of criteria for judging the soundness of any research is part of the current methodological scene. Qualitative researchers may encounter debates and challenges from those with a more traditional take. However, with postmodern, feminist, action, and emancipatory thought, the more naturalistic and explicitly interpretive approach of qualitative research has gathered momentum and support in research communities with viable and strong contributions. Qualitative research is generally no longer tossed aside as simply an alternative or merely the pilot study. However, as noted in the Preface to this edition and discussed below, the qualitative researcher needs to be mindful of strong countervailing conservative forces. When facing debates and challenges about the soundness, validity, utility, and generalizability of qualitative methods, the researcher can draw on the deep conversations in the literature about the appropriate criteria for judging the soundness and rigor of qualitative research.

In the politics of knowledge, certain research is seen as the gold standard, the most dependable, the conventional and privileged way. Powerful and dominant groups work to maintain those conventions, sometimes marginalizing other forms or sources of knowledge (Lather, 1991; Marshall, 1997a; Scheurich, 1997). The U.S. Department of Education, to promote traditional designs, requests and supports studies by "qualified scientists" that "address causal questions" and that "employ randomized experimental designs" (Flinders, 2003, p. 380) as the way to transform the field. This focus on quantitative inquiry means that expanded exploration of issues do not qualify as research under these new restrictions. Although the realities of knowledge politics are not reassuring to the novice researcher, she needs to be prepared to be articulate about the interpretive paradigm. The essential considerations are articulated well by Patton (2002), who notes that the credibility of a qualitative report depends on the use of rigorous methods of fieldwork, on the credibility of the researcher, and on the "fundamental appreciation of naturalistic inquiry, qualitative methods, inductive analysis, purposeful sampling, and holistic thinking" (pp. 552–553).

Developing a logic that will solidly defend a proposal entails three large domains: (a) responding to criteria for the overall soundness of the project; (b) demonstrating the usefulness of the research for the particular conceptual framework and research questions; and (c) demonstrating the sensitivities and sensibilities to *be* the research instrument. Careful consideration of each will help the proposal writer develop a logic in support of the proposal.

❖ CRITERIA OF SOUNDNESS

All research must respond to canons of quality—criteria against which the trustworthiness of the project can be evaluated. These canons can be phrased as questions to which all social science research must respond (Lincoln & Guba, 2000). First, how credible are the particular findings of the study? By what criteria can we judge them? Second, how transferable and applicable are these findings to another setting or group of people? Third, how can we be reasonably sure that the findings would be replicated if the study were conducted with the same participants in the same context? And fourth, how can we be sure that the findings reflect the participants and the inquiry itself rather than a fabrication from the researcher's biases or prejudices? Postmodern and feminist challenges to traditional research assert that all discovery and truths emerge from the researcher's prejudgments and predilections. Those espousing these positions argue that such predispositions should be used "as building blocks . . . for acquiring new knowledge" (Nielson, 1990, p. 28).

In their historic work that shaped this discourse profoundly, Lincoln and Guba (1985) referred to these questions as establishing the "truth value" (p. 290) of the study, its applicability, consistency, and neutrality. Every systematic inquiry into the human condition must address these issues. Strategically, it may be useful to match these terms to the conventional positivist paradigm—internal validity, external validity, reliability, and objectivity. Lincoln and Guba then demonstrated the need to rework these constructs for interpretive qualitative inquiry.

They proposed four alternative constructs that have given qualitative researchers new terms with different connotations, ones that more accurately reflect the assumptions of the qualitative paradigm. The first is *credibility*, in which the goal is to demonstrate that the inquiry was conducted in such a manner as to ensure that the subject was appropriately identified and described. The inquiry should then be "credible to the constructors of the original multiple realities" (Lincoln & Guba, 1985, p. 296).

The credibility/believability of a qualitative study that aims to explore a problem or describe a setting, a process, a social group, or a pattern of interaction will rest on its validity. An in-depth description showing the complexities of processes and interactions will be so embedded with data derived from the setting that it is convincing to readers. Within the parameters of that setting and population and the limitations of the theoretical framework and design, the research will be credible. A qualitative researcher should therefore adequately state those parameters, thereby placing boundaries around and limitations on the study.

The second construct Lincoln and Guba (1985) propose is *transferability*, in which the researcher should argue that his findings will be useful to others in similar situations, with similar research questions or questions of practice. The burden of demonstrating that a set of findings applies to another context rests more with the researcher who would make that transfer than with the original researcher. Kennedy (1979) refers to this as the *second decision span* in generalizing. The first decision span allows the researcher to generalize the findings about a particular sample to the population from which that sample was drawn (assuming adequate population specification and random selection of the sample). The second decision span occurs when another researcher wants to apply the findings about a population of interest to a second population believed or presumed to be similar enough to the first to warrant that application. This second decision span entails making judgments about and an argument for the relevance of the initial study to the second setting.

A qualitative study's transferability or generalizability to other settings may be problematic, at least in the probabilistic sense of the terms. Generalizing qualitative findings to other populations, settings, and treatment arrangements—that is, its *external* validity—is seen by traditional canons as a weakness in the approach. To counter challenges, the researcher can refer to the original theoretical framework to show how data collection and analysis will be guided by concepts and models. By doing so, the researcher states the theoretical parameters of the research. Then, those who make policy or design research studies within those same (or sufficiently similar) parameters can determine whether the cases described can be generalized for new research policy and transferred to other settings. In addition, the reader or user of specific research can see how research ties into a body of theory.

For example, a case study of a new staff development program in a high school can be tied to theories of the implementation of innovations in organizations, leadership, personnel management, and adult career socialization. The research can then be used in planning program policy and further research in a variety of settings—not just the high school, school organizations, and staff development. It can be included with research about organizations and can contribute to the literature on organizational theory.

One additional strategic choice can enhance a study's generalizability: triangulating multiple sources of data. Triangulation is the act of bringing more than one source of data to bear on a single point. Derived from navigation science, the concept has been fruitfully applied to social science inquiry (see Richards, 2005; Rossman & Wilson, 1994). Data from different sources can be used to corroborate, elaborate, or illuminate the research in question (Rossman & Wilson, 1994). Designing a study in which multiple cases, multiple informants, or more than one data-gathering method is used can greatly strengthen the study's usefulness for other settings.

The third construct is *dependability,* in which the researcher attempts to account for changing conditions in the phenomenon chosen for study and changes in the design created by an increasingly refined under-standing of the setting. This represents a set of assumptions very dif-ferent from those shaping the concept of reliability. Positivist notions of reliability assume an unchanging universe where inquiry could, quite logically, be replicated. This assumption of an unchanging social world is in direct contrast to the qualitative/interpretative assumption that the social world is always being constructed and that the concept of replication is itself problematic.

The final construct, *confirmability,* captures the traditional concept of objectivity. Lincoln and Guba (1985) stress the need to ask whether the findings of the study could be confirmed by another. By doing so, they ask if the logical inferences and interpretations of the researcher make sense to someone else. Does that reader or critical friend see how inferences were made? Do they make sense? With this criterion, Lincoln and Guba are asserting that the logic and interpretive nature of qualitative inquiry can be made (somewhat) transparent to others, thereby increasing the strength of the assertions.

A qualitative research proposal may well need to respond to concerns about the natural subjectivity of the researcher shaping the research. Again, the researcher should assert the strengths of qualitative methods by showing how she will develop an in-depth understanding of, even empathy for, the research participants to better understand their worlds. The researcher's insights increase the likelihood that she will be able to describe the complex social system being studied. She should, however, build into the proposal strategies for limiting bias in interpretation. Such strategies could include the following:

- Planning to use a research partner or a person who plays the role of critical friend who thoughtfully and gently questions the researcher's analyses.

- Building in time for cross-checking, peer debriefing, and time sampling to search for negative instances.

- Describing how analysis will use, but not be limited by, previous literature and how it will include checking and rechecking the data and a purposeful examination of possible alternative explanations.

- Providing examples of explicitly descriptive, nonevaluative note taking: planning to take two sets of notes, one with description and another with tentative categories and personal reactions.

- Citing previous researchers who have written about bias, subjectivity, and data quality.

- Planning to conduct an audit trail of the data collection and analytic strategies (see Lincoln & Guba, 1985; Richards, 2005).

Clearly, criteria of goodness for qualitative research differ from the criteria developed for experimental and positivist research. Still, it is helpful to articulate the parallels and differences. Qualitative research does not claim to be replicable. The researcher purposefully avoids controlling the research conditions and concentrates on recording the complexity of situational contexts and interrelations as they occur naturally. The researcher's goal of discovering this complexity by altering research strategies within a flexible research design, moreover, cannot be replicated by future researchers nor should they attempt to do so.

Qualitative researchers can respond to the traditional social science concern for replicability, however, by taking the following steps. First, they can assert that qualitative studies by their nature (and, really, all research) cannot be replicated because the real world changes. Second, by planning to keep thorough notes and a journal or log that records each design decision and the rationale behind it, researchers allow others to inspect their procedures, protocols, and decisions. Finally, by planning to keep all collected data in well-organized, retrievable form, researchers can make them available easily if the findings are challenged or if another researcher wants to reanalyze the data.

For works emphasizing the interpretive strengths of qualitative inquiry, though, it is more important to embrace subjectivity. Triangulation is not so much about getting "truth" but rather about finding the multiple perspectives for knowing the social world. Another set of criteria derives from the assumption that research is good if it helps promote emancipatory change, derived from feminist theory and critical theory. Such goodness criteria support the value of research that highlights oppressive power relations and that empowers the participants, often with collaborative action research. Finally, and relatedly, we see an emerging trend toward judging research value through its presentation or its performance. Thus, one values the research effort for the aesthetics of its narrative, the theater, poetry, or other performance (McCall, 2000). Whichever philosophical assumptions ground one's proposal, the researcher should have good responses to the important question: How can you make sure that your earthy, thick, evocative finding is not, in fact, wrong? (Miles, 1979) The traditional, realist responses will be very different from those of the proposal writer doing critical ethnography. Each must be convincing in the arguments and strategies they propose for assuring goodness.

For some descriptive studies, aimed at presenting a thick description of reality, traditional scientific standards can be paralleled, as in using comparative analysis and in emphasizing rigor in data collection, in cross-checking, and in intercoder consistency, as explicated in, for example, Miles and Huberman's (1994) guidelines and Anfara, Brown, and Mangione's (2002) demonstration. However, continuing discussions of criteria for assessing the value and trustworthiness of qualitative research are quite persuasive. Qualitative inquiry, moving to a kind of "non-naïve realism" (Smith & Deemer, 2000), recognizes that understanding is relative and there are multiple understandings and that, at best, we present a report that is likely to be true given our existing knowledge. As Smith and Deemer put it, "Relativism is nothing more or less than the expression of our human finitude: we must see ourselves as practical and moral beings, and abandon hope for knowledge that is not embedded with our historical, cultural, and engendered ways of being" (p. 886). Finally, "criteria should not be thought of as an abstraction, but as a list of features that we think, or more or less agree at any given time and place, characterize good versus bad inquiry" (p. 894).

Planning ahead, thinking about how one's final research product will be judged as "good," is a useful exercise for proposal writers. Marshall (1985a, 1990) developed criteria to apply to written reports of qualitative research; we have adapted them here for proposal development. Attention to these issues assures a sound and convincing research proposal.

The Design and Methods Should Be Explicitly Detailed

The researcher explicates the design and methods so the reader can judge whether they are adequate and make sense. She includes a rationale for qualitative research generally and the specific genre in which the study is situated. She discusses the anticipated methods for attaining entry and managing role, data collection, recording, analysis, ethics, and exit. She describes how the site and sample will be selected. Data collection and analysis procedures will be made public, not remain magical.

The researcher states clearly any assumptions that may affect the study. Biases are expressed, and the researcher engages in some preliminary self-reflection to uncover personal subjectivities. She articulates, often drawing on the work of others, how she will be a finely tuned research instrument whose personal talents, experiential biases, and insights will be used consciously. She argues that she will be careful to be self-analytical and recognize when she is becoming overly subjective and not critical enough of her interpretations. As part of this process, she analyzes the conceptual framework for theoretical biases. Furthermore, the researcher articulates how she will reflexively engage with and discuss the value judgments and personal perspectives that are inherent in data collection and in analysis. She will, for example, exercise caution to distinguish between descriptive field notes ("The roofs had holes and missing tiles.") and judgmental ones ("Many houses were dilapidated.").

The researcher writes about her tolerance for ambiguity, how she will search for alternative explanations, check out negative instances, and use a variety of methods to ensure that the findings are strong and grounded (e.g., with triangulation). Methods are proposed for ensuring data quality (e.g., informants' knowledgeability, subjectivities, and candor) and for guarding against ethnocentric explanations by eliciting cross-cultural perspectives.

The researcher describes preliminary observations, a pilot study, or her first days in the field, demonstrating how the research questions have been generated from observation, not merely from library research. The researcher is careful about sensitivity of those being researched: Ethical standards are maintained. She argues that people in the research setting will likely benefit in some way (ranging from an hour of sympathetic listening to feeling empowered to take action to alter some facet of their lives).

Research Questions and the Data's Relevance Should Be Explicit and Rigorously Argued

The researcher discusses how there will be abundant evidence from raw data to demonstrate the connection between those data and her interpretations. She shows how data will be presented in readable, accessible form, perhaps aided by graphics, models, charts, and figures. She states the preliminary research questions clearly and argues that the data collected will allow her to respond to those questions and generate further questions. The relationship between the proposed study and previous studies is explicit. The researcher discusses how the study will be reported in a manner accessible to other researchers, practitioners, and policymakers. She argues that she will be able to make an adequate translation of findings so that others will be able to use them in a timely way.

The Study Should Be Situated in a Scholarly Context

The proposal acknowledges the limitations of generalizability while assisting the readers in seeing the potential transferability of findings. The study is tied into the big picture. The researcher will look holistically at the setting to understand linkages among systems and will trace the historical context to understand how institutions and roles have evolved.

While defining central concepts, with reference to previously identified phenomena, the researcher argues that this research will go beyond established frameworks, challenging old ways of thinking.

Records Should Be Kept

The researcher describes how the data will be preserved and available for other analyses. She documents any in-field analysis. Furthermore, there is explicit mention of a running record of procedures, perhaps an audit trail that will be included in an appendix to the final written report.

Attention to these criteria ensures a solid qualitative proposal that displays concern for issues of trustworthiness and shows how knowledgeable the proposal writer is regarding these issues. Many issues are addressed in the body of the proposal; others may be discussed in the meeting to defend the proposal or in response to the queries of funding agencies. (See Marshall, 1985b, 1990, for a discussion of the evolving set of "criteria of goodness" that cuts across scholarly and political debates.)

Finally, researchers need to allay the fears (both their own and those of their reviewers) that they might stay in the field or become stalled when faced with analyzing the data. They need to demonstrate their ability to move from data collection to analysis and interpretation to writing. Again, a pilot study, a hypothesized model, or an outline of possible data analysis categories can be appended to the proposal. Qualitative researchers should always caution that such models, outlines, and categories are primarily heuristic (tentative guides) to begin observation and analysis. They are reassuring, however, to those who are uncomfortable with the flexibility and ambiguity. Such guides assist in demonstrating that qualitative researchers are, indeed, guided by concrete and systematic processes in collecting and analyzing the data. Still, qualitative research cannot get bogged down by what Schwandt (1996) calls *criteriology:* lists that are too restrictive and preordained.

❖ DEMONSTRATING THE ESSENTIAL QUALITATIVENESS OF THE QUESTIONS

Many discussions about criteria of goodness for qualitative research emphasize the transparency of the data collection and analysis and the "systematic-ness" of procedures for gathering and presenting evidence. Other standards matter as well. The real-world significance of the questions asked, the practical value of potential findings, and the degree to which participants in the study may benefit are emerging criteria. Frequently still, in attempting to make a proposed design efficient and conform to traditional research, reviewers recommend alterations in the original design. They may argue that the time for exploration is wasteful or just a pilot study; they may try to change the nature of the study from ethnographic exploration and description to a more traditional design. They may worry that the design is not "tight." Researchers' explanations, therefore, must sway their audiences with the power of their methodologies for the kinds of unanswered questions they will explore. Also, they must allay fears about design "looseness," the immersion in the natural setting, and the time expended in exploration.

❖ THE VALUE OF THE QUALITATIVE APPROACH

In Chapter 1, and throughout this book, we discuss the matching of methodology with research questions. When presenting a proposal, this kind of matching constitutes the most essential and potentially convincing argument. *It is not enough to give a nod to this by citing Lincoln and Denzin and Marshall and Rossman!*

The researcher must be eloquent about the need for research methodologies that are culturally sensitive, that, in the real world, can identify contextually generated patterns. She must be able to speak and write effectively about why nonmeasurable soft data are so very valuable. Her extensive critique of previous research that left unanswered questions, that made clear the need to observe naturally or to elicit emic perspectives substantiate her assertions. Demonstrating how persistent problems continue unresolved can substantiate her proposal to toss aside the survey with the wrong questions and to instead explore the narratives of people involved with the problems. Demonstrating the value of qualitative inquiry's "toolbox that enables researchers to develop concepts" (Morse, 2004) in fields with inadequate conceptualizing and theory building can buttress her proposal. Using humorous analogies and wit can be effective, if done judiciously. For example, she might use Morse's criticism of the research in medicine that demands quantitative methods even for qualitative questions as being like "trying to put in a nail using a chainsaw" (Morse, 2004, p. 1030).

Feminist, postmodern, and critical theorists invite us to engage in research that does not "Otherize" participants and has liberatory potential. They seek to discover and create, often collaboratively, knowledge that benefits those usually marginalized from the mainstream. Thus, emerging criteria lend special credence and value to proposals that challenge dominant (and *dominating*) practice or that include participants whose meaning making was overlooked in previous policy and research (Carspecken, 1996; Harding, 1987; Lather, 1991; Marshall, 1997b: Scheurich, 1997). And increasingly, the practical utility of research is becoming a valued criterion, especially for action research and when immediate pressing problems need research-based recommendations (Hammersley, 1990).

Thus, the value to be derived from using a qualitative approach needs to be convincingly explicated. Proposal writers need to anticipate reviewers' concerns and walk them through with rationales and examples. The following vignettes show how two researchers developed rationales for their work. Vignette 27 describes how a proposal writer anticipated a funding agent's challenge to the usefulness of qualitative research. Vignette 28 shows how a doctoral student successfully withstood challenges to his right to alter the design during fieldwork if it became necessary or prudent.

VIGNETTE 27

Justifying Time for Exploration

A proposal to conduct three in-depth case studies of high schools undergoing change (Rossman, Corbett, & Firestone, 1984) had received favorable internal review, although one administrator had quite a few worries about the value of qualitative research. The proposal had been transmitted to a federal agency where it would receive close scrutiny as a major portion of the group's work over the next 5 years.

As the research team sat on a train heading south, they pondered the type of questions they would be required to answer. Surely their sampling plan would be challenged: The criterion of "improvement" would have to be quite broadly construed to locate the kinds of high schools they wanted. The notion of studying a school's culture was new to many in the research community, never mind the Washington bureaucrats. The team anticipated questions about the usefulness of that concept, as well as the presentation of theoretical ideas on cultural change and transformation.

It struck the researchers as prudent to develop a rationale grounded in the applied research of others rather than relying on anthropological constructs. As they reviewed that logic, three points seemed most salient. First, the research proposal assumed that change in schools could not be adequately explored through a snapshot approach. Rather, the complexity of interactions among people, new programs, deeply held beliefs and values, and other organizational events demanded a long-term, in-depth approach. Second, at that time, little was known about change processes in secondary schools. Most of the previous research focused on elementary schools and had been generalized, perhaps inappropriately, to secondary schools. The proposed research was intended to fill the gap. Finally, much had been written about teachers' resistance to change. The rationale for and significance of the study would be in uncovering some of that construct, in delving beneath the surface and exploring the meaning perspectives of teachers involved in profound change.

The proposal called for long-term engagement in the social worlds of the three high schools selected for study. The team anticipated a challenge to that time allocation and decided to defend it through the rationale presented above as well as with the idea that complex processes demand adequate time for exploration, that interactions and changes in belief systems occur slowly.

After the 2-hour hearing, the team felt it had done a credible job but realized that the funding agent had not yet come to accept the longer time frame of qualitative research. In the negotiations, the research team had to modify the original plan to engage in participant observation over the course of a single school year. To save the project from rejection, they had agreed to 6 months of data collection, over the winter and spring terms.

In this vignette, the researchers developed a sound logic for the major aspects of the study. Justification for the substantive focus grew from the conceptual framework and the significance of the study. The major research approach—long-term engagement in the social world— could best be justified through demonstrating the need for exploration.

The quest for cultural understandings requires intense and lengthy involvement in the setting and design flexibility. For example, in their research in Fijian communities, Laverack and Brown (2003) discuss their need to adapt, given different cultural styles of group dynamics, facilitative, spatial arrangements, gender dynamics, and protocols and perceptions of time. Without making adaptations of traditional Western assumptions, their research would have flopped. Convincing the uninitiated critic that design flexibility is crucial can be a tough hurdle for the proposer of qualitative research. The next vignette shows how a fictitious doctoral student in economics successfully countered challenges to the need for design flexibility.

VIGNETTE 28

Defending Flexibility

Katz had been fascinated with families' financial decisions long before he first took a course in microeconomics as a college sophomore. That exposure to theory crystallized his interest and gave it an intellectual home. During his doctoral course work, however, he had pursued this interest from a cross-cultural perspective, enrolling in as many anthropology courses as his adviser would permit.

Katz's interest grew as he read case studies of families in other cultures. Quite naturally, he became interested in the methods anthropologists used to gather their data; they seemed so very different from econometrics or even economic history methods. As he immersed himself in these methods, his fascination grew. Now, about to embark on his dissertation, he had convinced one committee member to support his proposal to engage in a long-term, in-depth study of five families in very different socioeconomic circumstances. As he prepared for a meeting with the other two committee members, he reviewed the strengths of his proposal.

First, he was exploring the inner decision-making processes of five families—something no economics research had done. The value of the research would rest, in part, on the contribution this would make to understanding the beliefs, values, and motivations of certain financial behaviors. Second, he was contributing to methodology because he was approaching a topic using new research methods. He could rely on the work of two or three other qualitative economists, well-established scholars in their fields, to demonstrate that others had undertaken such risky business and survived!

Third, he had thoroughly combed the methodological literature for information that would demonstrate his knowledge of many of the issues that would arise: The design section of the proposal was more than 60 pages long and addressed every conceivable issue. He had not attempted to resolve them all but, rather, to show that he was aware that they might arise, knowledgeable about how others had dealt with them, and sensitive to the trade-offs represented by various decisions.

During the committee meeting, the thoroughness and richness of the design section served him well. The fully documented topics and sensitive discussion revealed a knowledge and sophistication not often found in doctoral students. What Katz had not anticipated, however, was the larger question brought up by one committee member: With such a small sample, how could the research be useful?

Fortunately, Katz recalled the argument developed by Kennedy (1979) about generalizing from single case studies. He had conceptualized his study as a set of family life histories from which would be drawn analytic categories, with relationships among them carefully delimited. Not unlike a multisite case study, Katz's proposal could be evaluated from that perspective. This logic proved convincing enough that Katz's committee approved his proposal.

In these vignettes, each proposal demanded a well-thought-out, thorough, logical defense. When the proposal is considered as an argument, the need to provide a clear organization, document major design

Table 7.1   Questions From Reviewers With Little Qualitative Experience

"I'm not used to this; could you explain this *qualitative* approach you're taking?"

"Why don't you include any surveys in this research study?"

"I don't see any numbers here—how is this real research?"

"What is your control group?"

"How can this be generalized?"

"If you're the one collecting *and* analyzing the data, how will we know you're right?"

"How can you be objective?"

"How can you verify your findings?"

"Can you explain this idea of 'grounded theory'"?

"Explain this concept of emergent sampling (or emergent data analysis)."

"It looks like you're using stories as part of your data collection. Are stories really data?"

"How can you start this research without knowing what you're looking for?"

"How will you use any of these findings? How will you explain how this small sample can be OK?"

"I think this will be a fun study but I worry about whether you'll be able to publish it in journals."

Table 7.2   Questions From Reviewers Attuned to Qualitative Methodology

"I like your research design but what's the significance of your findings?"

"How have you made a good match of topic and qualitative or quantitative approaches?"

"Is it feasible to believe you can finish this study in a year?"

"What processes will you go through to categorize your data?"

"How will you talk about and handle validity and reliability in this qualitative research?"

"Could you give me an example of going from concepts to data collection? Going from interpretations to generalizable findings? What about other naturalistic inquiries or dealing with negative instances?"

"What if you don't get access to your study population? What if people won't talk to you?"

"What is the final product going to look like?"

"Can you give me some examples of comparable work?"

"How can you condense your qualitative research to a publishable 12-page journal article?"

"How will you make time in your life to focus on this research?"

"Are you going to go out 'in the field,' never to be seen again?"

"How will you know when to stop collecting data?"

"How will policy makers or practitioners make use of your findings?"

"What philosophical assumptions guide you in your efforts to assure the 'goodness' of your research?"

decisions, and demonstrate the overall soundness of the study becomes clear. Following the advice we provide here will help the qualitative research proposal writer think through the conceptual and methodological justifications and rationales for the proposed study. In planning a defense of the proposal, we suggest that the researcher anticipate questions that may come from a funding agency or from a dissertation committee. Having well-prepared and rehearsed answers will facilitate the defense. Tables 7.1 and 7.2 present types of questions that we have encountered. Those in Table 7.1 come from reviewers with little experience with qualitative methods; those in Table 7.2 are from those who are familiar with the methods and seek justifications for the decisions in the proposal.

Although some of these questions may never be articulated, they may be present in the minds of foundation officials or dissertation committee members. Building a logic in support of the proposed qualitative study will help reassure skeptics and strengthen the argument.

And, to ease worries and tense questioning, the proposer can tell stories. For example, to explain the flexibility and reflectiveness of the human research instrument, she might read a bit from Narayan's (1993) account of fieldwork in the Himalayan foothills—how she was variously identified as being from her mother's village, from Bombay, as native, as outsider. But when she appeared at weddings, "where a splash of foreign prestige added to the festivities, I was incontrovertibly stated to be 'from America' . . . she came *all* the way from there for this function, yes, with her camera and her tape recorder" (p. 674). Thus she was viewed as an honored guest, even though many people present thought Americans were savages because television revealed that they didn't wear many clothes.

❖ DEMONSTRATING PRECEDENTS

Now, in the 21st century, with academic journals and handbooks devoted to qualitative inquiry, with doctoral programs sometimes requiring qualitative skills, researchers have plentiful resources to draw upon. While we honor old traditions, like that of Margaret Mead and other classical ethnographers going into the field and inventing strategies, the budding researcher now can, and should, draw upon the wisdom from those inventions. Further, he can often cite scholars in his own field whose use of qualitative methodology has led to important new understandings.

Qualitative research has proliferated in the practice disciplines like nursing and those dealing with health, illness, and life transitions (Sandelowski & Barroso, 2003). In psychology, the field traditionally associated with the controlled experiment and the statistical analysis creating mathematical models of psychological processes, some scholars recognize the need for qualitative inquiry as a way to delve into "the personal 'lifeworlds' . . . and the range of social interpretations of events" (Ashworth, 2003, p. 4; see also Michell, 2003). The fields of social work and journalism are naturals for qualitative inquiry and are developing literatures and courses to hone skills and goodness criteria (Shaw & Ruckdeschel, 2002; Shaw, 2003; Morse, 2003).

Probably the best strategy for demonstrating the value of one's proposed qualitative study is to share copies of important qualitative books and journal articles from one's own or similar fields with a possibly skeptical committee member or reviewer. While some (quantitative) sociologists might still challenge the understandings of professional enculturation in *Boys in White* (Becker, Geer, Hughes, &

Strauss, 1961) or *The Silent Dialogue* (Olesen & Whittaker, 1968), or see little value in the methodological carefulness demonstrated in the detailed appendices of *Work and the Family System* (Piotrkowski, 1979) or Lareau's (1989) *Home Advantage,* others would be open to learning. While some might wonder how Kanter (1977) would want to spend so much time studying one business, others would find her representation of the effects of stunted career mobility in *Men and Women of the Corporation* valuable for individuals, for women and minorities, and for personnel managers, too. Citing such books and even showing copies of such well-managed and significant qualitative studies may impress and reassure evaluators and reviewers.

Being well read in qualitative methodological approaches and in final research reports, in one's own discipline and in the books and articles of prestigious and well-known scholars, provides excellent support for arguing the value of a proposal and reassuring those who worry about whether it can be done. Precedents are useful, too, for demonstrating that conducting qualitative inquiry is a viable career choice for a budding academic. Wolcott (2005) finds that academic presses are more likely to be open to qualitative publications in the following fields: African studies, anthropology, art history, Asian studies, classical studies, cultural studies, European history, film, fine arts, gender studies, geography, Jewish studies, Latin American studies, law, linguistics, literary studies, Middle Eastern studies, music, natural history, philosophy, photography, political science, religious studies, science, sociology, and women's studies. Ironically, even as the federal government devalues qualitative genres, universities are advertising professorial positions for teaching them!

❖ A FINAL WORD

The process of developing a qualitative research proposal—the revisions necessitated by the interrelatedness of the sections—will create a final product that convinces readers and develops a rationale for the researcher's own guidance. It will justify the selection of qualitative methods and demonstrate the researcher's ability to conduct the study. The writing and creating processes will help the researcher to develop a logic and a plan that will guide and direct the research. The time, thought, and energy expended in writing a proposal will reap rewards. A proposal that is theoretically sound, methodologically ethical, efficient, and thorough will be impressive. One that demonstrates the researcher's capacity to articulate the arguments for "goodness" to conduct the fieldwork; and to find sound, credible, and convincing ways to analyze and present the research will truly prepare you for your research endeavor.

DIALOGUE BETWEEN LEARNERS

Melanie,

I thought I'd raise another issue that relates to the focus question that I responded to this morning. When people ask me what I do, I often respond that I'm a professional student. As much as I enjoy the freedoms of being a full-time student, one cannot stay this way forever. I want my dissertation to be a strong one (after all, I'm only planning on writing one). I like the idea of creating a dissertation work group with friends that are working on their dissertations at the same time. This seems like a good way to create a support group and help each other along through this process. However, I'm also finding that the more I move into the process of the dissertation, the more isolated I am from my peers. If it weren't for my assistantships, I might not be on campus at all. I could easily be in the field for a prolonged period of time and lose contact with the people I used to take classes with. What do you think? Anything to be concerned about?

Hope all is well,

Aaron

Hi Aaron,

I think isolation is a huge issue for graduate students (possibly professors, as well?). In fact, this is one issue I've been conscious of since day one of graduate school. How can I specialize my own interests while staying generalizable enough to my peers?

I'm with you on dissertation support groups. I have tried to establish writing groups or reading groups or just plain support groups through my years here but I've had very little success.

Everyone is *so* busy, with *so* many other claims on their time; without a true commitment to group meetings, it just falls by the wayside. I wonder if a dissertation group would meet with the same fate. It does carry more weight than a reading group, after all, and there's a definite product to introduce into the meetings. I feel like I need that human connection during this process. In some ways, research is very dehumanizing to the researcher. You can spend days on end with audio files, articles, scraps of field notes, computer printouts but yet have no actual human contact. Surrounded by people on paper but none in physical actuality! As much as I would like someone to read through my drafts and question my methods, I also want someone to talk to about the daily issues: writer's block, writing for a committee, work locations, forgetting to eat dinner. I really value the human connection, which is why my research interests so often hinge on relationships, and I would like that connection as a support throughout the research process.

So, there's my two cents. Talk to you soon,

Melanie

* * * * * *

References

Aberbach, J. D., & Rockman, B. A. (2002). Conducting and coding elite interviews. *PS: Political Science & Politics, 35*(4), 673–676.

Adler, P. A., & Adler, P. (1994). Observational techniques. In N. K. Denzin & Y. S. Lincoln (Eds.), *Handbook of qualitative research* (pp. 377–392). Thousand Oaks, CA: Sage.

Alexander, B. K. (2005). Performance ethnography: The reenacting and inciting of culture. In N. K. Denzin & Y. S. Lincoln (Eds.), *The SAGE handbook of qualitative research* (3rd ed., pp. 411–441). Thousand Oaks, CA: Sage.

Alvarez, R. (1993). *Computer mediated communications: A study of the experience of women managers using electronic mail.* Unpublished manuscript, University of Massachusetts Amherst.

Alvesson, M. (2003). Methodology for close up studies—Struggling with closeness and closure. *Higher Education, 46,* 167–193.

Anderson, E. (1976). *A place on the corner.* Chicago: University of Chicago Press.

Anderson, G. (1989). Critical ethnography in education: Origins, current status, and new directions. *Review of Educational Research, 59,* 249–270.

Anderson, G. L., & Herr, K. (1993). The micro-politics of student voices: Moving from diversity of voices in schools. In C. Marshall (Ed.), *The new politics of race and gender* (pp. 58–68). Washington, DC: Falmer.

Anderson, T., & Kanuka, H. (2003). *E-research: Methods, strategies, and issues.* Boston: Allyn & Bacon.

Anfara, V. A. Jr., Brown, K. M. & Mangione, T. L. (2002). Qualitative analysis on stage: Making the research process more public. *Educational Researcher, 31,* 28–38.

Argyris, C., & Schön, D. A. (1974). *Theory in practice.* San Francisco: Jossey-Bass.

Argyris, C., & Schön, D. A. (1991). Participatory action research and action science compared: A commentary. In W. F. Whyte (Ed.), *Participatory action research* (pp. 85–96). Newbury Park, CA: Sage.

Asch, T. (Producer). (1970). *The feast* [Motion picture]. Washington, DC: U.S. National Audiovisual Center.

Ashcroft, B., Griffiths, G., & Tiffin, H. (2000). *Post-colonial studies: The key concepts.* London: Routledge.

Ashworth, P. (2003). The origins of qualitative psychology. In J. A. Smith (Ed.), *Qualitative psychology-A practical guide to research methods* (pp. 4–24). London: Sage.

Atkinson, P., & Delamont, S. (2005). Analytic perspectives. In N. K. Denzin & Y. S. Lincoln (Eds.), *The SAGE handbook of qualitative research* (3rd ed., pp. 821–840). Thousand Oaks, CA: Sage.

Atkinson, P., Delamont, S., & Hammersley, M. (1988). Qualitative research traditions: A British response to Jacob. *Review of Educational Research, 58,* 231–250.

Atkinson, R. (1998). *The life story interview.* Thousand Oaks, CA: Sage.

Banks, M. (2001). *Visual methods in social research.* London: Sage.

Bargar, R. R., & Duncan, J. K. (1982). Cultivating creative endeavor in doctoral research. *Journal of Higher Education, 53,* 1–31.

Baron, R. S., & Kerr, N. L. (2003). Social dilemmas. In *Group process, group decision, group action* (2nd ed., pp. 139–154). Philadelphia: Open University Press.

Barzun, J., & Graff, H. F. (2004). *The modern researcher* (6th ed.). Belmont, CA: Thomson/Wadsworth.

Basit, T. (2003). Manual or electronic? The role of coding in qualitative data analysis. *Educational Research, 45*(2), 143–154.

Bateman, B. E. (2002). Promoting openness toward culture learning: Ethnographic interviews for students of Spanish. *Modern Language Journal, 86*(3), 318–331.

Baucom, D. H., & Kerig, P. K. (2004). Coding couples' interactions: Introduction and overview. In P. K. Kerig & D. H. Baucom (Eds.), *Couple observational coding systems* (pp. 3–10). Mahwah, NJ: Lawrence Erlbaum.

Baym, N. (2000). *Tune in, log on.* Thousand Oaks, CA: Sage.

Becker, H. S., Geer, B., Hughes, E. C., & Strauss, A. L. (1961). *Boys in white: Student culture in medical culture.* Chicago: University of Chicago Press.

Becker, T. M., & Meyers, P. R. (1974–1975). Empathy and bravado: Interviewing reluctant bureaucrats. *Public Opinion Quarterly, 38,* 605–613.

Benbow, J. T. (1994). *Coming to know: A phenomenological study of individuals actively committed to radical social change.* Unpublished doctoral dissertation, University of Massachusetts Amherst.

Bennis, W. G., & Nanus, B. (2003). *Leaders: Strategies for taking charge.* New York: Harper & Row.

Berelson, B. (1952). *Content analysis in communication research.* Glencoe, IL: Free Press.

Berg, B. L. (2004). *Qualitative research methods for the social sciences* (5th ed). Boston: Pearson/Allyn & Bacon.

Berger, M. T. (2003). Dealing with difficult gatekeepers, vulnerable populations, and hooks that go awry. In M. S. Feldman, J. Bell, & M. T. Berger (Eds.), *Gaining access* (pp. 65–68). Walnut Creek, CA: AltaMira Press.

Best, S. J., & Krueger, B. S. (2004). *Internet data collection.* Thousand Oaks, CA: Sage.

Birdwhistell, R. L. (1970). *Kinesics and content: Essays on body motion communication.* Philadelphia: University of Pennsylvania Press.

Bloom, L. R., & Munro, P. (1995). Conflicts of selves: Non-unitary subjectivity in women administrators' life history narratives. In J. A. Hatch & R. Wisniewski (Eds.), *Life history and narrative* (pp. 99–112). London: Falmer.

Bogdan, R. C., & Biklen, S. K. (2003). *Qualitative research in education: An introduction to theory and methods* (4th ed.). Boston: Allyn & Bacon.

Botherson, M. J. (1994). Interactive focus group interviewing: A qualitative research method in early intervention. *Topics in Early Childhood Special Education, 14*(1), 101–118.

Bowen, E. S. (1964). *Return to laughter.* Garden City, NY: Doubleday.

Brainard, J. (2001). The wrong rules for social science? *Chronicle of Higher Education, 47*(26), A21–A23.

Brantlinger, E. A. (1997, April). *Knowledge, position, and agency: Activism and inward gaze as a natural next step in local inquiry.* Paper presented at the annual meeting of the American Educational Research Association, San Diego, CA.

Brice Heath, S., & McLaughlin, M. (1993). *Identity and inner-city youth: Beyond ethnicity and gender.* New York: Teachers College Press.

Briggs, J. (2000). *Fire in the crucible: Understanding the process of creative genius.* Grand Rapids, MI: Phanes.

Brizuela, B. M., Stewart, J. P., Carrillo, R. G., & Berger, J. G. (Eds.). (2000). *Acts of inquiry in qualitative research.* Cambridge, MA: Harvard Educational Review, Reprint Series No. 34.

Brock, K., & McGee, R. (2002). *Knowing poverty: Critical reflections on participatory research and policy.* Sterling, VA: Earthscan Publications.

Bronfenbrenner, U. (1980). Ecology of childhood. *School Psychology Review, 9,* 294–297.

Brooks, P. C. (1969). *The use of unpublished primary sources.* Chicago: University of Chicago Press.

Browne, A. (1987). *When battered women kill.* New York: Free Press.

Buchanan, E. A. (Ed.). (2004). *Readings in virtual research ethics: Issues and controversies.* Hershey, PA: Information Science Publication.

Bull, P. (1983). *Body movement and interpersonal communication.* New York: John Wiley.

Burrell, G., & Morgan, G. (1979). *Sociological paradigms and organisational analysis.* London: Heineman.

Campbell-Nelson, K. (1997). *Learning the land: A local hermeneutic for indigenous education in West Timor, Indonesia.* Unpublished research proposal to the U.S. Information Agency. Fullbright-Hays Doctoral Support Program. University of Massachusetts Amherst.

Cancian, F. M., & Armstead, C. (1992). Participatory research. In E. F. Borgatta & M. Borgatta (Eds.), *Encyclopedia of sociology* (Vol. 3, pp. 1427–1432). New York: Macmillan.

Cappello, M. (2005). Photo interviews: Eliciting data through conversations with children. *Field Methods, 17*(2), 170–184.

Capra, F. (1975). *The Tao of physics.* Berkeley, CA: Shambhala.

Capra, F. (1982). *The turning point: Science, society and the rising culture.* New York: Simon and Schuster.

Capra, F. (1996). *The web of life.* New York: Doubleday.

Carspecken, P. F. (1996). *Critical ethnography in educational research: A theoretical and practical guide.* New York: Routledge & Kegan Paul.

Castelloe, P., & Legerton, M. (1998). *Learning together: Children and caregivers getting ready for school. A two-year report and evaluation for the Learning Together Project.* Lumberton, NC: Center for Community Action.

Charmaz, K. (2000). Grounded theory: Objectivist and constructivist methods. In N. K. Denzin & Y. S. Lincoln (Eds.), *Handbook of qualitative research* (2nd ed., pp. 509–535). Thousand Oaks, CA: Sage.

Charmaz, K. (2001). Grounded theory. In R. M. Emerson (Ed.), *Contemporary field research* (2nd ed., pp. 335–352). Prospect Heights, IL: Waveland.

Charmaz, K. (2005). Grounded theory in the 21st century: Applications for advancing social justice studies. In N. K. Denzin & Y. S. Lincoln (Eds.), *The SAGE handbook of qualitative research* (3rd ed., pp. 507–535). Thousand Oaks, CA: Sage.

Chase, S. E. (1995). *Ambiguous empowerment—The work narratives of women school superintendents.* Amherst: University of Massachusetts.

Chaudhry, L. N. (1997). Researching "my people," researching myself: Fragments of a reflexive tale. *Qualitative Studies in Education, 10*(4), 441–453.

Cheek, J. (2000). An untold story? Doing funded qualitative research. In N. K. Denzin & Y. S. Lincoln (Eds.), *Handbook of qualitative research* (2nd ed., pp. 401–420). Thousand Oaks, CA: Sage.

Cheek, J. (2004). At the margins? Discourse analysis and qualitative research. *Qualitative Health Research, 14*(8), 1140–1150.

Chen, S. L., Hall, G. J., Johns, M. D. (Eds.). (2003) *Online social research: Methods, issues, and ethics.* New York: Peter Lang.

Chessman, C. (1954). *Cell 2455 death row.* Englewood Cliffs, NJ: Prentice Hall.

Christians, C. G. (2000). Ethics and politics in qualitative research. In N. K. Denzin & Y. S. Lincoln (Eds.), *Handbook of qualitative research* (2nd ed., pp. 133–155). Thousand Oaks, CA: Sage.

Christians, C. G. (2005). Ethics and politics in qualitative research. In N. K. Denzin & Y. S. Lincoln (Eds.), *The SAGE handbook of qualitative research* (3rd ed., pp. 139–164). Thousand Oaks, CA: Sage.

Clandinin, D. J., & Connelly, F. M. (2000). *Narrative inquiry: Experience and story in qualitative research.* San Francisco: Jossey-Bass.

Clarricoates, K. (1980). The importance of being Ernest, Emma, Tom, Jane. In R. Deem (Ed.), *Schooling for women's work* (pp. 26–41). London: Falmer.

Clarricoates, K. (1987). Child culture at school: A clash between gendered worlds? In A. Pollard (Ed.), *Children and their primary schools* (pp. 188–206). London: Falmer.

Cohen-Mitchell, J. B. (2005). *Literacy and numeracy practices of market women in Quetzaltenango, Guatemala.* Unpublished doctoral dissertation, University of Massachusetts Amherst.

Cole, R. E. (1991). Participant observer research. In W. F. Whyte (Ed.), *Participatory action research* (pp. 159–166). Newbury Park, CA: Sage.

Cole, A. L., & Knowles, J. G. (2001). *Lives in context—The art of life history research.* Walnut Creek, CA: AltaMira Press.

Coles, R. (1971). *Children of crisis: Migrants, sharecroppers, mountaineers.* Boston: Little, Brown.

Coles, R. (1977). *Privileged ones: The well-off and the rich in America.* Boston: Little, Brown.

Coley, S. M., & Scheinberg, C. A. (2000). *Proposal writing* (2nd ed.). Thousand Oaks, CA: Sage.

Collier, J., & Collier, M. (1986). *Visual anthropology: Photography as a research method.* Albuquerque: University of New Mexico Press.

Collins, M., Shattell, M., & Thomas, S. P. (2005). Problematic interviewee behaviors in qualitative research. *Western Journal of Nursing Research, 27*(2), 188–199.

Collins, P. H. (1990). *Black feminist thought: Knowledge, consciousness, and the politics of empowerment.* New York: Routledge & Kegan Paul.

Conle, C. (2000). Narrative inquiry: Research tool and medium for professional development. *European Journal of Teacher Education, 23*(1), 49–54.

Conle, C. (2001). The rationality of narrative inquiry in research and professional development. *European Journal of Teacher Education, 24*(1), 21–33.

Connelly, F. M., & Clandinin, D. J. (1990). Stories of experience and narrative inquiry. *Educational Researcher, 19,* 2–14.

Connor, S. (1989). *Postmodernist culture: An introduction to theories of the contemporary.* Oxford, UK: Blackwell.

Cooke, B., & Kothari, U. (Eds.) (2001). *Participation: The new tyranny?* London: Zed Books.

Cooper, H. M. (1988). Organizing knowledge syntheses: A taxonomy of literature reviews. *Knowledge in Society, 1,* 104–126.

Cox, J. (1996). *Your opinion, please: How to build the best questionnaires in the field of education.* Thousand Oaks, CA: Corwin.

Crabtree, B. F., & Miller, W. L. (Eds.). (1992). *Doing qualitative research: Multiple strategies.* Newbury Park, CA: Sage.

Creswell, J. W. (1998). *Qualitative inquiry and research design: Choosing among five traditions.* Thousand Oaks, CA: Sage.

Creswell, J. W. (2003). *Research design: Qualitative, quantitative, and mixed methods approaches* (2nd ed.). Thousand Oaks, CA: Sage.

Crites, S. (1986). Storytime: Recollecting the past and projecting the future. In T. R. Sarbin (Ed.), *Narrative psychology: The storied nature of human conduct* (pp. 152–173). New York: Praeger.

Crivos, M. (2002). Narrative and experience: Illness in the context of an ethnographic interview. *Oral History Review, 29*(2), 13–15.

Czaja, R., & Blair, J. (2005). *Designing surveys: A guide to decisions and procedures* (2nd ed.). Thousand Oaks, CA: Pine Forge.

Daniels, D. H., Beaumont, L. J., & Doolin, C. A. (2002). *Understanding children: An interview and observation guide for educators.* Boston: McGraw-Hill Higher Education.

Davis, A., Gardner, B. B., & Gardner, M. R. (1941). *Deep South: A social anthropological study of caste and class.* Chicago: University of Chicago Press.

Delamont, S. (1992). *Fieldwork in educational settings: Methods, pitfalls and perspectives.* London: Falmer

Delamont, S. (2001). *Fieldwork in educational settings: Methods, pitfalls, and perspectives* (2nd ed.). London: RoutledgeFalmer.

deMarrais, K. B. (Ed.) (1998). *Inside stories: Qualitative research reflections.* Mahwah, NJ: Lawrence Erlbaum.

Denzin, N. K. (1970). *The research act: A theoretical introduction to sociological methods.* New York: McGraw-Hill.

Denzin, N. K. (1989). *The research act: A theoretical introduction to sociological methods* (3rd ed.). Englewood Cliffs, NJ: Prentice Hall.

Denzin, N. K. (1997). *Interpretive ethnography: Ethnographic practices for the 21st century.* Thousand Oaks, CA: Sage.

Denzin, N. K. (2005). Indians in the park. *Qualitative Inquiry, 5*(1), 9–33.

Denzin, N. K., & Lincoln, Y. S. (Eds.). (1994). *Handbook of qualitative research.* Thousand Oaks, CA: Sage.

Denzin, N. K., & Lincoln, Y. S. (Eds.). (2000). *Handbook of qualitative research* (2nd ed.). Thousand Oaks, CA: Sage.

Denzin, N. K., & Lincoln, Y. S. (Eds.). (2005). *The SAGE handbook of qualitative research* (3rd ed.). Thousand Oaks, CA: Sage.

DeWalt, K. M., & DeWalt, B. R. (2001). *Participant observation: A guide for fieldworkers.* Walnut Creek, CA: AltaMira Press.

Dewing, J. (2002). From ritual to relationship: A person-centered approach to consent in qualitative research with older people who have dementia. *Dementia, 1*(2), 157–171.

Dilevko, J. (2000). *Unobtrusive evaluation of reference service and individual responsibility: The Canadian experience.* Westport, CT: Ablex.

Dobbert, M. L. (1982). *Ethnographic research: Theory and application for modern schools and societies.* New York: Praeger.

Dollard, J. (1935). *Criteria for the life history.* New Haven, CT: Yale University Press.

Doppler, J. (1998). *The costs and benefits of gay-straight alliances in high schools.* Unpublished doctoral dissertation proposal. University of Massachusetts Amherst.

Douglas, J. D. (1976). *Investigative social research: Individual and team field research.* Beverly Hills, CA: Sage.

Edgerton, R. B. (1979). *Alone together: Social order on an urban beach.* Berkeley: University of California Press.

Edgerton, R. B. (1973). Method in psychological anthropology. In R. Naroll & R. Cohen (Eds.), *A handbook of method in cultural anthropology* (2nd ed., pp. 338–353). New York: Columbia University Press.

Edgerton, R. B., & Langness, L. L. (1974). *Methods and styles in the study of culture.* San Francisco: Chandler & Sharp.

Edmondson, R. (2005). Wisdom in later life: Ethnographic approaches. *Ageing and Society, 25*(3), 339–356.

Edson, C. H. (1998). Our past and present: Historical inquiry in education. In R. R. Sherman & R. B. Webb (Eds.), *Qualitative research in education: Focus and methods* (pp. 44–57). New York: Falmer.

Eek, D. (n.d.). *To work or not to work? A social dilemma analysis of health insurance.* Retrieved June 29, 2005, from http://www.psy.gu.se/download/gpr983.pdf

Eisner, E. W. (1988). The primacy of experience and the politics of method. *Educational Researcher, 20,* 15–20.

Eisner, E. W. (1991). *The enlightened eye: Qualitative inquiry and the enhancement of educational practice.* New York: Macmillan.

Elliott, J. (2005). *Using narrative in social research—Qualitative and quantitative approaches.* Thousand Oaks, CA: Sage.

Ellis, C., & Bochner, A. P. (2000). Autoethnography, personal narrative, reflexivity. In N. K. Denzin & Y. S. Lincoln (Eds.), *Handbook of qualitative research* (2nd ed., pp. 733–768). Thousand Oaks, CA: Sage.

Ellis, C., & Bochner, A. P. (Eds.). (1996). *Composing ethnography: Alternative forms of qualitative writing.* Walnut Creek, CA: AltaMira.

Emerson, R. M., Fretz, R. I., & Shaw, L. L. (1995). *Writing ethnographic fieldnotes.* Chicago: University of Chicago Press.

Esposito, N. (2001). From meaning to meaning: The influence of translation techniques on non-English focus group research. *Qualitative Health Research, 11*(4), 568–579.

Etter-Lewis, G., & Foster, M. (1996). *Unrelated kin: Race and gender in women's personal narratives.* New York: Routledge.

Everhart, R. B. (2005). Toward a critical social narrative of education. In W. T. Pink & G. W. Noblit (Series Eds.) & G. W. Noblit, S. Y. Flores & E. G. Murillo, Jr. (Book Eds.), *Understanding education and policy: Postcritical ethnography.* Cresskill, NJ: Hampton Press.

Faller, K. C. (2003). Research and practice in child interviewing. *Journal of Interpersonal Violence, 18*(4), 377–389.

Fals-Borda, O., & Rahman, M. A. (1991). *Action and knowledge: Breaking the monopoly with participatory action-research.* New York: Apex Press.

Fan Yihong. (2000). *Educating to liberate: Cross-boundary journeys of educators toward integration and innovation.* Unpublished doctoral dissertation proposal, University of Massachusetts Amherst.

Feldman, M. S., Bell, J., & Berger, M. T. (Eds.). (2003). *Gaining access: A practical and theoretical guide for qualitative researchers.* Walnut Creek, CA: AltaMira Press.

Fine, G. A., & Sandstrom, K. L. (1988). *Knowing children: Participant observation with minors.* Newbury Park, CA: Sage.

Flanders, N. A. (1970). *Analyzing teaching behavior.* Reading, MA: Addison-Wesley.

Flinders, D. J. (2003). Qualitative research in the foreseeable future: No study left behind? *Journal of Curriculum and Supervision, 18*(4), 380–390.

Fraser, N. (1997). *Justice interruptus: Critical reflections on the "postsocialist" condition.* New York: Routledge & Kegan Paul.

Freedman, J. (1975). *Crowding and behavior.* New York: Viking.

Freiberg, H. J. (1981). Three decades of the Flanders Interaction Analysis System. *Journal of Classroom Interaction, 16*(2), 1–7.

Friere, P. (1970). *Pedagogy of the oppressed*. New York: Seabury.

Frow, J., & Morris, M. (2000). Cultural studies. In N. K. Denzin & Y. S. Lincoln (Eds.), *Handbook of qualitative research* (2nd ed., pp. 315–346). Thousand Oaks, CA: Sage.

Gall, M. D., Borg, W. R., & Gall, J. P. (1996). *Educational research: An introduction* (6th ed.). White Plains, NY: Longman.

Gardner, R. (1974). *Rivers of sand* [Motion picture]. New York: Phoenix Films.

Gee, J. P. (1999). *An introduction to discourse analysis: Theory and method*. London: Routledge.

Geer, B. (1969). First days in the field. In G. McCall & J. L. Simmons (Eds.), *Issues in participant observation* (pp. 144–162). Reading, MA: Addison-Wesley.

Geertz, C. (1973). Thick description: Toward an interpretive theory of culture. In C. Geertz (Ed.), *The interpretation of culture: Selected essays* (pp. 3–30). New York: Basic Books.

Gerstl-Pepin, C. I. (1998). *Cultivating democratic educational reform: A critical examination of the A+ schools program*. Unpublished doctoral dissertation, University of North Carolina at Chapel Hill.

Gilligan, C. (1982). *In a different voice: Psychological theory and women's development*. Cambridge, MA: Harvard University Press.

Gitlin, A. (Ed.). (1994). *Power and method: Political activism and educational research*. New York: Routledge.

Glaser, B., & Strauss, A. (1967). *The discovery of grounded theory*. Chicago: Aldine.

Glazier, J. A. (2004). Collaborating with the "other": Arab and Jewish teachers teaching in each other's company. *Teachers College Record, 106*(3), 611–633.

Glesne, C. (1999). *Becoming qualitative researchers: An introduction* (2nd ed.). New York: Longman.

Gluck, S. B., & Patai, P. (Eds.). (1991). *Women's words: The feminist practice of oral history*. New York: Routledge.

Goldman, R., Hunt, M. K., Allen, J. D., Hauser, S., Emmons, K., Maeda, M., et al. (2003). The life history interview method: Applications to intervention development. *Health Education & Behavior, 30*, 564–581.

Goode, W. J. (1960). A theory of role strain. *American Sociological Review, II*(1), 483–496.

Gottschalk, L. A. (1969). *Understanding history*. New York: Knopf.

Gough, S., & Scott, W. (2000). Exploring the purposes of qualitative data coding in educational enquiry: Insights from recent research. *Educational Studies, 26*, 339–354.

Greenwald, J. (1992). *Environmental attitudes: A structural development model*. Unpublished doctoral dissertation, University of Massachusetts Amherst.

Griffin, C. (1985). *Typical girls?* London: Routledge & Kegan Paul.

Groth-Marnat, G. (2003). *Handbook of psychology assessment* (4th ed.). Hoboken, NJ: John Wiley.

Grumet, M. R. (1988). *Bitter milk: Women and teaching.* Amherst: University of Massachusetts Press.

Guba, E. G. (1978). *Toward a methodology of naturalistic inquiry in educational evaluation* (Monograph 8). Los Angeles: UCLA Center for the Study of Evaluation.

Gubrium, J. F., & Holstein, J. A. (Eds). (2002). *Handbook of interview research.* Thousand Oaks, CA: Sage.

Guerrero, L. K., DeVito, J. A. & Hecht, M. L. (Eds.). (1999). *The nonverbal communication reader: Classic and contemporary readings* (2nd ed.). Prospect Heights, IL: Waveland.

Hall, E. T. (1966). *The hidden dimension.* Garden City, NY: Doubleday.

Hall, E. T., & Hall, M. R. (1977). Nonverbal communication for educators. *Theory Into Practice, 16,* 141–144.

Hammersley, M. (1990). *Reading ethnographic research: A critical guide.* London: Longman.

Harding, S. (Ed.). (1987). *Feminism and methodology.* Bloomington: Indiana University Press.

Harper, D. (1994). On the authority of the image. In N. K. Denzin & Y. S. Lincoln (Eds.), *Handbook of qualitative research* (pp. 403–412). Thousand Oaks, CA: Sage.

Harry, B., Sturges, K. M., & Klingner, J. K. (2005). Mapping the process: An exemplar of process and challenge in grounded theory analysis. *Educational Researcher, 34*(2), 3–13.

Hart, R. A. (1997). *Children's participation: The theory and practice of involving young citizens in community development and environmental care.* London: Earthscan.

Hatch, J. A., & Wisniewski, R. (Eds.). (1995). *Life history and narrative.* London: Falmer.

Hatch, J. A. & Wisniewski, R. (1995). Life history and narrative: Questions, issues, and exemplary works. In J. A. Hatch & R. Wisniewski (Eds.), *Life history and narrative* (Qualitative Studies Series, pp. 113–135). London: Falmer.

Heron, J. (1996). *Co-operative inquiry: Research into the human condition.* Thousand Oaks, CA: Sage.

Hertz, R., & Imber, J. B. (1995). *Studying elites using qualitative methods.* Thousand Oaks, CA: Sage.

Hewson, C., Yule, P., Laurent, D., & Vogel, C. (2003). *Internet research methods: A practical guide for the social and behavioural sciences.* Thousand Oaks, CA: Sage.

Hickey, S., & Mohan, G. (Eds.) (2004). *Participation: From tyranny to transformation?* London: Zed Books.

Hine, C. (2001). *Virtual ethnography.* Thousand Oaks, CA: Sage.

Hockings, P. (Ed.). (1995). *Principles of visual anthropology.* New York: Mouton de Gruyter.

Hodder, I. (2000). The interpretation of documents and material culture. In N. K. Denzin & Y. S. Lincoln (Eds.), *Handbook of qualitative research* (2nd ed., pp. 703–716). Thousand Oaks, CA: Sage.

Hoffman, B. (1972). *Albert Einstein: Creator and rebel.* New York: Viking.

Hollingshead, A. B. (1975). *Elmtown's youth and Elmtown revisited.* New York: John Wiley.

Hollingsworth, S. (Ed.). (1997). *International action research: A casebook for educational reform.* London: Falmer.

Holman Jones, S. (2005). Autoethnography: Making the personal political. In N. K. Denzin & Y. S. Lincoln (Eds.), *The SAGE handbook of qualitative research* (3rd ed., pp. 763–791). Thousand Oaks, CA: Sage.

Holmes, R. M. (1998). *Fieldwork with children.* Thousand Oaks, CA: Sage.

Holstein, J. A., & Gubrium, J. F. (1995). *The active interview.* Thousand Oaks, CA: Sage.

Holstein, J. A., & Gubrium, J. F. (1997). Active interviewing. In D. Silverman (Ed.), *Qualitative research: Theory, method, and practice* (pp. 113–129). London: Sage.

Home Box Office Project Knowledge. (1992). *Educating Peter* [Motion picture]. New York: Ambrose Video Publishing (Distributors).

Hood, Jr., R. W. (2000). A phenomenological analysis of the anointing among religious serpent handlers. *International Journal for the Psychology of Religion, 10*(4), 221–240.

hooks, b. (1994). *Teaching to transgress.* New York: Routledge.

Jackson, B. (1978). Killing time: Life in the Arkansas penitentiary. *Qualitative Sociology, 1,* 21–32.

Jacob, E. (1987). Qualitative research traditions: A review. *Review of Educational Research, 51,* 1–50.

Jacob, E. (1988). Clarifying qualitative research: A focus on traditions. *Educational Researcher, 17,* 16–24.

Janesick, V. J. (1994). The dance of qualitative research design. In N. K. Denzin & Y. S. Lincoln (Eds.), *Handbook of qualitative research* (pp. 209–219). Thousand Oaks, CA: Sage.

Jensen, B. (2004). The case for non-intrusive research: A virtual reference librarian's perspective. *Reference Librarian, 85,* 139–149.

Jick, T. D. (1979). Mixing qualitative and quantitative methods: Triangulation in action. *Administrative Science Quarterly, 24,* 602–661.

Jones, D. M. (2004). *Collaborating with immigrant and refugee communities: Reflections of an outsider.* Unpublished doctoral dissertation, University of Massachusetts Amherst.

Jones, M. C. (1983). *Novelist as biographer: The truth of art, the lies of biography.* Unpublished doctoral dissertation, Northwestern University.

Jorgensen, D. L. (1989). *Participant observation: A methodology for human studies.* Newbury Park, CA: Sage.

Josselson, R. (Ed.). (1996). *Ethics and process in the narrative study of lives.* Thousand Oaks, CA: Sage.

Josselson, R., & Lieblich, A. (Eds.). (1993). *The narrative study of lives.* Newbury Park, CA: Sage.

Kahn, A. (1992). *Therapist initiated termination to psychotherapy: The experience of clients.* Unpublished doctoral dissertation, University of Massachusetts Amherst.

Kahn, R., & Cannell, C. (1957). *The dynamics of interviewing.* New York: John Wiley.

Kalnins, Z. G. (1986). *An exploratory study of the meaning of life as described by residents of a long-term care facility.* Project proposal, Peabody College of Vanderbilt University, Nashville, TN.

Kanter, R. (1977). *Men and women of the corporation.* New York: Basic Books.

Kanuha, V. K. (2000). "Being native" versus "going native": Conducting social work research as an insider. *Social Work, 45*(5), 339–447.

Kaplan, A. (1964). *The conduct of inquiry.* San Francisco: Chandler.

Katz, J. (2001). Analytic induction revisited. In R. M. Emerson (Ed.), *Contemporary field research* (2nd ed., pp. 331–334). Prospect Heights, IL: Waveland.

Keddie, N. (1971). Classroom knowledge. In M. F. D. Young (Ed.), *Knowledge and control* (pp. 133–160). London: Collier-Macmillan.

Kelle, E. (Ed.). (1995). *Computer-aided qualitative data analysis.* Thousand Oaks, CA: Sage.

Kelly, D., & Gaskell, J. (Eds.). (1996). *Debating dropouts: Critical policy and research perspectives.* New York: Teachers College Press.

Kemmis, S., & McTaggart, R. (Eds.). (1982). *The action research reader.* Geelong, Victoria, Australia: Deakin University Press.

Kemmis, S., & McTaggart, R. (2005). Participatory action research: Communicative action and the public sphere. In N. K. Denzin & Y. S. Lincoln (Eds.), *The SAGE handbook of qualitative research* (3rd ed., pp. 559–603). Thousand Oaks: CA: Sage.

Kendall, L. (2002). *Hanging out in the virtual pub: Masculinities and relationships online.* Berkeley: University of California Press.

Kennedy, M. M. (1979). Generalizing from single case studies. *Evaluation Quarterly, 12,* 661–678.

Kerig, P. K., & Baucom, D. H. (Eds.). (2004). *Couple observational coding systems.* Mahwah, NJ: Lawrence Erlbaum.

Kiegelmann, M. (1997). *Coming to terms: A qualitative study of six women's experiences of breaking the silence about brother-sister incest.* Ann Arbor: University of Michigan Press.

Kincheloe, J. L. (1991). *Teachers as researchers: Qualitative inquiry as a path to empowerment.* London: Falmer.

Knight, P. T. (2002). *Small-scale research: Pragmatic inquiry in social science and the caring professions.* Thousand Oaks, CA: Sage.

Kopal, M., & Suzuki, L.A. (Eds.). (1999). *Using qualitative methods in psychology.* Thousand Oaks, CA: Sage.

Kortesluoma, R. L., Hentinen, M., & Nikkonen, M. (2003). Conducting a qualitative child interview: Methodological considerations. *Journal of Advanced Nursing, 42*(5), 434–441.

Koski, K. (1997). *Interviewing.* Unpublished manuscript, University of Massachusetts Amherst.

Krieger, S. (1985). Beyond subjectivity: The use of self in social science. *Qualitative Sociology, 8,* 309–324.

Krippendorf, K. (2004). *Content analysis: An introduction to its methodology* (2nd ed). Thousand Oaks, CA: Sage.

Krueger, R. A. (1988). *Focus groups: A practical guide for applied research.* Newbury Park, CA: Sage.

Krueger, R. A., & Casey, M. A. (2000). *Focus groups: A practical guide for applied research* (3rd ed.). Thousand Oaks, CA: Sage.

Kvale, S. (1996). *InterViews: An introduction to qualitative research interviewing.* Thousand Oaks, CA: Sage.

Kwon, T. H., & Zmud, R. W. (1987). Unifying the fragmented models of information systems implementation. In R. J. Boland & R. Hirschheim (Eds.), *Critical issues in information systems research* (pp. 227–262). New York: John Wiley.

Lackey, N. R., Gates, M. F., & Brown, G. (2001). African American women's experiences with the initial discovery, diagnosis, and treatment of breast cancer. *Oncology Nursing Forum, 28*(3), 519–517.

Ladson-Billings, G. (1990). Like lightning in a bottle: Attempting to capture the pedagogical excellence of successful teachers of black students. *Qualitative Studies in Education, 3*(4), 335–344.

Ladson-Billings, G. (1995). Toward a theory of culturally relevant pedagogy. *American Educational Research Journal, 32*(3), 465–491.

Ladson-Billings, G. (2000). Racialized discourses and ethnic epistemologies. In N. K. Denzin & Y. S. Lincoln (Eds.), *Handbook of qualitative research* (2nd ed., pp. 257–277). Thousand Oaks, CA: Sage.

Ladson-Billings, G., & Donnor, J. (2005). The moral activist role of critical race theory scholarship. In N. K. Denzin & Y. S. Lincoln (Eds.), *The SAGE handbook of qualitative research* (3rd ed., pp. 279–301). Thousand Oaks, CA; Sage.

Lareau, A. (1989). *Home advantage: Social class and parental intervention in elementary education.* New York: Falmer.

Lather, P. (1991). *Getting smart: Feminist research and pedagogy with/in the postmodern.* London: Routledge & Kegan Paul.

Lather, P., & Smithies, C. (1997). *Troubling the angels: Women living with HIV/AIDS.* Boulder, CO: Westview.

Laverack, G. R., & Brown, K. M. (2003). Qualitative research in a cross-cultural context: Fijian experiences. *Qualitative Health Research, 13,* 333–342.

Lawless, E. J. (1991). Methodology and research notes: Women's life stories and reciprocal ethnography as feminist and emergent. *Journal of Folklore Research, 28,* 35–60.

LeCompte, M. D. (1993). A framework for hearing silence: What does telling stories mean when we are supposed to be doing science? In D. McLaughlin & W. G. Tierney (Eds.), *Naming silenced lives: Personal narratives and processes of educational change.* New York: Routledge & Kegan Paul.

Lee, R. M. (1995). *Dangerous fieldwork.* Thousand Oaks, CA: Sage.

Lee, R. M. (2000). *Unobtrusive methods in social research.* Philadelphia: Open University.

Leedy, P. D. (Ed.). (1997). *Practical research: Planning and design* (6th ed.). Upper Saddle River, NJ: Merrill.

Lees, S. (1986). *Losing out.* London: Hutchinson.

Lerum, K. (2001). Subjects of desire: Academic armor, intimate ethnography, and the production of critical knowledge. *Qualitative Inquiry, 7,* 466–483.

Lewis, A., & Porter, J. (2004). Interviewing children and young people with learning disabilities. *British Journal of Learning Disabilities, 32*(4), 191–197.

Libby, W. (1922). The scientific imagination. *Scientific Monthly, 15,* 263–270.

Lieblich, A., Tuval-Mashiach, R., & Zilber, T. (1998). *Narrative research: Reading, analysis, and interpretation.* Thousand Oaks, CA: Sage.

Lincoln, Y. S. (2005). Institutional Review Boards and methodological conservatism: The challenge to and from phenomenological paradigms. In N. K. Denzin & Y. S. Lincoln (Eds.), *Handbook of qualitative research* (3rd ed., pp. 165–181). Thousand Oaks, CA: Sage.

Lincoln, Y., & Guba, E. (1985). *Naturalistic inquiry.* Beverly Hills, CA: Sage.

Lincoln, Y. S. & Guba, E. G. (2000). Paradigmatic controversies, contradictions, and emerging confluences. In N. K Denzin & Y. S. Lincoln (Eds.), *The SAGE handbook of qualitative research* (2nd ed., pp. 163–188). Thousand Oaks, CA: Sage.

Lincoln, Y. S. & Tierney, W. G. (2004). Qualitative research and institutional review boards. *Qualitative Inquiry, 10*(2), 219–234.

Linhorst, D. M. (2002). A review of the use and potential of focus groups in social work research. *Qualitative Social Work, 1*(2), 208–228.

Locke, L. F., Spirduso, W. W., & Silverman, S. J. (2000). *Proposals that work: A guide for planning dissertations and grant proposals* (4th ed.). Thousand Oaks, CA: Sage.

Lofland, J., & Lofland, L. H. (1995). *Analyzing social settings: A guide to qualitative observation and analysis* (3rd ed.). Belmont, CA: Wadsworth.

Lutz, F., & Iannaccone, L. (1969). *Understanding educational organizations: A field study approach.* Columbus, OH: Charles Merrill.

MacJessie-Mbewe, S. (2004). *Analysis of a complex policy domain: Access to secondary education in Malawi.* Unpublished doctoral dissertation, University of Massachusetts Amherst.

Madison, D. S. (2005). *Critical ethnography: Method, ethics, and performance.* Thousand Oaks, CA: Sage.

Maguire, P. (2000). *Doing participatory research: A feminist approach.* Amherst, MA: Center for International Education.

Mandelbaum, D. G. (1973). The study of life history: Gandhi. *Current Anthropology, 14,* 177–207.

Mann, C., & Stewart, F. (2000). *Internet communication and qualitative research: A handbook for researching online.* London: Sage.

Manning, P. K. (1972). Observing the police: Deviants, respectables, and the law. In J. Douglas (Ed.), *Research on deviance* (pp. 213–268). New York: Random House.

Marcus, G., & Fischer, M. (1986). *Anthropology as cultural critique: An experimental moment in the human sciences.* Chicago: University of Chicago Press.

Markham, A. N. (2004). Internet communication as a tool for qualitative research. In D. Silverman (Ed.), *Qualitative research: Theory, method, and practice* (pp. 95–124). Thousand Oaks, CA: Sage.

Markham, A. N. (2005). The methods, politics, and ethics of representation in online ethnography. In N. K. Denzin & Y. S. Lincoln (Eds.), *Handbook of qualitative research* (3rd ed., pp. 793–820). Thousand Oaks, CA: Sage.

Marshall, C. (1979). *Career socialization of women in school administration.* Unpublished doctoral dissertation, University of California at Santa Barbara.

Marshall, C. (1981). Organizational policy and women's socialization in administration. *Urban Education, 16,* 205–231.

Marshall, C. (1984). Elite, bureaucrats, ostriches, and pussycats: Managing research in policy settings. *Anthropology and Education Quarterly, 15,* 235–251.

Marshall, C. (1985a). Appropriate criteria of trustworthiness and goodness for qualitative research on education organizations. *Quality and Quantity, 19,* 353–373.

Marshall, C. (1985b). The stigmatized woman: The professional woman in a male sex-typed career. *Journal of Educational Administration, 23,* 131–152.

Marshall, C. (1987). *Report to the Vanderbilt Policy Education Committee.* Vanderbilt University, Nashville, TN.

Marshall, C. (1990). Goodness criteria: Are they objective or judgment calls? In E. Guba (Ed.), *The paradigm dialog* (pp. 188–197). Newbury Park, CA: Sage.

Marshall, C. (1991). Educational policy dilemmas: Can we have control and quality and choice and democracy and equity? In K. M. Borman, P. Swami, & L. D. Wagstaff (Eds), *Contemporary issues in U.S. education* (pp. 1–21). Norwood, NJ: Ablex.

Marshall, C. (1992). School administrators' values: A focus on atypicals. *Educational Administration Quarterly, 28,* 368–386.

Marshall, C. (1993). *The unsung role of the career assistant principal* [Monograph]. Reston, VA: National Association of Secondary School Principals.

Marshall, C. (1997a). Dismantling and reconstructing policy analysis. In C. Marshall (Ed.), *Feminist critical policy analysis: A perspective from primary and secondary schooling* (Vol. 1, pp. 1–34). London: Falmer.

Marshall, C. (Ed.). (1997b). *Feminist critical policy analysis: A perspective from primary and secondary schooling.* London: Falmer.

Marshall, C., Mitchell, D., & Wirt, F. (1985). Assumptive worlds of education policy makers. *Peabody Journal of Education, 62*(4), 90–115.

Marshall, C., Mitchell, D., & Wirt, F. (1986). The context of state level policy formulation. *Educational Evaluation and Policy Analysis, 8,* 347–378.

Marshall, C., Patterson, J., Rogers, D., & Steele, J. (1996). Caring as career: An alternative model for educational administration. *Educational Administration Quarterly, 32,* 271–294.

Martin, R. R. (1995). *Oral history in social work: Research, assessment, and intervention.* Thousand Oaks, CA: Sage.

Matsuda, M. J., Delgado, R., Lawrence, C. R., & Crenshaw, K. W. (1993). *Words that wound: Critical race theory, assault speech, and the First Amendment.* Boulder, CO: Westview.

Maxwell, J. A. (1996). *Qualitative research design: An interactive approach.* Thousand Oaks, CA: Sage.

Maxwell, J. A. (2005). *Qualitative research design: An interactive approach* (2nd ed.). Thousand Oaks, CA: Sage.

Maynard-Tucker, G. (2000). Conducting focus groups in developing countries: Skill training for local bilingual facilitators. *Qualitative Health Research, 10*(3), 396–410.

McCall, M. M. (2000). Performance ethnography: A brief history and some advice. In N. K. Denzin & Y. S. Lincoln (Eds.), *Handbook of qualitative research* (2nd ed., pp. 421–433). Thousand Oaks, CA: Sage.

McCracken, G. (1988). *The long interview.* Newbury Park, CA: Sage.

McCrea, H. (1993). Valuing the midwife's role in the midwife/client relationship. *Journal of Clinical Nursing, 2*(1), 47–52.

McKernan, J. (1991). *Curriculum action research: A handbook of methods and resources for the reflective practitioner.* London: Routledge & Kegan Paul.

McLarty, M. M., & Gibson, J. W. (2000). Using video technology in emancipatory research. *European Journal of Special Needs Education, 15*(2), 138–139.

McNiff, J., & Whitehead, J. (2003). *Action research: Principles and practice.* London: Routledge.

McTaggart, R. (Ed.). (1997). *Participatory action research: International contexts and consequences.* Albany: State University of New York Press.

Meloy, J. M. (1994). *Writing the qualitative dissertation: Understanding by doing.* Hillsdale, NJ: Lawrence Erlbaum.

Mental measurements yearbook. (1992). Lincoln: Buros Institute of Mental Measurements of the University of Nebraska-Lincoln.

Merriam, S. B. (1998). *Qualitative research and case study applications in education.* San Francisco: Jossey-Bass.

Mertens, D. M. (2005). *Research and evaluation in education and psychology: Integrating diversity with quantitative, qualitative, and mixed methods.* Thousand Oaks, CA: Sage.

Meyer, A. D., & Goes, J. B. (1988). Organizational assimilation of innovations: A multilevel contextual analysis. *Academy of Management Journal, 31,* 897–923.

Meyer, J. W., & Rowan, B. (1992). Institutionalized organizations: Formal structure as myth and ceremony. In J. W. Meyer & W. R. Scott (Eds.), *Organizational environments: Ritual and rationality* (Updated ed., pp. 21–44). Newbury Park, CA: Sage.

Meyer, J. W., Scott, R. W., & Deal, T. W. (1992). Institutional and technical sources of organizational structure: Explaining the structure of educational organizations. In J. W. Meyer & W. R. Scott (Eds.), *Organizational environments: Ritual and rationality* (Updated ed., pp. 45–67). Newbury Park, CA: Sage.

Michell, J. (2003). The quantitative imperative: Positivism, naïve realism and the place of qualitative methods in psychology. *Theory & Psychology, 13,* 5–31.

Miles, M. B. (1979). Qualitative data as an attractive nuisance: The problem of analysis. *Administrative Science Quarterly, 24,* 590–601.

Miles, M. B., & Huberman, A. M. (1994). *Qualitative data analysis: An expanded sourcebook* (2nd ed.). Thousand Oaks, CA: Sage.

Miller, D., & Slater, D. (2000). *The Internet: An ethnographic approach.* Oxford, UK: Berg.

Miller, J. L. (1990). *Creating spaces and finding voices: Teachers collaborating for empowerment.* Albany: State University of New York Press.

Miller, R. L. (1999). *Researching life stories and family histories.* Thousand Oaks, CA: Sage.

Mills, G. E. (1993). Levels of abstraction in a case study of educational change. In D. J. Flinders & G. E. Mills (Eds.), *Theory and concepts in qualitative research: Perspectives from the field* (pp. 103–116). New York: Teachers College Press.

Mishna, F. (2004). A qualitative study of bullying from multiple perspectives. *Children & Schools, 26*(4), 234–247.

Mitchell, D., Wirt, F., & Marshall, C. (1986). *Alternative state policy mechanisms for pursuing educational quality, equity, efficiency, and choice* (Final report to the U.S. Department of Education, Grant No. NIE-G-83 0020). Washington, DC: U.S. Department of Education.

Mitchell, W. J. (Ed.). (1981). *On narrative.* Chicago: University of Chicago Press.

Montgomery, L. (2004). "It's just what I like": Explaining persistent patterns of gender stratification in the life choices of college students. *International Journal of Qualitative Studies in Education, 17*(6), 785–802.

Mooney, R. L. (1951). Problems in the development of research men. *Educational Research Bulletin, 30,* 141–150.

Morgan, D. L. (1997). *Focus groups as qualitative research* (2nd ed.). Thousand Oaks, CA: Sage.

Morrow, R. A., with Brown, D. D. (1994). *Critical theory and methodology.* Thousand Oaks, CA: Sage.

Morse, J. M. (1994). *Designing funded qualitative research.* In N. K. Denzin & Y. S. Lincoln (Eds.), *Handbook of qualitative research* (pp. 220–235). Thousand Oaks, CA: Sage.

Morse, J. M. (2003). A review committee's guide for evaluating qualitative proposals. *Qualitative Health Research, 13,* 833–851.

Morse, J. M. (2004). Using the right tool for the job [Editorial]. *Qualitative Health Research, 14,* 1029–1031.

Morse, J. M., & Richards, L. (2002). *Read me first for a user's guide to qualitative methods.* Thousand Oaks, CA: Sage.

Moss, G., & McDonald, J. W. (2004). The borrowers: Library records as unobtrusive measures of children's readings preferences. *Journal of Research in Readings, 27*(4), 401–412.

Mouffe, C., & LeClau, E. (1985). *Hegemony and socialist strategy: Towards a radical democratic politics.* New York: Verso.

Narayan, K. (1993) How native is a "native" anthropologist? *American Anthropologist, 95*(3), New Series, 671–686.

National Research Council. (2002). *Scientific research in education. Committee on Scientific Principles for Education Research* (R. J. Shavelson & L. Towne, Eds.). Center for Education, Division of Behavioral and Social Sciences and Education. Washington, DC: National Academy Press.

Nielson, J. (Ed.). (1990). *Feminist research methods: Exemplary readings in the social sciences.* Boulder, CO: Westview.

Noblit, G. W., Flores, S. Y., & Murillo, E. G., Jr. (Eds.). (2005). *Postcritical ethnography: Reinscribing critique.* Cresskill, NJ: Hampton Press.

Nordstrom, C., & Robben, A. (1995). *Fieldwork under fire: Contemporary studies of violence and survival.* Berkeley: University of California Press.

Noyes, A. (2004). Video diary: A method for exploring learning dispositions. *Cambridge Journal of Education, 34*(2), 193–209.

O'Hearn-Curran, M. (1997). *First days in the field: Lessons I learned in kindergarten.* Unpublished manuscript, University of Massachusetts Amherst.

O'Neill, J., Small, B. B., & Strachan, J. (1999). The use of focus groups within a participatory action research environment. In M. Kopala & L. A. Suzuki (Eds.), *Using qualitative methods in psychology* (pp. 199–209). Thousand Oaks, CA: Sage.

Odendahl, T., & Shaw, A. M. (2002). Interviewing elites. In J. F Gubrium & J. A. Holstein (Eds.), *Handbook of interview research* (pp. 299–316). Thousand Oaks, CA: Sage.

Olesen, V. L., & Whittaker, E. W. (1968). *The silent dialogue: A study in social psychology of professional socialization.* San Francisco: Jossey-Bass.

Page, S. (2000). Community research: The lost art of unobtrusive methods. *Journal of Applied Social Psychology, 30*(10), 2126–2136.

Park, P., Brydon-Miller, M., Hall, B., & Jackson, T. (Eds.). (1993). *Voices of change: Participatory research in the United States and Canada.* Ontario, Canada: Ontario Institute for Studies in Education Press.

Patton, M. Q. (1990). *Qualitative research and evaluation methods* (2nd ed.). Thousand Oaks, CA: Sage.

Patton, M. Q. (2002). *Qualitative research and evaluation methods* (3rd ed.). Thousand Oaks, CA: Sage.

Peace, S. D., & Sprinthall, N. A. (1998). Training school counselors to supervise beginning counselors: Theory, research, and practice. *Professional School Counseling, 1*(5), 2–9.

Pelto, P., & Pelto, G. H. (1978). *Anthropological research: The structure of inquiry* (2nd ed.). New York: Cambridge University Press.

Pepler, D. J., & Craig, W. M. (1995). A peek behind the fence: Naturalistic observations of aggressive children with remote audiovisual recording. *Developmental Psychology, 31*(4), 548–553.

Phaik-Lah, K. (1997). The environments of action research in Malaysia. In S. Hollingsworth (Ed.), *International action research: A casebook for educational reform* (pp. 238–243). London: Falmer.

Piantanida, M., & Garman, N. B. (1999). *The qualitative dissertation: A guide for students and faculty.* Thousand Oaks, CA: Corwin Press.

Pink, S. (2001). More visualizing, more methodologies: On video, reflexivity and qualitative research. *Sociological Review, 49*(4), 586–599.

Piotrkowski, C. S. (1979). *Work and the family system: A naturalistic study of working-class and lower-middle-class families.* New York: Free Press.

Platt, J. (1981). On interviewing one's peers. *British Journal of Sociology, 32,* 75–85.

Polsky, N. (1969). *Hustlers, beats, and others.* Garden City, NY: Doubleday Anchor.

Powdermaker, H. (1966). *Stranger and friend.* New York: Norton.

Prosser, J. (1998). *Image-based research: A sourcebook for qualitative researchers.* London: Falmer.

Punch, M. (1994). Politics and ethics in qualitative research. In N. K. Denzin & Y. S. Lincoln (Eds.), *Handbook of qualitative research* (pp. 83–97). Thousand Oaks, CA: Sage.

Qualis Research Associates. (1987). *The ethnograph* [Computer program]. Littleton, CO: Author.

Rager, K. B. (2005). Self-care and the qualitative researcher: When collecting data can break your heart. *Educational Researcher, 34*(4), 23–27.

Raingruber, B. (2003). Video-cued narrative reflection: A research approach for articulating tacit, relational and embodied understandings. *Qualitative Health Research, 13*(8), 1155–1169.

Rallis, S. F., & Goldring, E. B. (2000). *Principals of dynamic schools: Taking charge of change* (2nd ed.). Thousand Oaks, CA: Corwin.

Reardon, K., Welsh, B., Kreiswirth, B., & Forester, J. (1993). Participatory action research from the inside: Community development practice in East St. Louis. *American Sociologist, 24,* 69–91.

Reason, P. (Ed.). (1994). *Participation in human inquiry.* Thousand Oaks, CA: Sage.

Richards, L. (2005). *Handling qualitative data: A practical guide.* Thousand Oaks, CA: Sage.

Richards, T. J., & Richards, L. (1994). Using computers in qualitative research. In N. K. Denzin & Y. S. Lincoln (Eds.), *Handbook of qualitative research* (pp. 445–462). Thousand Oaks, CA: Sage.

Richardson, L. (1990). *Writing strategies: Reaching diverse audiences.* Newbury Park, CA: Sage.

Richardson, L. (1994). Writing: A method of inquiry. In N. K. Denzin & Y. S. Lincoln (Eds.), *Handbook of qualitative research* (pp. 516–529). Thousand Oaks, CA: Sage.

Richardson, L. (2000). Writing: A method of inquiry. In N. K. Denzin & Y. S. Lincoln (Eds.), *Handbook of qualitative research* (2nd ed., pp. 923–948). Thousand Oaks, CA: Sage.

Richardson, L., & St. Pierre, E. A. (2005). Writing: A method of inquiry. In N. K. Denzin & Y. S. Lincoln (Eds.), *The SAGE handbook of qualitative research* (3rd ed., pp. 959–978). Thousand Oaks, CA: Sage.

Riessman, C. K. (1993). *Narrative analysis.* Newbury Park, CA: Sage.

Riessman, C. K. (2002). Analysis of personal narratives. In J. F. Gubrium & J. A. Holstein (Eds.), *Handbook of interview research* (pp. 695–710). Thousand Oaks, CA: Sage.

Rizzuto, A. (1979). *The birth of a living God: A psychoanalytic study.* Chicago: University of Chicago Press.

Rodler, C., Kirchler, E., & Holzl, E. (2001). Gender stereotypes of leaders: An analysis of the contents of obituaries from 1974 to 1998. *Sex Roles,* 45(11/12), 827–844.

Rollwagen, J. (Ed.). (1988). *Anthropological filmmaking.* New York: Harwood Academic.

Rosenau, P. M. (1992). *Post-modernism and the social sciences: Insights, inroads, and intrusions.* Princeton, NJ: Princeton University Press.

Ross, M., & Conway, M. (1986). Remembering one's own past: The construction of personal histories. In R. Sorrentino & E. T. Higgins (Eds.), *Handbook of motivation and cognition: Foundations of social behavior* (pp. 122–144). New York: Guilford.

Rossman, G. B. (1984). I owe you one: Notes on role and reciprocity in a study of graduate education. *Anthropology and Education Quarterly, 15,* 225–234.

Rossman, G. B. (1994, November). *External evaluation report: Designing schools for enhanced learning.* Unpublished report. Andover, MA: Regional Laboratory for New England and the Islands.

Rossman, G. B., & Rallis, S. F. (1998). *Learning in the field: An introduction to qualitative research.* Thousand Oaks, CA: Sage.

Rossman, G. B., & Rallis, S. F. (2003). *Learning in the field: An introduction to qualitative research* (2nd ed.). Thousand Oaks, CA: Sage.

Rossman, G. B., & Wilson, B. L. (1994). Numbers and words revisited: Being shamelessly eclectic. *Quality and Quantity, 28,* 315–327.

Rossman, G. B., Corbett, H. D., & Firestone, W. A. (1984). *Plan for the study of professional cultures in improving high schools.* Philadelphia: Research for Better Schools.

Rubin, H. J., & Rubin, I. S. (2005). *Qualitative interviewing: The art of hearing data* (2nd ed.). Thousand Oaks, CA: Sage.

Rutter, D. R. (1984). *Aspects of nonverbal communication.* Amsterdam: Swets & Zeitlinger.

Ryan, G. W., & Bernard, H. R. (2000). Data management and analysis methods. In N. K. Denzin & Y. S. Lincoln (Eds.), *Handbook of qualitative research* (2nd ed., pp. 769–802). Thousand Oaks, CA: Sage.

Ryave, A. L., & Schenkein, J. N. (1974). Notes on the art of walking. In R. Turner (Ed.), *Ethnomethodology* (pp. 265–274). Baltimore: Penguin.

Safman, R. M., & Sobal, J. (2004). Qualitative sample extensiveness in health education research. *Health Education & Behavior, 31,* 9–21.

Sagor, R. (2005). *Action research handbook: A four-step process for educators and school teams.* Thousand Oaks, CA: Corwin.

Sampson, H. (2004). Navigating the waves: The usefulness of a pilot in qualitative research. *Qualitative Research, 4*(3), 383–402.

Sandelowski, M., & Barroso, J. (2003). Writing the proposal for a qualitative research methodology project. *Qualitative Health Research, 13,* 781–820.

Sanjek, R. (1990). On ethnographic validity. In R. Sanjek (Ed.), *Fieldnotes: The makings of anthropology* (pp. 385–418). Ithaca, NY: Cornell University Press.

Sarbin, T. R. (Ed.). (1986). *Narrative psychology: The storied nature of human conduct.* New York: Praeger.

Sariyant, T. P. (2002). *Knowing and understanding through auto/ethnography: Narrative on transformative learning experience of an international graduate student.* Unpublished doctoral dissertation, University of Massachusetts Amherst.

Schatzman, L., & Strauss, A. (1973). *Field research: Strategies for a natural sociology.* Englewood Cliffs, NJ: Prentice Hall.

Scherer, K. R., & Ekman, R. (Eds.). (1982). *Handbook of methods in nonverbal behavior research.* New York: Cambridge University Press.

Scheurich, J. (1997). *Research methods in the postmodern.* London: Falmer.

Schutt, R. K. (2001). *Investigating the social world: The process and practice of research.* Thousand Oaks, CA: Pine Forge.

Schwandt, T. A. (1996). Farewell to criteriology. *Qualitative Inquiry, 2,* 72.

Schwartz, H., & Jacobs, J. (1979). *Qualitative sociology: A method to the madness.* New York: Free Press.

Sechrest, L. (Ed.). (1979). *Unobtrusive measurement today.* San Francisco: Jossey-Bass.

Seidman, I. E. (1998). *Interviewing as qualitative research: A guide for researchers in education and the social sciences* (2nd ed.). New York: Teachers College Press.

Selener, D. (1997). *Participatory action research and social change.* Cornell, NY: Cornell Participatory Action Research Network.

Selwyn, N. (2002). Telling tales on technology: The ethical dilemmas of critically researching educational computing. In T. Welland & L. Pugsley (Eds.), *Ethical dilemmas in qualitative research* (pp. 42–56). Hants, England: Ashgate.

Senge, P. (1990). *The fifth discipline: The art and practice of the learning organization.* New York: Doubleday.

Seymour, W. S. (2001). In the flesh or online? Exploring qualitative research methodologies. *Qualitative Research, 1*(2), 147–168.

Sfard, A., & Prusak, A. (2005). Telling identities: In search of an analytic tool for investigating learning as a culturally shaped activity. *Educational Researcher, 34*(4), 14–22.

Shadduck-Hernandez, J. (1997). *Affirmation, advocacy, and action: Refugee/immigrant student education and community building in higher education.* Research proposal to the Spencer Foundation, University of Massachusetts Amherst.

Shadduck-Hernandez, J. (2005). *"Here I am Now!" Community service learning with immigrant and refugee undergraduates: The use of critical pedagogy, situated learning and funds of knowledge.* Unpublished doctoral dissertation, University of Massachusetts Amherst.

Sharp, R., & Green, A. (1975). *Education and social control.* London: Routledge & Kegan Paul.

Shaw, I. & Ruckdeschel, R. (2002). Qualitative social work: A room with a view. *Qualitative Social Work, 1,* 5–23.

Shaw, I. (2003). Qualitative research and outcomes in health, social work and education. *Qualitative Research, 3,* 57–77.

Shostak, M. (1983). *Nisa: The life and words of a !Kung woman.* New York: Random House.

Siegman, A. W., & Feldstein, S. (Eds.). (1987). *Nonverbal behavior and communication* (2nd ed.). Hillsdale, NJ: Lawrence Erlbaum.

Silverman, D. (1993). *Interpreting qualitative data: Methods for analysing talk, text and interaction.* London: Sage.

Silverman, D. (2000). Analyzing talk and text. In N. K. Denzin & Y. S. Lincoln (Eds.), *Handbook of qualitative research* (2nd ed., pp. 821–834). Thousand Oaks, CA: Sage.

Silverman, D. (2005). *Doing qualitative research* (2nd ed.). Thousand Oaks, CA: Sage.

Simpson, B. (2003). Sex, fear, and greed: A social dilemma analysis of gender and cooperation. *Social Forces, 82*(1), 35–52.

Sixsmith, J., & Murray, C. D. (2001). Ethical issues in the documentary data analysis of internet posts and archives. *Qualitative Health Research, 11*(3), 423–432.

Slim, H., & Thompson, P. (1995). *Listening for a change: Oral testimony and community development.* Philadelphia: New Society Publishers.

Smelser, N. J., & Erickson, E. H. (1980). *Themes of work and love in adulthood.* Cambridge, MA: Harvard University Press.

Smith, A. B., Taylor, N. J., & Gollop, M. M. (Eds.). (2000). *Children's voices: Research, policy and practice.* Auckland, NZ: Pearson Education.

Smith, C. D., & Kornblum, W. (Eds.). (1996). *In the field: Readings on the field research experience.* Westport, CT: Praeger.

Smith, C. S., & Faris, R. (2002). *Religion and the life attitudes and self-images of American adolescents.* Chapel Hill, NC: National Study of Youth and Religion.

Smith, J. K. (1988, March). *Looking for the easy way out: The desire for methodological constraints in openly ideological research.* Paper presented at the annual meeting of the American Educational Research Association, New Orleans.

Smith, J. K., & Deemer, D. K. (2000). The problem of criteria in the age of relativism. In N. K. Denzin & Y. S. Lincoln (Eds.), *Handbook of qualitative research* (2nd ed. pp. 877–896). Thousand Oaks, CA: Sage.

Smith, M. (1999). Researching social workers' experiences of fear: Piloting a course. *Social Work Education, 18*(3), 347–354.

Soloway, I., & Walters, J. (1977). Workin' the corner: The ethics and legality of ethnographic fieldwork among active heroin addicts. In R. S. Weppner (Ed.), *Street ethnography* (pp. 159–178). Beverly Hills, CA: Sage.

Sorenson, E. R. (1968). The retrieval of data from changing cultures. *Anthropological Quarterly, 41,* 177–186.

Sparks, A. (1994). Self, silence, and invisibility as a beginning teacher: A life history of lesbian experience. *British Journal of Sociology of Education, 15,* 92–118.

Spradley, J. P., & Mann, B. J. (1975). *The cocktail waitress—Woman's work in a man's world.* New York: John Wiley.

Spradley, J. S. (1979). *The ethnographic interview.* New York: Holt, Rinehart & Winston.

Spradley, J. S. (1980). *Participant observation*. New York: Holt, Rinehart & Winston.

Steedman, P. H. (1991). On the relations between seeing, interpreting and knowing. In S. Frederick (Ed.), *Research and reflexivity* (pp. 53–62). London: Sage.

Stewart, D. W., & Shamdasani, P. N. (1990). *Focus groups: Theory and practice*. Newbury Park, CA: Sage.

Storey, W. K. (2004). *Writing history: A guide for students*. New York: Oxford University Press.

Strauss, A., & Corbin, J. (1990). *Basics of qualitative research*. Newbury Park, CA: Sage.

Strauss, A., & Corbin, J. (Eds.). (1997). *Grounded theory in practice*. Thousand Oaks, CA: Sage.

Stringer, E. T. (1996). *Action research: A handbook for practitioners*. Thousand Oaks, CA: Sage.

Stringer, E. T. (1999). *Action research: A handbook for practitioners* (2nd ed.). Thousand Oaks, CA: Sage.

Stubbs, M. (1983). *Discourse analysis: The sociolinguistic analysis of natural language*. Oxford: Basil Blackwell.

Sutherland, E. H., & Conwell, C. (1983). *The professional thief*. Chicago: University of Chicago Press.

Szto, P., Furman, R., & Langer, C. (2005). Poetry and photography. *Qualitative Social Work, 4*, 135–156.

Tanaka, G. (1997). Pico College. In W. G. Tierney & Y. S. Lincoln (Eds.), *Representation and the text: Re-framing the narrative voice* (pp. 259–304). Albany: State University of New York Press.

Taylor, S. J., & Bogdan, R. (1984). *Introduction to qualitative research methods: The search for meanings* (2nd ed.). New York: John Wiley.

Temple, B., & Young, A. (2004). Qualitative research and translation dilemmas. *Qualitative Research, 4*(2), 161–178.

Tesch, R. (1990). *Qualitative research: Analysis types and software tools*. New York: Falmer.

Thomas, R. (1993). Interviewing important people in big companies. *Journal of Contemporary Ethnography, 22*(1), 80–96.

Thomas, W. I. (1949). *Social structure and social theory*. New York: Free Press.

Thompson, E. (Ed.). (1939). *Race relations and the race problem*. Durham, NC: Duke University Press.

Thompson, P. R. (2000). *The voice of the past: Oral history* (3rd ed.). Oxford, UK: Oxford University Press.

Thorne, B. (1983). Political activists as participant observer: Conflicts of commitment in a study of the draft resistance movement of the 1960s. In R. Emerson (Ed.), *Contemporary field research: A collection of readings* (pp. 216–234). Prospect Heights, IL: Waveland.

Thornton, S. J. (1993). The quest for emergent meaning: A personal account. In D. J. Flinders & G. E. Mills (Eds.), *Theory and concepts in qualitative research: Perspectives from the field* (pp. 68–82). New York: Teachers College Press.

Tierney, W. G., & Lincoln, Y. S. (Eds.). (1997). *Representation and the text: Re-framing the narrative voice.* Albany: State University of New York Press.

Tilley, S. A. (2003). "Challenging" research practices: Turning a critical lens on the work of transcription. *Qualitative Inquiry, 9*(5), 750–773.

Titchen, A., & Bennie, A. (1993). Action research as a research strategy: Finding our way through a philosophical and methodological maze. *Journal of Advanced Nursing, 18,* 858–865.

Toma, J. D. (2000). How getting close to your subjects makes qualitative data better. *Theory Into Practice, 39*(3), 177–184.

Tong, R. (1989). *Feminist thought: A comprehensive introduction.* San Francisco: Westview.

Tripp-Riemer, T., & Cohen, M. Z. (1991). Funding strategies for qualitative research. In J. M. Morse (Ed.), *Qualitative nursing research: A contemporary dialogue* (pp. 243–256). Newbury Park, CA: Sage.

Tsing, A. L. (1990). The vision of a woman shaman. In J. M. Nielsen (Ed.), *Feminist research methods* (pp. 147–173). San Francisco: Westview.

Tuchman, G. (1994). Historical social science. In N. K. Denzin & Y. S. Lincoln (Eds.), *Handbook of qualitative research* (pp. 306–323). Thousand Oaks, CA: Sage.

Tucker, B. J. (1996). *Teachers who make a difference: Voices of Mexican-American students.* Unpublished thesis proposal, Harvard University Graduate School of Education.

Turner, W. L., Wallace, B. R., Anderson, J. R., & Bird, C. (2004). The last mile of the way: Understanding caregiving in African American families at the end-of-life. *Journal of Marital & Family Therapy, 30*(4), 427–488.

Van Lange, P. A. M., Van Vugt, M., Meertens, R. M., & Ruiter, R. A. C. (1998). A social dilemma analysis of commuting preferences: The roles of social value orientation and trust. *Journal of Applied Social Psychology, 28*(9), 796–820.

Van Maanen, J. (1988). *Tales of the field: On writing ethnography.* Chicago: University of Chicago Press.

Van Maanen, J. (Ed.). (1995). *Representation in ethnography.* Thousand Oaks, CA: Sage.

Van Manen, M. (1990). *Researching lived experience: Human science for an action sensitive pedagogy.* Buffalo: State University of New York Press.

Van Vugt, M. (1997). Concerns about the privatization of public goods: A social dilemma analysis. *Social Psychology Quarterly, 60*(4), 355–367.

Villenas, S. (1996). Chicana ethnographer: Identity, marginalization, and co-optation in the field. *Harvard Educational Review, 66*(4), 711–731.

Viney, L. L., & Bousefield, L. (1991). Narrative analysis: A method of psychosocial research for AIDS-affected people. *Social Science and Medicine, 23,* 757–765.

Warren, C. A. B. (2001). Gender and fieldwork relations. In R. M. Emerson (Ed.), *Contemporary field research: Perspectives and formulations* (2nd ed., pp. 203–223), Prospect Heights, IL: Waveland.

Wax, R. (1971). *Doing fieldwork: Warnings and advice.* Chicago: University of Chicago Press.

Webb, E., Campbell, D. T., Schwartz, R. D., & Sechrest, L. (1966). *Unobtrusive measures: Nonreactive research in the social sciences.* Chicago: Rand McNally.

Webb, J., & Foddy, M. (2004). Vested interests in the decision to resolve social dilemma conflicts. *Small Group Research, 35*(6), 666–697.

Weick, K. E. (1976). Educational organizations as loosely coupled systems. *Administrative Science Quarterly, 21,* 1–19.

Weis, L. (1990). *Working class without work: High school students in a de-industrializing economy.* New York: Routledge.

Weis, L., & Fine, M. (2000). *Speed bumps: A student-friendly guide to qualitative research.* New York: Teachers College Press.

Weis, L., & Fine, M. (Eds.) (2000). *Construction sites: Excavating race, class, and gender among urban youth.* New York: Teachers College Press.

Weiss, R. S. (1994). *Learning from strangers: The art and method of qualitative interview studies.* New York: Free Press.

Weitzman, E. A. (2000). Software and qualitative research. In N. K. Denzin & Y. S. Lincoln (Eds.), *Handbook of qualitative research* (2nd ed., pp. 803–820). Thousand Oaks, CA: Sage.

Weitzman, E. A., & Miles, M. B. (1995). *Computer programs for qualitative data analysis.* Thousand Oaks, CA: Sage.

Wengraf, T. (2001). *Qualitative research interviewing: Biographic narrative and semi-structured methods.* London: Sage.

Weppner, R. S. (1977). *Street ethnography: Selected studies of crime and drug use in natural settings.* Beverly Hills, CA: Sage.

Westley, W. A. (1967). The police: Law, custom, and morality. In P. I. Rose (Ed.), *The study of society* (pp. 766–779). New York: Random House.

Whyte, W. F. (1980). *The social life of small urban spaces.* Washington, DC: Conservation Foundation.

Whyte, W. F. (1984). *Learning from the field: A guide from experience.* Beverly Hills, CA: Sage.

Whyte, W. F. (Ed.). (1991). *Participatory action research.* Newbury Park, CA: Sage.

Wilber, K. (1996). *Eye to eye: The quest for a new paradigm.* Berkeley: Shambhala.

Wilson, J. C., & Powell, M. (2001). *A guide to interviewing children: Essential skills for counsellors, police, lawyers and social workers.* New York: Routledge.

Wilson, S. (1977). The use of ethnographic techniques in educational research. *Review of Educational Research, 47,* 245–265.

Winter, R. (1982). Dilemma analysis: A contribution to methodology for action research. *Cambridge Journal of Education, 12,* 161–174.

Wiseman, F. (Director). (1969). *High school* [Motion picture]. Boston: Zippora Films.

Wolcott, H. F. (1973). *The man in the principal's office: An ethnography.* Walnut Creek, CA: AltaMira.

Wolcott, H. F. (1985). On ethnographic intent. *Educational Administration Quarterly, 3,* 187–203.

Wolcott, H. F. (1994). *Transforming qualitative data: Description, analysis, and inter-pretation*. Thousand Oaks, CA: Sage.

Wolcott, H. F. (2001). *Writing up qualitative research*. Thousand Oaks, CA: Sage.

Wolcott, H. F. (2002). *Sneaky kid and its aftermath: Ethics and intimacy in fieldwork*. Walnut Creek, CA: AltaMira.

Wolcott, H. F. (2005). *The art of fieldwork* (2nd ed.). Walnut Creek, CA: AltaMira.

Yablonsky, L. (1965). *The tunnel back: Synanon*. Baltimore: Penguin.

Yin, R. K. (1984). *Case study research: Design and methods*. Beverly Hills, CA: Sage.

Yin, R. K. (2003). *Case study research: Design and methods* (3rd ed.). Thousand Oaks, CA: Sage.

Young, M. F. D. (Ed.). (1971). *Knowledge and control*. London: Collier-Macmillan.

Yow, V. R. (1994). *Recording oral history: A practical guide for social scientists*. Thousand Oaks, CA: Sage.

Zelditch, M. (1962). Some methodological problems of field studies. *American Journal of Sociology, 67*, 566–576.

Ziller, R. C., & Lewis, D. (1981). Orientations: Self, social and environmental precepts through auto-photography. *Personality and Social Psychology Bulletin, 7*, 338–343.

Zinsser, W. (1990). *On writing well: An informal guide to writing nonfiction* (4th ed.). New York: Harper.

Zuckerman, H. (1972). Interviewing an ultra-elite. *Public Opinion Quarterly, 36*(5), 159–175.

Index

About the Authors

Catherine Marshall is Professor in the Department of Educational Leadership at the University of North Carolina at Chapel Hill and previously taught at the University of Pennsylvania and Vanderbilt University. She has published extensively about the politics of education, qualitative methodology, women's access to careers, and the socialization, language, and values in educational administration. Professor Marshall is also author or editor of numerous other books, including: *Rethinking Educational Politics*, with Cynthia Gerstl-Pepin, and *Leadership for Social Justice: Making Revolutions in Education*, with Maricela Oliva. Earlier volumes include *Feminist Critical Policy Analysis, Vols. I and II*; *Culture and Education Policy in the American States*, with Douglas Mitchell and Frederick Wirt; *The Assistant Principal: Doing It Differently: The Administrative Career*, with Katharine Kasden; and *The New Politics of Race and Gender*.

While an officer in the American Educational Research Association (AERA), Marshall pushed the field of education politics to do more to incorporate issues of race and gender. She also leads scholars and practitioners who push equity research into action as part of an initiative she calls Leadership for Social Justice. In 2003, AERA bestowed the Willystine Goodsell Award on Dr. Marshall for her career of scholarship and activism in behalf of women and girls. She is now analyzing qualitative interviews for a book on educator activists who courageously engage in social movements.

Early in her scholarly career, while chairing dissertation committees for numerous doctoral students, she recognized a need and began to develop this book. As this 4th edition appears, she will have been teaching qualitative methodology courses for 25 years.

Gretchen B. Rossman is Professor of Education at the University of Massachusetts at Amherst. She received her Ph.D. in education from the University of Pennsylvania with a specialization in higher education administration. She has served as Visiting Professor at Harvard University's Graduate School of Education. Before coming to the University of Massachusetts, she was Senior Research Associate at Research for Better Schools in Philadelphia. Prior to 1995, her research focused on the local impact of changes in federal, state, and local policy, studying school-based restructuring efforts to include students with disabilities and those from refugee and immigrant families. Since 1995, she has worked internationally, serving as research and evaluation specialist for projects on strengthening the education of girls in India and on capacity building in the education sector through a university linkages project with Chancellor College of the University of Malawi, Southern Africa.

Professor Rossman has coauthored three books based on her research: *Change and Effectiveness in Schools: A Cultural Perspective*, with Dick Corbett and Bill Firestone; *Mandating Academic Excellence: High School Responses to State Curriculum Reform*, with Bruce Wilson; and *Dynamic Teachers: Leaders of Change*, with Sharon Rallis. In addition, she and Sharon Rallis have published the second edition of their introductory qualitative research text, *Learning in the Field: An Introduction to Qualitative Research*. In addition to her teaching and research responsibilities, she consults regularly on reform both internationally and domestically and has served as a qualitative evaluation specialist to several educational organizations.